Byron and Beth Borger have l
Unapologetic champions of the life of the mind, their work has been a
ministry to generations of Christians who have discovered that God's joy and
delight is as wide as the world itself. Curators of the imagination, stewards of
the tradition, priests of print, they have always done more than sold books:
they have furnished faithful minds and hearts. This book is a lovely
testimony to that good work.
   —James K.A. Smith, Calvin College, author of *You Are What You Love:*
      The Spiritual Power of Habit

When I want to know how to think about the things that matter most,
I trust Byron Borger to point me in the right direction—never telling me
what to think, but ready with endless resources to help me discover how
to think in the best ways. He and Beth have made me, on countless occasions,
feel like the most treasured writer and person in the world, as I suspect they
have done for many of the contributors to this volume. Their impact in
hearts and minds is now multiplied, through these pages and in the lives
of countless readers they've guided and nurtured through the years.
May this smart personal volume make you curious enough to buy a book—
this book!—for readers you love, at Hearts & Minds Bookstore.
   —Margot Starbuck, author of *Small Things with Great Love:*
      Adventures in Loving Your Neighbor

Byron Borger is a true believer. Like the lineup of insightful essayists who
contributed to this book in his honor, Borger believes that reading the right
book at the right time can supply just the kind of provocation, insight, or
solace we need, when we need it.
   —Cameron J. Anderson, author of *The Faithful Artist:*
      A Vision for Evangelicalism and the Arts

Byron Borger spent his life making us all richer by introducing us to authors
and ideas that helped us flourish. Some of his suggested readings made us
laugh, made us angry, made us wrestle—but each made us better people. We
honor you and we are indebted to you. Thank you for discovering the good
and true and beautiful and spending your life generously sharing it with us.
   —Margaret Feinberg, author of *Flourish: Live Free, Live Loved*

While living and teaching in New York City I had been hearing about the Hearts & Minds Bookstore for some time. And then one day I was lured to a speaking engagement for The Row House in Lancaster, PA with the promise of a visit to the bookstore. How could I say no?

My expectations were high and, boy, were they met. I felt like a gambling addict stumbling into a casino. Suffice it to say that on my return trip to the city I traveled back home with far more baggage than I had left with. This book is a tantalizing taste of what it is like to visit that magical place. It makes me dream of returning there to restock!

—Harry Bleattler, chair of the Media, Culture, and the Arts
program at The King's College, New York City

Byron Borger represents everything that is right with bookstores. He is a thoughtful and winsome curator of ideas and prose in moment when most booksellers are crass consumerists. Thank God for Byron, and thank God for Hearts & Minds!

—Jonathan Merritt, contributing writer for *The Atlantic* and author of
Learning to Speak God from Scratch

How fitting this splendid collection is as a tribute to Byron and Beth Borger, partners and booksellers extraordinaire whose life-long vision and ambitions exemplify the idea of Christian vocation and faithful living. Featuring an array of writers commenting on influential works in their fields, this volume represents the fruit of the Hearts & Minds enterprise and will no doubt encourage the same lively discourse we've come to associate with Bryon's own booklists.

—William D. Romanowski, Calvin College, author of *Reforming
Hollywood: How American Protestants Fought for Freedom at the Movies*

I thank God for Byron and Beth Borger—they are such solid gold people, and friends as well. Without them, many a thoughtful Christian writer would be on the endangered species list in the face of the tsunami of Big Data recommended reading. While Hearts & Minds exists, serious Christian books can live too."

—Os Guinness, author of *Impossible People: Christian Courage
and the Struggle for the Soul of Civilization*

A Book for Hearts & minds

What You Should Read & Why

—A FESTSCHRIFT HONORING THE
WORK OF HEARTS & MINDS BOOKSTORE

A Book for HEARTS & MINDS

What You Should Read & Why

—A FESTSCHRIFT HONORING THE
WORK OF HEARTS & MINDS BOOKSTORE

Edited by Ned Bustard

In Christian art, the square halo identified a living person presumed to be a saint. Square Halo Books is devoted to publishing works that present contextually sensitive biblical studies and practical instruction consistent with the Doctrines of the Reformation. The goal of Square Halo Books is to provide materials useful for encouraging and equipping the saints.

First Edition 2017
Copyright ©2017 Square Halo Books
P.O. Box 18954, Baltimore, MD 21206
www.SquareHaloBooks.com

ISBN 978-1-941106-07-5
Library of Congress Control Number: 2017956191

All rights reserved. No part of this book may be reproduced without permission from the author, except by a reviewer who may quote brief passages in a review; nor may any part of this book be reproduced, stored in a retrieval system or transmitted in any form by any means (electronic, mechanical, photocopying, recorded or other), without permission from the author.

Printed in the United States of America.

Obviously, this book is dedicated to Byron & Beth Borger. *What would we have read without you?*

SOLI DEO GLORIA

Contents

READING
Byron Borger 11

ART
Ned Bustard 17

BIBLICAL STUDIES
Calvin Seerveld 29

COOKING
Andi Ashworth 41

CREATION CARE
Byron Borger 51

CREATIVE NONFICTION
Gregory Wolfe 57

EDUCATION
G. Tyler Fischer 67

ETHICS
David P. Gushee 77

FANTASY
Matthew Dickerson 89

FILM
Denis Haack 99

HISTORY
Daniel Spanjer 107

LAW
Mike Schutt 117

LITERATURE
Karen Swallow Prior 133

NEW TESTAMENT STUDIES
N.T. Wright 143

POETRY
Aaron Belz 155

POLITICS
Eric Bryan 165

SCIENCE
Michael Kucks 177

SOCIOLOGY
Bradshaw Frey 189

URBAN PLANNING
Tom Becker 199

VOCATION
Steve Garber 209

OVERSTOCK
About the Authors 219

reading

Byron Borger

MY WIFE AND I STARTED A BOOKSTORE. We're still trying to figure out how to keep it afloat, but overall it's been a long and fun journey.

In the late seventies, I worked in campus ministry and part of what it emphasized was working with students. I worked with students at a small branch campus of Penn State, mostly engineering majors. I would invite them to think Christianly, as we say, and talk about the relationship of their faith to their sense of calling. I was always passing out books—you're a Christian nurse, here's something on healthcare, you're going to be a scientist analyzing evolution, here's a Christian philosophy on this or that—and students would say to me, you should have a bookstore! Finally I realized they were right. Part of my passion was connecting people with resources they might use in their own spiritual development, but particularly as that related to living out their faith in the work world.

In my experience with bookstores, there were big broad chains that carried everything with a secular, anti-godly mood, but you still got a lot of good stuff. Then you had Christian bookstores that were oriented toward my people, with little trinkets and stupid artwork and maybe a book or two. And then you had seminary bookstores that were either liberal or conservative—and the liberals had better bookstores! Nothing in between. There wasn't a thoughtful but broad bookstore carrying books on every topic (without the specialty of only serving the academy or theologians or pastors) anywhere to be found. Being theologically Reformed, I believe that moms and artists and politicians and businesspeople all need to think through their vocation with a Christian perspective. Martin Luther is said to have asserted that the milkmaid and the beer barrel-maker were just as important to the kingdom of God as the clergy. We have people who've come into our store over the years and seen Science, Ecology, Education, and then the arts—and they take a look around and say, "We thought this was supposed to be a Christian bookstore." On the other hand, you have other people who come in and they look around and say, "What is this place?"

What I'd like to talk about today is reading as a spiritual discipline. And I'd like to tell a couple of stories from history to remind us about how books can make a great difference in people's lives. These are the kinds of stories we can tell our children and our neighbors and our parishioners In the history of redemption, books have played a serious part. Not that God needs only books to do His work, but in God's grace He has chosen to manifest Himself through the printed page and that's an important part of Western history and of redemptive history. After that, we'll look at reasons that books are important today and then the unique quandary we have in a postmodern world.

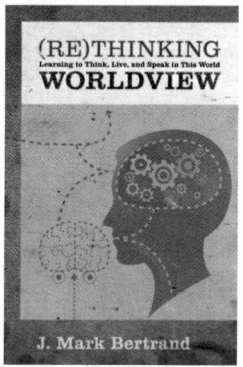

One of the places I like to start is after the exile when the prophets of hope started reminding the people that one day they would go back to a restored Jerusalem. Nehemiah is building the wall and they find the Scriptures, and they're so excited about the rediscovery of the printed page that they have the Feast of Booths. They make everyone stay up all night in tents just so they can read. The priests assign people to stand up and read the text to everybody. And we still celebrate that. Reading the book out loud is important to do. In preaching and teaching, we need to hear the text aloud.

It is no accident that Jesus is Word, and that the circulation of letters around the New Testament was the printed page. People would gather together and read these sometimes contraband letters. In some of these house churches you could get arrested if you were reading one of these letters that said that the King was Jesus. Making copies and distributing those handwritten letters is seminal to who we are. It helped shape the formation of the early church. The early church shared Eucharist together, they sang, they shared with the poor, but they also read. Reading the text out loud was an important part of who the church became. (Paul is ordering books at the end of his life—telling Timothy to send him more books!) That's part of who we are.

Think of Augustine, one of the great figures of the early church. He's a hungover, worldly guy (whose Godly mom is praying for him). But one day, he comes out of a hangover and he's looking outside and hears a little girl singing "Take up and read." and the first book he sees is a Bible and he grabs it and opens it up and his life is transformed.

You probably also know the story of Saint Patrick. Patrick is taken to the rough, ugly areas of Ireland by barbarians as a slave, when he is about ten years old. He escapes, comes back to the continent, becomes a Christian, and then feels led by God to go back and share the Gospel with his captors. And he realizes he can't preach the text because they can't read—they don't have a written language yet. He realizes he needs to teach them to read and teach them to write so that he can teach the Bible. A big part of evangelism was literacy. The Irish fell in love with letters and one out-

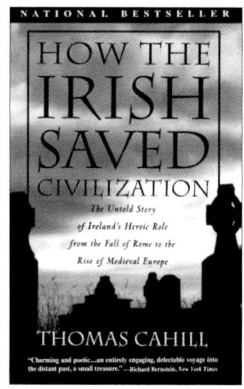

come of that was the Book of Kells. Another outcome was that while the barbarians are destroying Europe, the Irish are busy making copies of the great books of Western literature, and that is *How the Irish Saved Civilization.*

In contrast to the book-loving monks in Ireland, today our culture has in many ways abandoned books and reading in favor of tweets, commercials, and videos. In such a context it is no wonder that people have a hard time with the depth and logical flow of, for example, the book of Romans. I have a friend who was in the process of writing a book a few years ago on the loss of print culture in the postmodern world. I asked him about this situation and he said, maybe your kids won't understand the book of Romans, but perhaps they'll understand John more than you ever will. Ours is a visual, fast-paced, episodic culture. Can reading be a sprutual discipline in such an age as ours? I believe that it can.

William Wilberforce—an English politician, philanthropist, and leader of the movement to stop the slave trade—became a Christian in part by his relationship with John Newton, who wrote "Amazing Grace." How did Newton become a Christian? By reading *The Imitation of Christ.* He was a slave trader. (When he writes, "Saved a wretch like me," he was.)

And he read this Medieval classic and it changed his life. Newton became a Christian, and Newton befriended Wilberforce, who was a politician who embraced the abolitionist movement. Wilberforce had been thinking about becoming a missionary, but Newton challenged Wilberforce to serve God right there in England through English politics.

One of the reasons they read so widely in those periods is because John Wesley, the great revival preacher, had a method of reading medieval classics in order to disciple people. Wesley kept books in his carriage (like our audiobooks today) so that he could "redeem the time." And then after he finished them, he would pass the books around.

Founder of the Reformed Churches in the Netherlands and the Free University of Amsterdam, journalist, statesman, and neo-Calvinist theologian Abraham Kuyper said that Calvinism extends to all vocations and corners of life—the arts, science, law, politics, and the rest. Kuyper became a pastor in the late 1800s but was not really a believer at the time. A woman in his congregation gave him a George MacDonald novel about a pastor who is struggling with doubt, and Kuyper committed his life to Christ. Another example is Luther reading Erasmus, and Calvin reading Luther. So whether it's "take up and read" with Augustine, or Luther reading Erasmus, or Wilberforce and Newton reading *The Imitation of Christ,* or Kuyper reading this goofy novel, reading and passing books on can transform culture.

Another example is Chuck Colson. Colson went to jail, but the night before he went to prison he wept and realized his own sin because he read C.S. Lewis' *Mere Christianity.* How did Lewis become a Christian? He was reading George MacDonald. (When the Inklings would gather together, Tolkien would say to Lewis, "We write these fairy tales and grand stories, but if you're an atheist, why should good win over evil? You know that good has to win over evil, but without God,

Reading as a Spiritual Discipline 15

you can't have a story, let alone a good story!" And slowly, Lewis' ideas changed. He was reading a fairy tale by MacDonald on the train, and as he says, "I knew I was a Christian when I got off that train.")

Colson also said that R.C. Sproul's *Holiness of God* series changed his life. Increasingly throughout his life Colson is talking about Christianity as a worldview. He got that idea from Kuyper. So all these people are passing books on to each other and that can make a huge difference in someone's life. Is this an apologetic to buy books and give them away? Absolutely.

You can affect people's lives and change history. That's a taste of why bookselling is a ministry for me and why passing books around to people can make a big, big difference.

There are a few points I'll make from here on out to remind us of how God has used books and to have stories under our belts: reading is an act of *worship*, reading is an act of *spiritual formation*, reading is an act of *discipleship*, and reading is an act of *mission*.

I believe reading is *worship*. God tells us that we are called to love Him with all our minds. So the mandate to use our minds is not just for intellectuals or scholarly types or philosophers, it's a mandate to all of us to use the gray matter God has given us to think well and read well to His glory. It's an act of worship

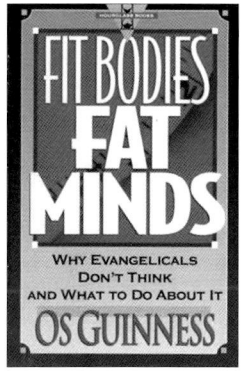

and an act of love. (Os Guinness has a little book called *Fit Bodies, Fat Minds,* where he traces the history of why evangelicals have "sold the farm" on the development of the mind.) Reading is a way to love God with our minds and therefore reading can become an act of worship.

I'll go further and say that reading is an act of *spiritual formation*. In the Middle Ages, they had something called *Lectio Divina,* a Latin word that basically means that you read slowly to see God speak. I often skim books for my job, but in my personal life I read rather slowly. Now you mostly do this with the Scriptures. But the early monks would say you can

practice *Lectio Divina* with any literature. Not to read too fast for content, but to gently mull over what God wants to say. It's like a reading with the heart, if you will. If we read carefully we can hear the voice of God.

Reading is also an act of *discipleship*. In Timothy, Paul writes, "Study to show thyself approved." We are mandated to know our stuff. So there is not only a gentle formation of our heart by slow, careful reading, there is also some sense that we have to master the content. For instance, reading theology and knowing about the doctrine of Creation—is Bauer right about Genesis in *The Beginning: A Second Look at the First Sin*? Does God care about ecology? Are the visual arts important to God?—these things matter. If we're going to be disciples that are approved by God for good works, we have to know what it is that God wants us to do. So a little bit of reading, a little bit of arguing, a little bit of study. We need to know our stuff to tell the wheat from the tares in our culture.

And lastly, reading is an act of *mission*. Think of how the apostle Paul on Mars Hill goes to the think tank of his day where people gather to intellectually talk about ideas. To reach that audience he uses books he had read (specifically quoting from *Phenomena* by Aratus in Acts 17:28). His ability to reference these great thinkers and philosophers gives him clout with their followers as he shares the true Gospel.

Books transform our lives and the lives of our friends and neighbors. There's a reason Jesus is called the Word. He was made flesh and dwelt among us. God has given us words from the beginning—words that inspire, inform, and instruct us. All we need to do is take up and read. And then pass it on.

Adapted from a lecture given in May 2004 at *The New Humanity: A Biblical View of the Fall and Cultural Renewal*—a Square Halo Books theological conference.

aRT

Ned Bustard

WHAT COLOR SHOULD YOU PAINT A FLYING ELEPHANT? For many of my early years I felt like that query had as much relevancy within my Christian circles as did a question like, *"What art books should you read and why?"* Perhaps a better question would have been, *"Should elephants fly?"* That was a more basic question parallel to my internal conflict over whether a Christian should be in the arts or not. Yes, there were flying elephants, and yes, they had been painted, but why bring them up? Painted flying elephants are statistically negligible and (to date) only animated.[1]

Therefore, it would be helpful to first ask: *Is the Bible opposed to the visual arts?* Wheaton professor Clyde S. Kilby responded to this concern when he wrote:

> Many Christians, I believe, sincerely think so. It seems more nearly correct, however, to say that [the Bible] is opposed only to the wrong use of [the arts]. Aaron used the gold jewelry of the Israelites to fashion a golden calf underneath Sinai, but Moses used their jewelry as part of the stuff of the tabernacle.[2]

As gold jewelry could be used in a blasphemous way to sculpt a golden idol but also be used by Bezalel to build the Ark of the Covenant (the very seat of God), so the arts can be used to rail against God or to bring glory to God. From the perspective of the craftsman, there is not a big difference between sculpting a gold calf and sculpting a gold cherubim.[3] The difference between them is that one brings life and one brings death. After reading the description of the art God wanted Bezalel to make in Exodus, it is clear that the Bible is not antagonistic to the visual arts. Indeed, the first person to be described as filled by the Spirit in the Bible was an artist. But I didn't learn that in church. I had to wait to find that out until my college years when I read a book called *Art and the Bible*.

Francis Schaeffer in *Art and the Bible* worked together with Madeleine L'Engle in *Walking on Water* to give me a theology that valued art and inspired me to be a maker of art.[4] Without those books on art and faith, I would never have made it to this point in my life where I am working as a professional artist and running an art gallery. And while I still think *Art and the Bible* and *Walking on Water* should both be required reading universally, nowadays I often direct folks to read *Art for God's Sake: A Call to Recover the Arts* by Philip Graham Ryken as a primer for understanding the issues related to art and faith.

WHY ART NEEDS NO JUSTIFICATION[5]

Calvin Seerveld wrote: "While not every believer needs to specialize in art, every believer does need to support its ongoing christian production . . . other-wise we have been immature and unwise as a communion of saints."[6] Why? Because we are a body. Our educational system encourages isolating knowledge in strata of understanding through separate classes covering separate concepts in separate periods. And our culture generally sets up silos of ideas and disciplines, isolating them from each other. But the Bible teaches that even if the hand is different in shape and function from the mouth, they are both needed and interdependent. For many in our society, the assumption that all truth is scientific truth goes nearly unchallenged. But the Bible resists the scientific method and yet claims both truth and authority. The Christian knows that all of Creation was made by God and proclaims His glory.[7] Both biological truth and biblical truth can be embraced. Not only can they be embraced, but they can inform and illuminate understanding in their respective spheres. Therefore, believers need to support art and artmaking for the maturation and wisdom of the communion of saints. That is why books on art, artists, and artmaking should be read. This is not to make everyone an artist, but so that everyone can understand their part of the Body of Christ and their corner of Creation better thanks to the insights offered by art.

I have seen this played out in several relationships. My friend Dr. James Romaine will often share with me his observations about art and history. He does not make art himself, but he is an avid reader and careful observer. Through his insights I can see and understand art history better as well as my own artmaking. My friend Dr. Annalisa Crannell has also shared with me her work about art and math. Although I am highly allergic to anything related to numbers, she has pulled back the curtains on many occasions to show how the visual distortions I see from various points of view are computationally recreatable with pencil and paper. And my friend Rev. Luke LeDuc often describes the process of crafting a sermon in such a way that I see the practice and craft of artmaking reflected time and time again in his labors.

It may be fairly easy to see how the hand benefits the mouth but less obvious at first glance how the mouth benefits the hand. Likewise, it might be challenging to imagine how art can benefit the church. The first and possibly most important service art provides to the Body is that of seeing and teaching to see. Everyone looks but most people do not see. Art is about learning to see. "Art is a means of renewing our eyes and our hearts. [... It is] a God-given way, for us to recognize His voice and His world."[8] It is proverbial that we need to stop and smell the roses. Or as John Calvin said it, "But as the greater part of mankind, enslaved by error, walk blindfold in this glorious theatre."[9] So much goodness, truth, and beauty are commonly ignored in day-to-day life. It is one of art's jobs therefore to arrest us in our mad scurrying and turn our heads so that we can really see what God has made and what God is doing. Vincent Van Gogh helps us to see stars in the night sky. Paul Cézanne helps us see apples on a table. Andrew Wyeth helps us see a lace curtain blown by a sea breeze.

In addition to helping us look down to earth to revel in quotidian delights, art also encourages us to look up to the heavens to see transcendent truths. It has been observed that

> [a]rt encouraged by the church can have a profound positive impact on our lives as believers. It can serve to remind us of the faith's great mysteries: the immanence and transcendence of God, the humanity and deity of Christ, the great difference in a life dedicated to God and one lived in selfishness, the need for quiet and reflection amid our hectic daily lives, and the simple nobility of an ordinary life in Christ.[10]

As with all of life and the created order, ultimately art is not simply for our betterment as human beings or even as spiritual beings. Art is for the glory of God. Dick Staub wrote that "Art's single, unifying purpose is to glorify the creator, God.... The highest and best motivation for art is the artist's desire to enjoy and glorify God." But this unified purpose does not lead to uniformity, Staub says that "[b]eyond this overriding purpose, artists' works will be as diverse as God's own creation, with each specific work of art serving one or more subsidiary purposes."[11] Not only is there no restriction on style and form, there aren't even thematic or spiritual constraints. All of creation is open to the artist's palette. "The Reformation emphasized the truth that God had become human, bringing dignity to earthly, secular life," explains Michael Horton. "One need not 'sanctify' art by demanding that it serve the religious or moral interests of the church. Creation is a legitimate sphere in its own right."[12]

Such freedom in style, form, theme, and spiritual intent might worry some in the Church. And even if these freedoms were embraced, coming face to face with the actual art might bring all truth claims into question. Art is not propositional like the epistle to the Romans and is not quantifiable like the eruption cause by combining Diet Coke and Mentos. So how can there be any true knowing derived from art? Calvin Seerveld wrote:

> Art is not vague because it is not analytically precise, and it is not confused because it is not articulated clearly in some language with dictionary references. Art is also neither ineffable nor mysterious nor more subjective a knowledge than analytic philosophical statements or straight-forward English sentences about the weather. Artistic painting and sculpture simply have a different set of formative elements defining their existence, as art products, and one needs to learn how to read such artistic elements in order to understand that kind of genuine knowledge, knowledge characterized by the quality of suggestion and allusion.[13]

Art is a real and helpful source of knowledge if you possess the tools and education to understand it, just as a thermometer is a real and helpful source of knowledge if someone has explained what the fluid in the tube is doing, why it is doing it, and what all the little lines and numbers are supposed to mean.

COFFEE-TABLE BOOKS, ETC.

Hopefully these meandering musings on the value and importance of art have given birth to a desire to read some books about art and faith. So, what color should you paint a flying elephant? Perhaps blue would be a good choice. Ahh, but what *shade* of blue? Do you want the elephant to be Cerulean, Cornflower Blue, Federal Blue, Indigo, International Klein Blue, Midnight Blue, Navy Blue, Non-photo Blue, Parrish Blue, Periwinkle, Sky bBlue, Steel Blue, Ultramarine, Zaffre ... the list goes on and on. In the same way, to now suggest a book on art and faith to read it becomes necessary to discuss the different shades of books to choose from.

Thankfully, the art community within the church has grown a great deal since the early 80s and now my bookshelf is overflowing with good books about art and faith.[14] The best thing about crafting this little essay is the bittersweetness of leaving out many books that I love. I never could have imagined back in high school and college that there would ever come a day that I wouldn't be

What Art Books You Should Read & Why

able to count on one hand the books in print about Christianity and the arts. For quite some time there were slim pickings. In the 60s you might have read *The Mind of the Maker* by Lord Peter Wimsey's creator, Dorothy L. Sayers. In the 70s there were a few more choices like Hans Rookmaaker's *Modern Art and the Death of a Culture* and Francis Schaeffer's *Art and the Bible*. By the 80s several classics had been penned like Calvin Seerveld's *Rainbows for the Fallen World,* Madeline L'Engle's *Walking on Water: Reflections on Faith and Art,* and Nicholas Wolterstorff's *Art in Action.*

During the 90s a few more titles came out, then after the turn of the century the options for books on art and faith exploded (relatively speaking). All these books are still in print and are still valuable to read.

Although still not a burned-over district, there are enough books about art from the vantage point of Christianity that they must be discussed in categories. After having read a basic on art and faith like *Art and the Bible* or *Art for God's Sake* (a mandatory first step), I propose that it would be valuable to read books on **art history, art making,** an **artist, art theory,** and **art and the Church.**

The Religious Art of Andy Warhol
by Jane Daggett Dillenberger

There are many commendable survey books on art history like *The Square Halo and Other Mysteries of Western Art*, E. John Walford's *Great Themes in Art, Journey Into Christian Art,* and *The Lion Companion to Christian Art,* but finding art history books from a Christian perspective that are in print is quite a challenge.

Finding books about contemporary art that honestly deal with Christianity is even more of a challenge.[15] The Art World has a story it tells about the history of art and its principal actors are not allowed to break out of character. For example, Tanner is the "first African-American painter" and history books point to *The Banjo Lesson* (a painting depicting an old black man teaching a young boy to play) as his definitive work. But a book like *Henry Ossawa Tanner: Modern Spirit* clearly shows that Biblical narrative paintings were the heart and the soul of that artist. In a similar way, Andy Warhol is the "quirky king of Pop art," and his advocates and historians ardently defend that persona. Yet the real artist was much more complicated and multifaceted than he is usually portrayed. *The Religious Art of Andy Warhol* is an excellent book that lifts the veil on the spiritual aspects of Warhol's life and art. In the two years before he died Warhol made over one hundred paintings, drawings, and prints based on Leonardo da Vinci's *The Last Supper*. Not only that, but Dillenberger shows that Warhol had a lifelong interest in the Faith and attended church multiple times a week. This important volume focuses on his Skull paintings, the prints based on Renaissance religious artwork, his Cross paintings, and *The Last Supper* series. Reading books like this is helpful in instilling a healthy dose of skepticism into those who would listen to The Art World's grand narrative and hear with discernment.[16]

It Was Good: Making Art to the Glory of God
edited by Ned Bustard

A Christian looks at the world through the eyes of one who has a restored relationship with the Creator, and receives a new vision affecting every area of life—including the creative process. So what does it mean to be a creative individual who is a follower of the creative God? This was the first in a series that set out to answer that question. Instead of casting a vision for Christians in the arts (which had been done in other books like *The Liberated Imagination: Thinking Christianly About the Arts* or *Imagine: A Vision for Christians in the Arts*), the essays in *It Was Good* offer theoretical and practical insights into actually making art from a Christian perspective. Byron Borger wrote that this title was "one of the few books that I can say with confidence is one of the best we have had the privilege of carrying in our 25 years here at Hearts & Minds [...and] it is the best collection of its kind in print."[17] And although it has been around for many years now, the impact of this book continues on, as attested to in this testimonial from artist Craig Hawkins:

> Back in my second year of undergrad, seeking a BFA in Fine Art, I gave my life to Christ. I became involved with a campus ministry and the campus pastor came across the book *It Was Good: Making Art to the Glory of God*. He bought the book and gave it to me as a gift. At that point I was trying to reconcile a passion for art and a passion for Christ not knowing if they were compatible. This book was a rich

encouragement and confirmation that my faith and my art could not only coexist but also become something far more than I was seeing at any Christian bookstore or other resource I could find. This book introduced me to contemporary artists of faith making art that was honest, authentic, and good. This book helped jumpstart my journey of pursuing God with the gifts he has given me. Acknowledging him as the Creator and rejoicing in the creative ability he has endowed me with. I am deeply thankful for this book.[188]

Golden Sea
by Makoto Fujimura

It is challenging to make a recommendation for a monograph for only one artist, because of all the fantastic artists I've been fortunate to get to know over the years. There is Edward Knippers' *Violent Grace,* Joel Sheesley's *Domestic Vision, Beauty Given by Grace: The Biblical Prints of Sadao Watanabe, The Art of Sandra Bowden, The Art of Guy Chase, Through Your Eyes: Dialogues on the Paintings of Bruce Herman, Mary McCleary: After Paradise,* Tim Lowly's *Trying to Get a Sense of Scale*—and that doesn't even take into consideration books featuring multiple artists like *Faith and Vision: Twenty-Five Years of Christians in the Visual Arts.* Any and all of these are wonderful books worth buying and spending extended time with, reflecting on the art and text.

But if there was to be only one book recommended, it would be a beautiful cloth-bound, gold-embossed volume about the art of an artist whose impact continues to be felt, both inside and outside of the Church. That book is *Golden Sea* by Makoto Fujimura. A major mid-career project, *Golden Sea* contains images of his paintings with accompanying essays—by Dan Siedell, Kei Tatejima, Robert Kushner, Nicholas Wolterstorff, Gregory Wolfe, Thomas Hibbs (from the now out-of-print book *Rouault-Fujimura: Soliloquies*), Julie Hamilton, and Roberta Ahmanson—and a biographical documentary film.

Fujimura's art and writing can be found in other books like *It Was Good: Making Art to the Glory of God, Objects of Grace: Conversations on Creativity and Faith, Refractions: A Journey of Faith, Art, and Culture, The Four Holy Gospels:*

ESV Bible, and *Culture Care: Reconnecting with Beauty for Our Common Life*, but nothing compares to *Golden Sea* for getting a full understanding of Mako's art. Fujimura's art must be seen in person to fully drink in the shimmering layers of trapped minerals, but the large pages in this book and its quality reproductions allow for the next best way to enjoy his semi-abstract *nihonga* artwork.

Objects of Grace: Conversations on Creativity and Faith edited by James Romaine

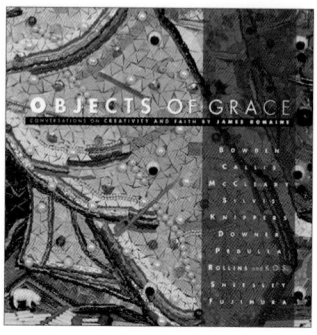

Kelly Crow, staff reporter of *The Wall Street Journal*, said during a CIVA (Christians in the Visual Arts) symposium at The King's College in New York that the Art World is like a cocktail party that has been going on for quite some time. Without question *Rainbows for the Fallen World: Aesthetic Life and Artistic Task* is a critical voice for Christians to hear in that conversation, and it is a classic that should be required reading for everyone. Byron Borger says: "Certainly one of the most widely respected writers about Christians in the arts, this eccentric book holds forth a vision of God's concern for nuance, suggestion, color and allusivity. Creatively written, serious and, at times, nearly stunning. Exceptional!"[19] Gideon Strauss, professor at the Institute for Christian Studies, confessed that no other pages outside of the Scriptures themselves "have more decisively and thoroughly shaped my understanding of God, the world, and myself than the introduction and first chapters of *Rainbows*."[200] When I first began working on *It Was Good*, William Edgar insisted that I read *Rainbows* to understand the art and faith conversation, and I am so glad that I did. But there are other conversations at the art cocktail party and, as in most professions, there is a peculiar language that must be learned in order to pick up the nuances and meanings in the discussions. How is the newcomer to the party to learn the vocabulary and begin to understand the accents at this party? *Art as Spiritual Perception* and *God in the Gallery* are both very helpful books in this regard. That being said, *Objects of Grace: Conversations on Creativity and Faith* stands out as a one-of-a-kind method to begin picking up "art speak."

Objects of Grace is a collection of conversations with some of today's most intriguing artists—Sandra Bowden, Dan Callis, Mary McCleary, John Silvis, Edward Knippers, Erica Downer, Albert Pedulla, Tim Rollins and K.O.S., Joel

Sheesley and Makoto Fujimura—along with beautiful reproductions of their art. It focuses on the intersection of Christianity and creativity. Gregory Wolfe of *Image* wrote:

> "*Objects of Grace* is the kind of book that I've been waiting twenty years to see. Here is a dynamic young art critic talking to a group of exceptionally talented visual artists about both contemporary art and Christian faith without a shred of self-consciousness or defensiveness.... To crown this achievement, the book is itself a work of art, lovingly and vividly designed. If church historians and cultural commentators want to find the cutting edge in American religion today, they should look no further than *Objects of Grace*."

Visual Faith: Art, Theology, and Worship in Dialogue by William Dyrness

The best mediator over the past several decades in the awkward relationship between Art and the Church has been Christians in the Visual Arts (CIVA). The beginning of their story was told beautifully in *Faith and Vision: Twenty-Five Years of Christians in the Visual Arts*. Between its covers are more than 200 images that showcase the work of CIVA's most accomplished artists and highlight the quality and breadth of its many traveling exhibitions, conferences, directories, and publications. One of that book's co-editors was Cameron J. Anderson, author of *The Faithful Artist: A Vision for Evangelicalism and the Arts*, which Anderson described to me once as "a kind of Venn diagram seeking to find common ground between evangelical Protestantism and the rise of modernism in the postwar period." There is no book that better captures the tensions and theological challenges that beset artists who found themselves caught between the Art World and the Church. It doesn't stay looking at the past, but also offers hope and vision for the future. Luci Shaw wrote that "Anderson opens up the mysteries of contemporary art, describing how works of art may operate as lenses through which to view the seen and unseen within culture." Other praiseworthy books in this vein are *For the Beauty of the Church: Casting a Vision for the Arts* and *The Next Generation: Contemporary Expressions of Faith*.

Possibly the most helpful book for those looking to engage both Art and the Church is *Visual Faith: Art, Theology, and Worship in Dialogue* by William Dyrness. In Hearts & Minds' *BookNotes* Byron Borger wrote, "Dyrness, as always, has an eye to everyday life and how an openness to allusiveness (as Seerveld puts it) and experiences of beauty can help us frame meaning, honor God, and move towards personal flourishing and social transformation."[211] In *Visual Faith* the reader will find a wonderful overview of art history from a Christian perspective, beginning with art in the Early Church and coming all the way up to Warhol, Pollock, and art today—like the exemplary works of Lynn Aldrich. There is also an entire chapter devoted to making and looking at art. If there was one book I'd give to people in my church who were interested in engaging with art (after *Art and the Bible* or *Art for God's Sake*), this would be it.

conclusion

"Saints are impractical; artists and philosophers are impractical. The world has room for only the practical."[222] And, for that matter, the Church often only has room for the practical. Yet that hasn't always been the case nor should it continue to be. Pope John Paul II wrote that

> ... the Church has not ceased to nurture great appreciation for the value of art as such. Even beyond its typically religious expressions, true art has a close affinity with the world of faith, so that, even in situations where culture and the Church are far apart, art remains a kind of bridge to religious experience. In so far as it seeks the beautiful, fruit of an imagination which rises above the everyday, art is by its nature a kind of appeal to the mystery. Even when they explore the darkest depths of the soul or the most unsettling aspects of evil, artists give voice in a way to the universal desire for redemption.[233]

Christians need to read books about art and , even more importantly, begin *looking* at art ("Seeing is the starting point!"[244] as art historian Linda Stratford once wisely exclaimed). To read books on art history, art making, artists, art theory, and art and the Church helps Christians glorify the Creator and better enjoy His Creation. And beyond delight, art serves as an agent for the proclamation of truth—it is a conduit for the understanding of some truths that cannot be reached any other way, because, at the end of the day, there are some ways of knowing, and some things that can only be grasped, by painting a flying elephant blue.

What Art Books You Should Read & Why 27

ENDNOTES

1 I'm referencing the fourth Disney animated feature film *Dumbo*, of course. But perhaps you might be thinking of "The Flying Elephant," a proposed super-heavy tank—planned but never built—by the British during World War I?
2 Clyde S. Kilby author and William Clyde S. Kilby, *The Arts and the Christian Imagination: Essays on Art, Literature and Aesthetics*, edited by William A. Dyrness (Brewster, MA: Paraclete Press, 2016), 87.
3 I write more about art used to the glory of God and used as an idol in *Revealed: A Storybook Bible for Grown-Ups*, 60, 62. And of course, there is an entire book on this topic: *It Was Good: Making Art to the Glory of God*.
4 I briefly described my personal struggle to reconcile art and faith in *Teaching Beauty: A Vision for Music & Art in Christian Education*, edited by G. Tyler Fischer (Baltimore, MD: Square Halo Books, 2016), 79-80.
5 See what I did there? I couldn't write this essay and leave Rookmaker out. His books *Art Needs No Justification* and *Modern Art and The Death of a Culture* were trailblazing texts in the conversation about faith and art in the 70s. And his impact is still being felt, as demonstrated in the recent publication *Modern Art and the Life of a Culture: The Religious Impulses of Modernism (Studies in Theology and the Arts)* by Jonathan A. Anderson and William A. Dyrness.
6 Calvin Seerveld, *Rainbows for the Fallen World: Aesthetic Life and Artistic Task*, (Toronto: Toronto Tuppence Press, 1980), 37.
7 "The heavens declare the glory of God, and the sky above proclaims His handiwork. Day to day pours out speech, and night to night reveals knowledge." Psalm 19:1-2.
8 Kilby, *Arts and the Christian Imagination*, 147.
9 Calvin's *Institutes* 1.5.8
10 from "The Reformation and the Visual Arts," an unpublished paper by Randy C. Randall.
11 Dick Staub, *The Culturally Savvy Christian: A Manifesto for Deepening Faith and Enriching Popular Culture in an Age of Christianity-Lite* (San Francisco, CA: Jossey-Bass, 2007), 186.
12 Michael S. Horton, *Where in the World Is the Church?: A Christian View of Culture and Your Role In It* (Phillipsburg, NV: Presbyterian and Reformed Publishing, 2002), 23.
13 Seerveld, *Rainbows for the Fallen World*, 79.
14 In *Teaching Beauty* I include a list of books I recommend reading on this topic, including Nicholas Wolterstorff's *Art in Action*, Jeremy S. Begbie's *Voicing Creation's Praise: Towards a Theology of the Arts*, Flannery O'Connor's *Mystery and Manners*, and more.
15 This is one of the reasons for the existence of ASCHA (pronounced "ash-uh"). Founded in 2010, ASCHA (The Association of Scholars of Christianity in the History of Art) is dedicated to the facilitation and promotion of scholarship that examines the historical and contemporary relationship between Christianity and the visual arts. ASCHA is international, non-partisan, and ecumenical; we invite the participation of scholars of all and no personal faith persuasions. ASCHA encourages the critical study of Christianity and the visual arts as that relationship is diversely manifested in all historical periods and world cultures. ASCHA is a forum for the advancement of research, dialogue, collaboration, and publication in the area of Christianity and the visual arts through the open and respectful exchange of knowledge and ideas among scholars. http://christianityhistoryart.org
16 *Art Rethought: The Social Practices of Art* by Nicholas Wolterstorff is a 2015 book by the author of *Art in Action*. In this work Wolterstorff discusses the *grand narrative* concerning art in the modern world, by which he means the generally agreed assumption that in the early

modern period the arts "came into their own," and that artworks became "works of art" that are transcendent objects set on pedestals as objects of disinterested attention. Wolterstorff argues that the grand narrative has to be rejected as too limiting and not able to honestly or helpfully deal with the full range of art that has been made or is being made today.

17 Byron Borger, review of *It Was Good: Making Art to the Glory of God* (Revised & Expanded), edited by Ned Bustard, *BookNotes*, March 2007, https://heartsandmindsbooks.com/2007/03/it_was_good_making_art_to_the/.
18 Craig Hawkins (craighawkinsart.com), personal correspondence with author, April 7, 2017.
19 http://www.heartsandmindsbooks.com/vocation/arts.htm
20 Byron Borger, "A Bona Fide Publishing Even: A Six-Volume Set of the Writings of Calvin G. Seerveld — All on Sale, 20% Off," *BookNotes*, December 20 2014, https://heartsandmindsbooks.com/2014/12/a_bone_fide_publishing_event_a/.
21 Byron Borger, review of *Poetic Theology: God and the Poetics of Everyday Life*, by William A. Dyrness, *BookNotes*, January 29, 2011, https://heartsandmindsbooks.com/2011/01/poetic_theology_dyrness_the_go/.
22 Jared M. Silvey, "The Role of Beauty in the Formation of Men as Men," *Crisis Magazine*, December 18, 2014, http://www.crisismagazine.com/2014/role-beauty-formation-men-men.
23 John Paul II, "Letter of His Holiness Pope John Paul II to Artists," The Holy See,1999, https://w2.vatican.va/content/john-paul-ii/en/letters/1999/documents/hf_jp-ii_let_23041999_artists.html.
24 During the Q&A, following her presentation at the 2017 ASCHA symposium: *A Strange Place Still? Religion in Contemporary Art*.

BIBLICAL THEOLOGY
Calvin Seerveld

"MOTHER, COULD WE READ JUST PSALM 117 TONIGHT?" That was a question we kids sometimes asked as the five o'clock suppertime was ending in our home on the rural South side of Long Island, New York, in the late 1930s, in early autumn, when there would still be enough fading sunlight outside, if you hurried a little, in which you could play a half hour of touch football.

In the family where I grew up, you read an actual Bible passage (not a devotional booklet) and prayed to finish every meal—breakfast, lunch, and supper. And before you went to bed, Mother would read a Bible story and a Grimm's fairy tale, and we children knew the difference between Cain and Abel and Hansel and Grethel.

As a sick teenager one night, I had to go downstairs from our bedroom to use the only toilet. It was about 4:00 AM, and I discovered my fishmonger father reading his Bible at the table and making notes, before he left to drive the truck a good hour in to the Fulton Fish Market by the Brooklyn Bridge in New York City, to get fresh fish caught from the Atlantic Ocean to sell in our store in Patchogue. I was surprised, and never forgot what my father was doing in what seemed like the middle of the night.

WHAT BIBLICAL THEOLOGY BOOKS SHOULD YOU READ?

Start with the Bible! My parents gave me my King James Bible on my eighteenth birthday (1948). My East German graduate student roommate in Basel, Switzerland, Gerhard Goebel, when I went to study there for a year with Oscar Cullmann and Karl Barth and to learn Hebrew (1955–56), gave me as a Christmas gift the *Zürcher Bibel* (Zwingli's Reformation translation, kept up-to-date by the Reformed Church of Switzerland from 1907 to 1931), which is especially fine on the Old Testament. The Hervormde Kerk in the Netherlands where my wife and I were married (1956), gave us the fairly new Revised Standard Version English translation of 1946/1952. In 1966-67, studying in Heidelberg with Gerhard von Rad and Claus Westermann, I bought two of the three volumes of Martin Buber's German translation of the Old Testament, *Die Schriftwerke* (1962) and *Bücher der Kundung* (1966) (translated jointly with Franz Rosenzweig, edited by Jacob Hegner). And my wife gave me the *New Revised Standard Version* of the Bible (1989) on our 35th wedding anniversary (1992).

All these Bibles are my basic tool kit, along with my third edition of Rudolph Kittel's edited *Biblia Hebraica*, and my old beaten-up Erwin Nestle critical edition of the *Novum Testamentum Graece,* the Köhler-Baumgartner *Lexicon in Veteris Testamenti Libros* (Leiden: E.J. Brill, 1958), and Joseph Henry Thayer's translation of *Grimm's Wilke's Clavis Novi Testamentui* (Chicago: American Book Company, 1899).

With Johann Gottfried Herder (1744-1803) I believe the best training in Biblical Theology is to make your own plodding translation of the original Hebrew (Aramaic) and Greek texts. Then you actually get to chew the cud of God's Word, as you struggle to read it slowly enough to let the Holy Spirit sink the writing deep down into your bottom consciousness, percolate there at heart-depth, till you hear God **speak** to you God's wisdom. If you cannot learn to read the Hebrew and Greek, then read a good modern translation in a language which is not your mother tongue, so you have to look up words in a dictionary and reflect on their varied meanings. The Bible has literary flexibility and flair in its God-breathed formulation. If you are born an American, why not try your hand at a Spanish or French Bible: Nueva Versión Internacional (Castilian) (2005), and *La Nouvelle Bible Segond* (2002).

Theological Dictionary of the New Testament
translated by Geoffrey W. Bromiley

The most thorough and exciting help I know for **studying** the Bible is Kittel's *Wörterbuch zum Neuen Testament,* eds. Gerhard Kittel and Gerhard Friedrich (Stuttgart: W. Kohljhammer, 1933-1979), ten volumes. Although I use the German edition, the work has also been translated into English by Geoffrey W. Bromily as *Theological Dictionary of the New Testament* (Grand Rapids: Eerdmans, 1964-1976),

What Biblical Theology Books You Should Read & Why 31

ten volumes (*the abridged edition is shown here*).

This "Dictionary" of words in the New Testament is really an encyclopedia which gives astute, condensed historical biographies of faith-important lingual expressions found in the Bible. Greek words and concepts have had their meanings altered in the one thousand years between Homer (c. 800 BC) and Gregory of Nyssa (c. 329–390 AD). The more than one hundred authors in these ten volumes are united in trying to document how the Greek language was used by pagan classical Greek writers and thinkers, then how the Jewish translators of the Septuagint coloured the same Greek word with Old Testament overtones, and also how rabbinic literature and the Patristics who lived after Jesus employed the same language. All this backgrounding and surrounding effort goes into pointing out precisely the special wrinkle given to the Greek in the New Testament because, although the language was ordinary spoken human language (as Hamann and Herder have argued), this New Testament Greek was breathed alive by God's Holy Spirit, and likely has a unique and "holy" import.

For example, ἐλπίς (hope) in the pagan Greek vocabulary was the last plague! to come out of Pandora's box; so "hope" meant a delusionary expectation to help one forget current troubles. The biblical Older Testament writings, however, turned hope (בטח) into a covenantal God-oriented trust in a Messianic certain future. So the Greek ἐλπίς in the Jewish-written New Testament comes to be the patient, comforted, sure expectation of a coming state of joy with the risen Lord Jesus Christ, quite different than Pandora's uncertain wishfulness.

Likewise, εἰρήνη ("peacefulness") in Plato and Epictetus denotes a condition of rest, of not fighting, a state of calm repose marking the end or absence of dispute. The Septuagint almost always uses εἰρήνη to translate שלום (shalom, "well-being"), and fills out the notion of "peace" with a positive shalom note of being a gift of God which is communal, full-bodied, and fruitful. So εἰρήνη ("peace") in the New Testament connotes a full-fledged, saved and restored wholesomeness (like the German *Heil!*) that Jesus Christ provides even in the face of persecution (John 16:33), not just absence of turmoil.

My two examples greatly oversimplify the often twenty pages of rich, nuanced exposition given jointly, say, by Rudolph Bultmann and Gerhard von Rad, or Julius Schniewind and Karl Ludwig Schmidt, on a single Greek word. And there are always surprising, sharp remarks which make you think twice: "Holy" (ἅγιος) does not mean "moral"!—which gives a quite different slant on human "sanctification." Or, John the Baptizer and Jesus do not report that there is a Kingdom of God and it consists in this or that; but they preach, "[t]he miraculous Kingdom-Rule of God is imminent! and only persecuted, humbled **children** can and shall receive its grace!" And there are six pages of text on the preposition "in." To be ἐν Χριστῷ Ἰησοῦ ("**in** Jesus Christ") is not a Hellenistic mystical union, but simply means "you **belong** to Jesus Christ." And so on.

Kittel's *Theological Dictionary* is a thesaurus, like being able to listen to a wise Methuselah about walking and talking with God. Years and years of deep reflection on the interconnected and special Old and New Testaments revealing God await you. As a reader you must naturally use discretion and remain a wary reader of its Existentialist "in-our-Now-crisis" bent, but this collection is an amazing source for biblical theology.

The standard old ICC (*International Critical Commentary on the Holy Scriptures*) is a horse of a different colour and (to mix my metaphor) it may not be your cup of tea. Like its German counterpart, *Die Schriften des Alten Testament*, eds. Gressman, Gunkel, Haller, Schmidt, Stærk and Volz (Göttingen: Vandenheck & Ruprecht, 1911–1925, three volumes), the ICC generally assumes the methodology of "historical criticism" along with the "documentary hypothesis." This means, as I see it, that ICC commentators put the biblical texts on trial, so to speak, and do painstaking philological, intricately grammatical, and lexical detective work to ferret out how and when the final edited writings got in front of us.

I can explain it best this way: when I read Genesis in one academic semester with Walter Baumgarten (1956), the last of the early "higher critics" still alive, he taught us that *Genesis* is composed of J (Yahwist), E (Elohim), P (the priests got in their licks), and D (the late Deuteronomist ephasizing LAW) sources. It is as if the Synoptic Gospel accounts—by Matthew, Mark, Luke, and John—were compressed into a single account. We will now disentangle Genesis into its different sources, and hear their distinctive sounds and contentions. We will not begin with Genesis 1, he said, because then we'll never finish the book. We start with the Isaac Geschichte (chapters 21–26), then the Abraham Geschichte (12–20), then the Jacob Geschichte (27–50), and finally the Ur-Geschichte (1–11).

Baumgarten was a superb teacher. You watched Genesis decompose into fragments before your very eyes, yet were fascinated by the different stylistic markings pointed out which made such analysis of sources plausible.

The ICC theologians—better, Rationalistic theo**logic**ians—are not interested in the Bible as God-speaking revelation to guide a communion of saints, so much as a puzzling traditioned document to be assiduously examined in excruciating detail so that you become aware of its packaging together disparate emphases. You notice artistic anomalies and dated cross-referencing correspondencies, and stand above the text to freely make second-guessing editorial judgments.

> "O Israel, hope in the Lord" (Psalm 130:7a) is a gloss because the phrase doesn't fit the meter of the psalm....
> A Maccabean editor added verses 17–18 to Psalm 132....
> Doubtless... a scribal error has been inserted....

I have used only a few of the 59 ICC commentaries (written 1836–2005; the whole Bible is not yet covered), but I consider their misguided contribution to biblical theology worth serious attention because you are forced to notice minute style variations telltale of subtle secondary meanings.

My own working methodology follows the lead of Brevard Childs' acceptance, rather than a questioning, of the Church-decided canonic text as starting point for exposition, and the Bible as authority for deepening our faith in Jesus Christ's rule acoming (see B. Childs, *Introduction to the Old Testament* [Philadelphia: Fortress Press, 1979]). But if you believe "without a doubt all things contained in the Scriptures" (*Belgic Confession of Faith,* article 5) as I do, then the ICC writers, who are completely immersed in the literary character of the Holy Scriptures and as nit-picking sticklers know the Bible books' styled formulations better than we do! can sharpen your biblical theology. It does not hurt but gives grit to one's amazed trust in the ongoing work of the Holy Spirit to realize that God had someone, possibly around Nehemiah's time, add the last two verses to David's Psalm 51 for use in the second temple liturgy.

A diametrically different approach than the *ICC* to Biblical Theology can be found in the work of the Hasidic German Jewish scholar Martin Buber (1878–1961). For Buber the Bible is not an IT-data one examines in detached fashion, but a live-wire, **living text** where the eternal person of **I**, God, is **speaking** directly to **YOU** now. The Bible by nature is proclamation, a calling-out to repent (turn around!), a cry embedded in a script. So listen, and come to find and meet the grace of the incomprehensible God.

In order to help contemporary people **hear** the oral character of God's Word, Buber, with Franz Rosenzweig (1886–1929), spent three and a half decades (1925–1961) translating the Hebrew text into German language that tried to get back behind Luther's superb effort, past the Vulgate and Septuagint versions, to the primal, sense-resonant Hebrew, minding even the breathing rhythm of a speaker. The result is a translation of crabbed, Hebraicized German, with compelling short phrases, and coinages, highlighting *Leitwörter* (key leading words) which bespeak the unity of the Bible. Buber and Rosenzweig meant to recapture and restore the original Eastern Jewish tonal meaning of God's revelation from Western intellectualized encrustation.

For example: תורה (torah) is translated as *Weisung* (Guidance) rather than as *Gesetz* (Law), since God's commandments are not legal stipulations so much as loving, protective injunctions. נבי (seer, prophet) like Amos or Jonah is not one who predicts the future, but is an announcing herald who faces the people of Israel, and us, with alternatives from which we must choose. ידע: "Adam knew Eve" (Genesis 4:1) is not pointing to intellectual comprehension nor is it a prudish euphemism; "knowing" in the Hebrew for Buber has earthy sense, the overtone of touch, encounter, mutual connectedness. To "know" the LORD God, as Jeremiah puts it, is to advocate what is just and reliable for the poor and those in dire need (c.f. Jeremiah 22:15–16). "Knowing" in the original Jewish Hebrew language of the Bible, Buber contends, is not an intellectual exercise, but is heart-involved and hands-on contact activity.

Buber's passion for concrete, mutual, respectful encounter leads him to supplement investigative IT-knowledge of things with this I-Thou meeting reception of an Other, in knowing glory-laden trees, toneful symphonies, a new human neighbour, as well as God. God's world is actually the burning bush Moses encountered as reported in Exodus 3:1–6: "Creation is not a hurdle on the road to God, it is the road itself."[1] Buber is asking us, with all our getting of detailed information and scientific advancement of facts, to also treat ordinary flowers with a humbled, meditating awareness of the flowers' identity breathing a creatural witness to its Almighty Creator. Then our ordinary life begins to bespeak what the Scriptures show and tell.

Right and Wrong: An Interpretation of Some Psalms
translated by Ronald Gregor Smith

To get a good firsthand taste of Buber's biblical theology, for those confined to English, a good little book is *Right and Wrong: An Interpretation of Some Psalms*, translated by Ronald Gregor Smith (London: SCM Press, 1952). Buber hears Psalm 12 telling us to wake up to the reality that we inhabit a culture of lies. Deceitful speech and lying deed are rampant, according to God's Word, and are destroying, disintegrating our very selves and neighbours. Psalm 14 does not exempt the nation of Israel and believers in God from being fools. "My people" (verse 4) is "the remnant" in Israel and elsewhere who truly follow God by doing justice and shunning self-righteousness. When we complainingly ask, "Why does the way of the wicked prosper?" (Jeremiah 12:1-4), Psalm 73 tells us that when we are stunned or flabbergasted by the apparent indecipherability of God's (in)action, know truly that in the (sinful) struggle one has before the mystery of God, you are indeed near to God.

And in Psalm 1 Buber neatly distinguishes *sinners* (הטאים), who have fits of doing evil and miss walking on God's way again and again—sinners are mixed within the company of the *tzaddiqim* ("the proven ones") too—*sinners* are distinct from the *wicked* (רשעים) who have a persistent disposition to be evil persons. Psalm 1 reassures those who have ears to hear that the ways of the godless wicked peter out, but those who stand in awe of the LORD God will be directed on the Way of Life and genuine happiness even amid the sorrows of Suffering Servant persecution.

A person who follows Jesus Christ will notice that Buber's biblical theology needs no mediator between God and humans, so sometimes a quasi-mystical attentive silence threatens to obtrude. And Buber's final apocalyptic horizon still ties the coming universe-wide Kingdom of God somehow to the actual land of Palestine, with his ("two-state" solution) enigmatic warning to the state of Israel: "Israel would lose its own self if it replaced Palestine by another land, and it would lose its own self if it replaced Zion by Palestine."[2] Yet Buber's reverence for the biblical text and prayerful scrutiny of God's spoken Word can help us read and hear the Bible on our knees.

Ethics by Dietrich Bonhoeffer

If you want a biblical theology that is truly Christ-centered, marked by a buoyant faith-certainty that God shall indeed come through, despite an increasingly evil constriction of daily life and a faltering, beleaguered Church, read Dietrich Bonhoeffer's (1906-1945) *Ethics. His Cost of Discipleship* (*Nachfolge*, 1937), *Life Together* (*Gemeinsames Leben*, 1939), and *Letters from Prison* (*Widerstand und Erbgebung*, 1955) cohere in a stirring testimony of a German Lutheran pastor who was gradually caught up in conspiratorial, double-agent activity for the Confessing Church[3] in Adolph Hitler's tyrannized Germany, which led to Bonhoeffer being hanged for treason a month before Germany capitulated to the Allied forces. The *Ethik* (c.1940-1943) is a series of unfinished fragments written during the Nazi turmoil of fear and palpable evil, posthumously edited together by his friend Eberhard Bethge, which shows unusual reflective courage pointing to Jesus Christ.

God's commandment of fully reconciling love revealed in Jesus Christ embraces the whole of life, says Bonhoeffer, and is permission to live as fully human creatures before God's face. Creation and redemption, the penultimate and the ultimate, both have their connected bona fide reality: God loves creation and has confirmed that love by marking history with the cross of Christ, whose resurrection testifies to God's will for a new world of shalom amid the darkest days. Jesus Christ's gracious action concretely unites the God-authorized mandates for the Church, marriage and family, human culture, and government.

The Church community, for Bonhoeffer, is officially set up by God to **proclaim the Word** of God, fearlessly to summon the whole world to submit to the saving dominion of Jesus Christ, **and** to **exercise the discipline of confessing sin** among the congregated faithful. The Church is to proclaim not the wickedness of the world, but the grace of Jesus Christ. The Church's earthly task, to match its worldly-wise and winsome proclamation of law **and** gospel, of repentance and grateful preparation for Jesus Christ's coming again to rule with blessed equity, is **diaconal deeds**.

Governance, government, says Bonhoeffer, has the God-ordained particular authority and power (ἐξουσία) to punish (backed up by "the sword," armed force) those who do wrong, and to protect and promote right-doing (I Peter 2:13-14). So what do Christians do when the governors violate their God-given office? Human societal problems are so historically entangled in guilt, says Bonhoeffer, that the attempt to find "solutions" may be unbiblical! And you don't ask yourself, "How can I do or be good?" Because Jesus Christ has become your conscience, you ask, "What is the will of God? Does my action help my neighbour become a human before God?"

Disobedience to the government—and pastor Bonhoeffer finally came to believe that assassination of Hitler was a necessary precondition to a successful *coup d'etat* that might deliver Germany from its militaristic mania— can only be "a concrete decision in a singular particular case" (which is not generalizable), and must be "a venture of responsibility... undertaken on one's own responsibility," ready to accept the guilt of criminality yourself. Becoming guilty sometimes becomes necessary in responsible action, says Bonhoeffer very soberly. And right here in the *Ethik* he notes the Codex D supplement to Luke 6:5: "Oh, man, if you really know what you are doing, you are blessed; but if you don't know what you are doing, you are accursed and a law-breaker." Christ's remark to Peter in Matthew 26:52 haunted Bonhoeffer: "all who take the sword will perish by the sword." But how can we followers of Christ be rid of Hitler's exterminating evil....

The biblically rich way Bonhoeffer encourages God's people to live in the world as followers of Jesus Christ is exemplified in the few pages of the *Ethics* in which he examines "[w]hat is meant by 'telling the truth.'" Telling the truth is not simply a matter of speech corresponding to facts, says Bonhoeffer, but must respect the participants and God's dimension of creational order and reconciliation along with our fallenness. For a child in his home to be questioned by Gestapo agents as to whether there be a Jew hidden behind the house walls, and to answer "Yes," would not be telling the truth. God's truth judges out of love, and the Nazi officer has no right to the knowledge requested. In our corruptible world some things are to remain concealed, and be confessed confidentially only to God, lest they become a Satanic "truth," the malicious, destructive LIE.

Bonhoeffer's biblical theology is not an academic exercise, but is a gutsy, joyful wrestling with the Scriptures to make concrete Jeremiah's counsel to the ancient Israelites: seek the shalom of the city where you have been exiled, and pray to the LORD on its behalf, for in its welfare you will find your shalom (Jeremiah 29:7, 11). Jesus Christ is the Lord of this very world we inhabit. So go! tell it to everybody, and serve the neighbour with the milk of the Gospel—God's reconciling love—and not with sugared water.

I'll mention briefly just one more provocative book that can help keep one's biblical theology alive and honest to God, before I conclude by mentioning the writings which have fostered my own biblical theology.

When the Gods Are Silent: On the Meaning of the Old Testament by Kornelis Heiko Miskotte

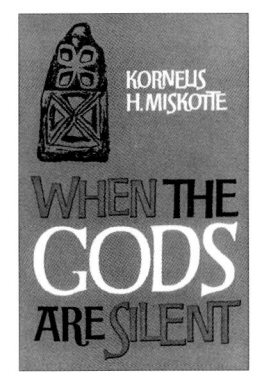

Kornelis Heiko Miskotte (1894–1976) was a Dutch scholar-pastor assigned in 1942 by the Hervormde Kerk of the Netherlands to preach to intellectuals estranged from the church (de buitenkerkelijke). I heard

him preach once in 1954, after he had become theology professor at Leiden University, and true to his reputation his proclamation captivated me with the honest, no-nonsense grit and certainty of God's being veritably at work in our very history today—God has been looking for me and has now found me! Like a caught fish, wiggle on God's line.

Miskotte's *When the Gods Are Silent: On the Meaning of the Old Testament*[4] is a book worth owning and rereading; Miskotte's writing surprises you, like Pascal's *Pensées*, and has the passion of Buber, Bonhoeffer and Karl Barth, to face us with the upside down éclat of the LORD God's salvaging outcasts. Both uptight "religious" and proudly irreligious people have one thing in common, says Miskotte: they are so bitterly, dryly serious. They both have great difficulty in understanding that in biblical faith one grasps and lives in joy! Joyfulness is the very nature of creaturely things, and in God too is an everlasting jubilation—that is the Old Testament Gospel. Old Testament writers do not downgrade death, chaos, and destruction of life into metaphors, but the *torah*, prophets, and psalms reveal that the inscrutable, merciful LORD God— God sometimes hides from us (Isaiah 45:15)—is conquering these elemental evil powers debilitating God's world. God is making things new (Isaiah 65:17). So live comforted in anticipation of that reality acoming, even if you experience the loneliness of Psalm 88. To be too sure of oneself is dangerous, says Miskotte, but to hold onto the childlike trust in God's restorative just-doing is to give the Old Testament backing to the New Testament promise of Jesus Christ's imminent return.

Although not all Miskotte's views may be kosher, endearing to me, for example, is his diary entry (August 1930) questioning the worth of conducting the time-consuming *huisbezoek* in the congregation (the Reformed Church practice of pastor and elders visiting families regularly in their homes to check up on the development of their faith): as God's royal priests (Exodus 19:3–6, I Peter 2:9–10—Miskotte sprinkles Scripture references throughout his writings), we must be vigilant not to turn God's Church into a cozy, ingrown fellowship, and remember Christ's admonition to be not honey in the world, but to be the "salt of the earth" (Matthew 5:13).

Introducing Biblical Hermeneutics: A Comprehensive Framework for Hearing God in Scripture by Craig G. Bartholomew

Although I am not a theologian by profession, the contours of my own biblical theology are well articulated by Gordon J. Spykman, *Reformational Theology: A New Paradigm for Doing Dogmatics* (Grand Rapids: Eerdmans, 1992) and by Craig G. Bartholomew, *Introducing Biblical Hermeneutics. A Comprehensive Framework for Hearing God in Scripture* (Grand Rapids: Baker Academic, 2015). Spykman and Bartholomew have wrestled with the Scriptures, and without jargon and cant present what I would call an Evangelical-Reformational-Catholic biblical vision for living our lives before the face of God: the marvelous good creation is a burning bush of the covenantal LORD God's glory; evil powers and our human sin historically obstruct God's gift of shalom; the saving lordship of Jesus Christ is indeed coming, so the Holy Spirited faithful followers of Jesus Christ gratefully work out their salvation, despite persecution, as we expectantly anticipate the Lord's return (Revelation 1:9).

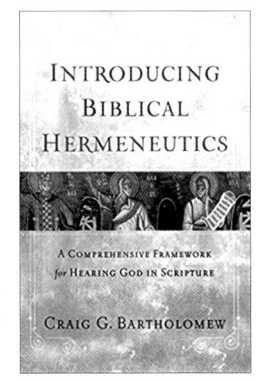

This biblical theology includes Augustine's self-incriminating, fraught confession: *Da mihi castitatem et continentiam, sed noli modo* ("Give me chastity and continence, [O Lord,] but not yet!") (*Confessions* 8.17). This biblical perspective breathes what I learned from the mouth of Karl Barth: "Don't talk Jesus, and then talk Christ. The truth is always Jesus Christ together, the mediating God-man Saviour of the world." And this committed biblical testimony of mine goes back to the truth of Jean Calvin's witness in the *Institutes of the Christian Religion*, written for ordinary believers and any curious not-yet believers: *Omnis recta dei cognitio ab obedientia nascitur* (I.6.2) "All right knowledge of God is born out of obedience."

Endnotes

1 Martin Buber, *Between Man and Man*, translated by Ronald Gregor Smith (New York: Macmillan, 1947), 52.
2 Buber, *Israel and Palestine. The History of an Idea* (London: East and West Library, 1952), 142.
3 "The Confessing Church" developed during the 1930s in opposition to the "German Christian" Protestant pastors who were pro National Socialist programs and regulations. Martin Niemoller and Karl Barth helped "the Confessing Church" take shape, and Bonhoeffer became a leader as the Nazi government increased punitive restrictions on its underground existence.
4 *Als de goden zwijgen. Over de zin van de Oud Testament* (1956), translated by John W. Doberstein (New York: Harper & Row, 1967). The English (and German) translation omits and expands sections of the original Dutch version, and is considered the definitive form of the work.

COOKING
Andi Ashworth

I LOVE TO ROAM THE FOOD WRITING SECTION of a bookstore, thumbing through cookbooks and looking for the latest cooking memoir. Though my kitchen shelves are nearly full, I can always squeeze in another book of recipes or something educational and fun to read like Michael Pollan's *Cooked*. I feel a kinship with people who work with food and spend untold hours in the kitchen. I'm drawn to their stories like a magnet. I savored *Bread and Wine*, Shauna Niequist's collection of essays about life around the table. I read *Blood, Bones and Butter* twice, Gabrielle Hamilton's memoir of becoming a chef and creating her restaurant, Prune. I remember the days after Christmas in 2006 because of Julia Child's *My Life in France*, written with her husband's grandnephew, Alex Prud'homme. I stayed in my pajamas and read on the couch, in front of the fire, tucked up in bed. I was sick and the book transformed my memories of that week. And when it seemed like everyone from church folks, to home cooks and chefs, to literary people were rediscovering the utterly delightful and unique *The Supper of the Lamb* by Episcopal priest and cook Robert Farrar Capon, I bought a copy. First published in 1969, it was chosen to be a part of the Modern Library Food Series and republished in 2002. I read it slowly, taking it in over months, underlining sentences, paragraphs, and whole pages, absorbing Father Capon's whimsical and wise love of creation and the pleasures of cooking and eating. In his preface to the second and third editions, he wrote,

> . . . it was God who invented dirt, onions and turnip greens; God who invented human beings, with their strange compulsion to cook their food; God who, at the end of each day of creation, pronounced a resounding "Good!" over his own concoctions . . . Food is not just some fuel we need to get us going toward higher things. Cooking is not a drudgery we put up with in order to get fuel delivered. Rather,

each is a heart's astonishment. Both stop us dead in our tracks with wonder. Even more, they sit us down evening after evening, and in the company that forms around our dinner tables, they actually create our humanity.[1]

One of the many reasons I'm drawn to Byron and Beth Borger is their insatiable appetite to read widely and expose their customers to books that range across the whole of life. In his *BookNotes* reviews, I love that Byron includes the latest books on home, cooking, creation care, food justice, sustainable agriculture, and hospitality, as well as referring readers to older classics. In the April 21, 2012 *BookNotes* post titled "Food, Faith, and Feasting: Books about Faith and Food," he wrote:

> Although I suppose some Christian bookstores don't have sections on creation care or even cookbooks, I sure can't imagine why. There is a lot in the Bible about food and feasting, about farming and famine. We simply must allow our faith to inform our principles and practices in this side of life.

In the same post Byron mentioned Edith Schaeffer's book, *The Hidden Art of Homemaking*, as "an early voice helping evangelicals, at least, see that homemaking and cooking and sustaining a household with creativity is serious, spiritual business, a human art, to be offered in hospitality to our loved ones, neighbors, and even strangers." Edith's books were crucial in helping me understand the meaning of caring for human life, and her inspiration was partly what led me to cookbooks. I needed help for the work God was calling me to.

I entered marriage at the age of nineteen, armed with only a green plastic file box of Betty Crocker recipe cards, and no knowledge of my future work. I was a blooming feminist and wannabe hippie, eating stir-fry with tofu cross-legged on the floor with my husband, clueless about the nurturing arts or the work of sustaining a household. But as marriage turned into motherhood, and family making turned into a vocation steeped in the work of hospitality, I grew into the challenge. I came to respect the kitchen as a powerful and healing place to labor, to understand that cooking skill and food knowledge are deeply connected to Christ's teachings about feeding the hungry, and to know that however God might lead me to participate in caring for His world, it would always begin in my own household.

In our mid-thirties, my husband and I moved our family from California to Nashville, and then to a century-old church we made into our home, recording studio, and community gathering space. Chuck named it The Art House and

What Cooking Books You Should Read & Why

we welcomed friends and strangers most days. In that beautiful place I became a unique version of family cook, bed and breakfast provider for houseguests, and caterer for in-house projects and events: recording sessions, artist retreats, songwriter weeks, video shoots, and special evenings open to our city. After twenty-five years of service, we now live in a different setting where large-scale hospitality is no longer my daily reality, but cooking remains, and with it my reliance on cookbooks.

Cookbooks are my tools, my inspiration, and my teachers. They help me answer the ever-present questions that travel with me through life: What should I make for dinner? What should I make for a birthday meal, for Thanksgiving, for dessert on the porch with friends?

The Breakfast Book by Marion Cunningham

One day this past April as the university school year was coming to a close, I got up early and went to the kitchen. As the coffee brewed I surveyed the counter where I'd laid out tools and baking ingredients the night before: bowls, wooden spoons, measuring cups, flour, butter, lemons, apples. My husband's songwriting students were coming later that morning and I'd instinctively thought of welcoming them with Raw Apple Muffins and Lemon Yogurt Muffins from *The Breakfast Book* by Marion Cunningham. I've made them both countless times for every kind of reason and they're always a hit. The apple muffins are especially easy to make with very little notice. I've pulled a rabbit out of the hat many times for a morning meeting in our living room or a tracking session in the studio. If I have two apples in the fridge, it's likely I have everything else on hand: sugar, eggs, oil, vanilla extract, flour, baking soda, salt, and cinnamon.

I bought *The Breakfast Book* soon after it was published in 1987 and began using it for my family and for special events. I made Classic Waffles, Bridge Creek Oatmeal Pancakes with buttermilk and oats, Fresh Ginger Muffins, and Apple Pancake, an eggy pancake with apples sautéed in butter that becomes golden and fluffy in the oven. When my daughter Molly was growing up, she often woke up early on Saturday mornings to create a family breakfast restaurant called Musician's Café. With the help of her little brother as wait staff, she made handwritten menus and used whatever she could find in the refrigerator and cupboards to feed us. She drew heavily from *The Breakfast Book* and always offered Cuban Orange Juice from the Breakfast Beverages chapter (1/2 cup orange juice, 1/2 milk, optional: 1 egg. Blend until smooth and frothy, and serve cold).

My well-loved copy of the book shows the marks of thirty years of use. Whole sections are loosed from the binding, favorite recipes are starred, and pages are crinkled and food-stained. The recipe for Cinnamon Butter Puffs, a muffin that tastes like a cinnamon-sugar donut, has a note at the top of the page referring to a family get-together for my husband and son-in-law: *Triple the recipe for 2013 August birthday brunch.*

Over the years I've added recipes from other sources to my list of breakfast standards, but I've never come across another cookbook quite like this one. The recipes range across every conceivable breakfast idea, from scones to granola, from omelets and frittatas to potato dishes, from meats and fish to fruit preserves, from breakfast beverages to Judith Jones' recipe for homemade yogurt. With its warm, inviting cover, its artful drawings of food and cooking scenes, and the wonderful quotes that are sprinkled throughout the pages, there is no other book I know of that so beautifully highlights the morning meal. Marion Cunningham's introduction explains why she chose to focus on breakfast:

> The deeper reason that breakfast inspires me is that we have become so busy maintaining our lives in the working world that we often find ourselves sharing the same house with strangers. The meaning of "home" has disappeared. Surveys report that families no longer sit down together for the evening meal. Eating is a lonely experience for many, and we can be lonely without even knowing it sometimes. Standing up by a microwave oven, or refrigerator, or in front of the TV, automatically eating, leaves out a precious human element from our lives...If it is true that dinner is becoming a solitary, fast-feed-yourself experience, I'm hoping that breakfast, with its easy, wholesome honesty, will be an opportunity to be with and share oneself with friends and family. There is no greater inducement to conversation than sitting around a table and sharing a good meal."[2]

The Family Dinner: Great Ways to Connect With Your Kids, One Meal at a Time by Laurie David

Thirty years after Ms. Cunningham wrote her introduction, the loss of the family table has become a national conversation, taken up in places as diverse as the *New York Times,* National Public Radio, the *Christian Science Monitor,* and the American College of Pediatricians website. A few years ago I was preparing to give a talk on "The Family Table" at a gathering inspired by Arthur Boer's book, *Living into Focus.* While I was in the note-taking stage I learned of Laurie David's book, *The Family Dinner: Great Ways to Connect With Your Kids One Meal at a Time.* I mention it briefly as a well-researched, warm, and fun resource on why the family table matters and how to create it. The book is chock-full of recipes (meals that can be put together quickly as well as those that take more time), conversation starters and games for the table, ideas for cooking with kids, tips on keeping a greener kitchen, discussion topics and possibilities for reading around the table, the importance of gathering with grandparents and extended family, and a thoughtful chapter on continuing mealtime rituals after a divorce. It's a book I would have gone crazy for when I was raising kids, but it still has so much to offer me as a grandmother. For anyone who struggles with keeping a family table given the pace and overwhelming nature of modern life, this book is a goldmine.

Chez Panisse Pasta, Pizza, and Calzone by Alice Waters

One weekend in the early 1980s as my eyes were opening to the creative and meaningful world of the culinary arts, I drove from Sacramento to San Francisco with my children to spend time with our dear friend, chef, and restaurant consultant, Kathi Riley Smith. After tucking the kids in the first night, I plucked Alice Waters' *Chez Panisse Pasta, Pizza, and Calzone* cookbook off Kathi's kitchen shelf and took it with me for bedtime reading. I'd never read through a cookbook before and only knew of Alice Waters through Kathi. I was intrigued and inspired by her writing. She encouraged readers to let the harvest of seasonal, fresh, and local ingredients inspire the menu. Alice and her restaurant Chez Panisse were early pioneers of what is now commonplace: the farm to table movement. As I turned the pages, I saw recipes with foods I hadn't yet heard of and sometimes couldn't pronounce: prosciutto, pancetta, tagliatelle, fava beans, pesto, Nicoise olives, radicchio, and chanterelles. She used virgin olive oil, fresh herbs, and fresh garlic. I only knew of dried herbs in a jar and garlic salt. Despite all that was foreign to me, the book was friendly to read and contained an explanation of ingredients and cooking terms in the back. I picked up a copy of my own when I went home and began to cook from it.

The Classic Italian Cookbook by Marcella Hazan

Soon after, I bought Marcella Hazan's *The Classic Italian Cookbook* through a cookbook-of-the-month club. As I read, I learned that the image of Italian food I'd grown up with (spaghetti, lasagna, and pizza) is only the tip of the iceberg. Italy's cooking is vast and changes from region to region, according to geography and climate, whether in the mountainous regions, valleys, or by the sea. Marcella placed the home cook at the center of the best Italian cooking. "There probably has been no influence, not even religion, so effective in creating a rich family life, in maintaining a civilized link between the generations, as this daily sharing of a common joy. Eating in Italy is essentially a family art, practiced for and by the family."[3]

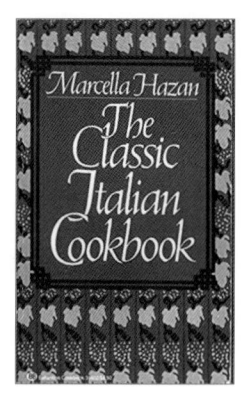

The Classic Italian Cookbook is organized by sauces, antipasti, first courses, second courses, vegetables, salads, the cheese course, desserts, and fruit. The instructions are clear, detailed, and easy to understand. As I moved through the book, I sautéed veal chops with sage and white wine, and tried Mushroom and Cheese Salad, a delicious but unlikely pairing of white mushrooms and Swiss cheese tossed with olive oil, lemon juice, salt, and pepper. I made Lentil Soup with pancetta or prosciutto, onion, celery, carrot, canned Italian tomatoes, and broth. I learned to make risotto and polenta, which became staples in our household. I tried the simple deliciousness of sautéing fresh spinach or Swiss chard in olive oil and garlic, and I stopped using bottled salad dressing. Instead, I learned to dress lettuces with salt, olive oil, good wine vinegar, and pepper, the way Marcella taught, sometimes substituting lemon juice for the vinegar.

What Cooking Books You Should Read & Why 47

These days, I often add a tiny smash of garlic, some fresh minced herbs, or a bit of Dijon mustard, but Marcella's method is always the foundation.

This cookbook contains some recipes I will most likely never try since the foods are too distant from what I know. I'll leave Sweetbreads Braised with Tomatoes and Peas, or Fried Calf's Brains, to someone whose family of origin or cultural experience predisposes them to a more courageous palate. But when I want an excellent meat sauce Bolognese style, or a simple pan-roasted chicken with garlic, rosemary, and white wine, I'll open *The Classic Italian Cookbook* and get to it.

After Marcella Hazan's death in 2013, David Sipress wrote a tribute to her in *The New Yorker*. He described her as a "short, compact lady, a tough biscotti with a raspy voice who didn't suffer fools gladly and had a surprising preference for Jack Daniels over a glass of wine. But in her books her voice is always warm and encouraging. This, and the fact that her recipes are consistently clear and straightforward, enabled me to overcome a lifetime of insecurity in the kitchen."[4]

The Classic Italian Cookbook is true to its name. It is a classic, worthy of the attention of anyone seeking to learn what the book's title page describes: the art of Italian cooking and the Italian art of eating. It's been an invaluable addition to my education and I return to it often.

The Art of Simple Food:
Notes, Lessons, and Recipes from
a Delicious Revolution by Alice Waters

Many years after opening *Chez Panisse Pizza, Pasta, and Calzone* for the first time, I was fully immersed in my Art House vocation, preparing to feed the crew for a live concert/video shoot my husband was directing in our home. As I often did when thinking through the menu for a crowd, I called Kathi to get precise directions for roasting large amounts of pork loin. After talking me through the steps she recommended Judy Rodgers' *The Zuni Café Cookbook* and Alice Waters' *The Art of Simple Food* as excellent and trustworthy resources for basic cooking instructions. I already owned *The Zuni Café Cookbook,* but I immediately bought *The Art of Simple Food.* It is now the book I turn to when I need to know how to do most anything: braise chicken legs, roast a piece of salmon, make croutons, pan fry a pork chop and make a quick pan sauce, or bake vanilla custard. *The Art of Simple Food* is not encyclopedic like *The Joy of Cooking* (still a fantastic and far-reaching resource), but I love its elegance and philosophy, the emphasis on starting with good ingredients, ideas for stocking the pantry and planning menus, the wealth of essential cooking techniques, and the pure pleasure of cooking and sharing food that comes through Alice's writing. It's a beautiful resource from a woman who's had a mighty influence on American cooking.

One fall when overcast days and lowering temperatures put me in the mood for comfort food, I looked through *The Art of Simple Food* for inspiration and found the beef stew recipe I've used ever since. It's deeply flavored, rich, and hearty. The recipe begins by browning cubed beef chuck in bacon fat, then sautéing onion quarters with two whole cloves inserted into the flesh, chunks of carrots, fresh thyme, savory, parsley, and a bay leaf. Next you add diced tomatoes (fresh or canned), a small head of chopped garlic, one thin strip of orange zest, red wine, and beef stock or chicken broth (homemade adds to the intensity of flavor). As one does when personalizing a recipe over time, I add my own touches: fresh rosemary and other vegetables like celery, potatoes, mushrooms, turnips, or rutabagas. Alice often gives a short list of variations at the end of her recipes, ideas for changing or adding ingredients. The first time I made this stew I stirred in small, pitted black olives at the end of cooking as she suggested, using briny Kalamatas. It sounds like an odd addition, but it is delicious. Last winter I made a pot to deliver to my neighbors down the street. Not knowing them well at the time, I packed the olives separately with a note: *throw them in if you feel adventurous!* They took me up on it, added the olives, and said it was the best stew they'd ever eaten.

The Barefoot Contessa Cookbook by Ina Garten

Along with Marion Cunningham, Alice Waters, and Marcella Hazan, Ina Garten's cookbooks have enjoyed a wide influence. I first came to know her through a column she wrote for *Martha Stewart Living* magazine titled "Entertaining is Fun." She provided tips and menus for a relaxed style of hospitality that I appreciated. I was always looking for more ideas to provide for the many people coming through our doors, so I quickly bought Ina's first book, *The Barefoot Contessa Cookbook*. Published in 1999, it was the first of what is now a line of ten cookbooks. Every other fall a new one appears just in time for Christmas. I own them all but I have my favorites, the ones that helped me through years of intense hospitality and whose recipes still remain classics in my cooking repertoire. *Barefoot Contessa Parties* and *Barefoot Contessa Family Style* have the marks of heavy usage, but *The Barefoot Contessa Cookbook* is where I often begin when I'm looking for ideas to host an occasion or make a menu for an ordinary week. It's impossible to say how many times I've made Ina's Homemade Granola, Roasted-Tomato Basil Soup, Perfect Roast Chicken, or Guacamole. Most weeks I roast seasonal vegetables tossed simply in olive oil, salt, and pepper, as I learned from her. I use Ina's recipe for Peach and Raspberry Crisp at least once a summer (freely substituting blackberries or blueberries). I've taken Indonesian Ginger Chicken to friends who just had a baby, and last fall it was the center of the menu for my granddaughter's thirteenth birthday dinner.

I return to the Barefoot Contessa cookbooks again and again because of Ina's no-fuss recipes and their easy-to-find ingredients. Though I've used the original book more than the others, I do view them all as a set, a wealth of ideas and recipes to draw from. I've made Strawberry Country Cake from *Barefoot Contessa Parties*, Lasagna with Turkey Sausage from *Barefoot Contessa Family Style*, Winter Slaw with kale, radicchio, and Brussels sprouts from *Make it Ahead*, Cheese Straws from *Barefoot in Paris*, and Herb-Marinated Loin of Pork from *Back to Basics*. I've tweaked some of the recipes to fit my preferences; for example, using less butter or oil when the amount asked for seems too heavy-handed, or leaving dried fruit out of the granola recipe after learning by experimentation that the granola would stay crunchier without it. For years I made double batches every few weeks, adding cinnamon, exchanging the sliced almonds for a mixture of chopped pecans, cashews, and almonds, and once in a while adding a little pure maple syrup to the honey and oil mixture. As I made small changes to fit my tastes, I came to think of it as Art House Granola, the perfect solution to the needs of our unique household.

My kitchen shelves contain cookbooks I'm just beginning to explore, like the beautiful, inspiring series *Canal House Cooking* by Christopher Hirsheimer and Melissa Hamilton, and Yotam Ottolenghi's vegetable cookbook *Plenty*. But I chose to highlight the cookbooks that have had a shaping influence in my life, and that I think are worthy of an important place in any cook's library. These books gave me clear instructions, helped form my palate, schooled me on foods and flavors that sit well together on the plate, gave me basic recipes from which to fly on my own, helped shape my imagination for the endless creativity surrounding one of life's most basic needs, and expressed care for the hospitality and joy of gathering people to the table.

Whether these cookbook writers have understood their love of food and cooking as Father Capon did, I don't know, but because of what I've learned from them, I understand his words more clearly. "It will be precisely because we loved Jerusalem enough to bear it in our bones that its textures will ascend when we rise; it will be because our eyes have relished the earth that the color of its countries will compel our hearts forever. The bread and the pastry, the cheeses, the wine, and the songs go into the Supper of the Lamb because we do: It is our love that brings the City home." [5]

Endnotes

1. Robert Farrar Capon, *The Supper of the Lamb: A Culinary Reflection* (New York: The Modern Library, 2002), xxvi.
2. Marion Cunningham, *The Breakfast Book* (New York: Alfred A. Knopf, 1987), xi-xii.
3. Marcella Hazan, *The Classic Italian Cook Book* (New York: Alfred A. Knopf, 1980), 5.
4. David Sipress, "Marcella Hazan Saved My Life," *The New Yorker*, September 30, 2013, http://www.newyorker.com/culture/culture-desk/marcella-hazan-changed-my-life.
5. Capon, *The Supper of the Lamb*, 190.

creation care

Byron Borger

IT WAS A YEAR AGO THAT THE MOMENTOUS OIL LEAK in the Gulf Coast exploded onto the national scene, with pictures and videos and news reports and prayer services and a stunning amount of day by day information. I am sure you, too, would say it was hard not to be upset about it. Like other similar, terrible days in our memory—the Exxon Valdez oil spill, Three Mile Island, Chernobyl, Bhopal—I had so many mixed emotions as the disasters were reported and the damage became known. This time, for me, I felt less righteous anger and more deep sadness. Less a desire to rise up for social change and more paralyzed fear and hopelessness (not cynicism or apathy, really, just inertia. Perhaps I yielded to what the ancients called the sin of sloth—not laziness, really, but an inability to trust God, to rouse one's self to faithfulness. I wanted to write a bit about it—it is at least something I could do, alerting our friends who read our *BookNotes* blog. Alas, I could not.

Now the Japanese nuclear reactors are spilling their poison all over the seas, the wind carrying the low-level radiation who knows where. There are the standard government cover-ups, the outright lies, the technological optimists who naturally have a gizmo for every social sin. And then there are the witless folks complaining about the media coverage, as if they know that radiation ain't that bad. They are wrong. Heaven help us.

And this week, those taken with a similar spirit of technological optimism and cavalier attitudes about poison-sharing are minimizing a crisis here in our own beloved state of Pennsylvania. Our backyard nuke plant, TMI, recently failed (another) safety test. One of our own Pennsylvania Congressmen helped lead the charge in Congress to weaken the Clean Water Act. And the natural gas industry has discovered quick and easy ways to obtain the natural gas deposits by "fracking." You most likely have heard of the documentary *Gasland* (some of it set in Pennsylvania) showing the dangers of this; the scene of fire coming out of the water spigot is enough to give anybody pause. What in the heck are these guys thinking, supposing that such groundwater pollution is acceptable? Our new governor, elected in part by beloved neighbors of mine, is giving these guys the green light for big time drilling—even in state game reserves.

That is, until last week when a blowout in Bradford County spilled tainted water into farmlands and streams. The most polluted was Towanda Creek, which runs directly into the mighty Susquehanna, which runs into the Chesapeake Bay. And as the spill in Pennsylvania continues its toxic flow (relatively small, compared to the large Gulf oil disaster), a bit of attention is now being given to the other unsavory practices of these slick natural gas guzzlers—like the controversial practice of dumping waste into rivers. Even our not-very-green Republican administration this week has called on drillers to stop, as an Associated Press journalist put it, "using riverside treatment plants to get rid of the millions of barrels of ultra-salty, chemically tainted wastewater that gush from gas wells."

You've seen *Erin Brockovitch*. You surely know that these sorts of tragedies do not happen in an ideological, political, or economic vacuum. The Bible teaches that there are "principalities and powers," and it is also clear that we shape cultures based on our deepest idols. For better or for worse, either we image the true Creator God or we reflect other false ideologies. Environmental accidents are not just technological mishaps, but are injustices that occur amidst political decisions, business practices, worldview assumptions, ethical choices, philosophical ideas, and leadership failures. They are results of our way of life, based on our ultimate beliefs about things. Former Dutch Parliament member and Christian economist Dr. Bob Goudzwaard and his co-authors in *Hope for Troubled Times: A New Vision for Confronting Global Crisis* are surely right to link ideology and idolatry as we discern the interrelatedness of the symptoms and the most root cause of social breakdown. Granted, often things are not simplistic and there aren't usually simple "good guys and bad guys" wearing their own white or black hats. That is not to say that there are not good and bad guys sometimes; there surely are. And sometimes they are one and the same.

All of which is to say, again and again, that as God's people, the church community must be aware of the issues of the day—*a la* the sons of Issachar of 1 Chronicles 12:23. We must be vigilant to be agents of gospel transformation, and must be voices of justice, also for the land itself. There are Christians these days on the front lines serving the poor, doing third world mission trips,

What Creation Care Books You Should Read & Why 53

and calling for a holistic faith lived out in action—but they have not been quite so active in engaging the complexities of public policy and structural reformation. Which is why we regularly recommend books about culture and social transformation, titles that help us think broadly about our involvement in God's world, like the aforementioned Goudzwaard title, Andy Crouch's truly delightful and very helpful *Culture Making*, and James Davison Hunter's much discussed *To Change the World*.

It should be evident that the Bible teaches what might be called a green theology—a strong emphasis on the doctrine of creation (what Calvin called "the theatre of God"). At Easter we recall that Christ's bodily resurrection points to a new creation that certainly includes a renewed call to care for the earth. N.T. Wright's *Surprised By Hope* gets at this, as do fine books like Albert Wolter's *Creation Regained* or Michael Witmer's very nice *Heaven Is A Place On Earth*. Stewardship and development of the potentials of a good (if fallen) creation are central to a Christian way of seeing life. As we celebrate God's good creation, confess our sinful role in adding to the dysfunction of a fallen world, and affirm that only Christ can rescue us (we cannot do it ourselves) and that He does His restoring work on the cross, we realize that at the very heart of Christian theology is a serious, nonnegotiable commitment to care for the world God has entrusted to us, the world that we messed up and that He has graciously saved. Empowered by the Spirit, under the authority of the now ascended King, we are to humbly go about our business, in deeds of humility, reclaiming God's world from brokenness and despair (and, yes, pollution and degradation.) We are to reclaim that original cultural mandate, nicely summarized in Genesis 2:15, to tend and keep the garden. Part of what it means to be human is to not only be a fellow-creature but to be a caretaker of it all.

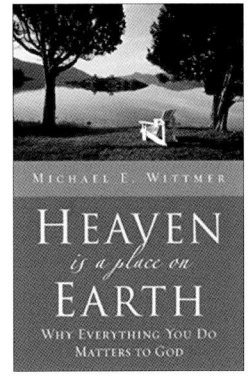

So, here are some books about all this. We have more. Too many, actually, for a sensible business, since so few sell. We hope you understand our desire to be known as a place that desires to glorify God by making available these kinds of books, because we believe they do glorify God; creation care pleases Jesus, who obviously spoke often of plants, and counseled us to "consider the lilies." This is faithful, urgent, important stuff.

Thanks for caring.

Surprises Around the Bend: 50 Adventurous Walkers edited by Richard Hasler

We've really enjoyed this nice collection of excerpts from journals written by famous hikers, naming their joy, their insight, their motivation, their struggles, and their discoveries. A spirituality of hiking? Check out these stories by Francis of Assisi, John Bunyan, Johnny Appleseed, John Muir, James Michener, Thomas Merton, Toyohiko Kagawa, Martin Luther King, Jr., Henry Thoreau, of course, and dozens more. Even includes reflections by Dietrich Bonhoeffer, Mother Teresa, and C.S. Lewis. Take this in your day pack on your next adventure.

All Creation Sings: The Voice of God in Nature by J. Ellsworth Kalas

Rev. Kalas is renowned as a basic Bible study leader, a prolific author of nice books used in adult ed classes or for basic Christian growth. He is the former President of Asbury Theological Seminary and is a fine writer. Here he turns his attention to what the Bible says—and, wow, does it say a lot—about the way in which creation speaks God's voice. Consider this, among other things, an extended meditation on Psalm 19:1. Or a reflection on the hymn "This Is My Father's World," from which the title is taken. It is a core Bible teaching that we don't hear much about. Very nice, with good discussion questions making it very appropriate for a study group, Bible class, reading group, or for adult Sunday school use.

To Garden With God by Christine Sine

My, how I respect Tom and Christine Sine, who have joyfully networked folks for years, forming and sustaining communities that think missionally, practice spiritual disciplines, serve the poor, create faithful liturgies, and—yep—garden like mad. This emerges out of more than fifteen years of gardening experience and offers practical advice, fascinating stories, and solid spiritual lessons about God's good creation.

Serve God, Save the Planet: A Christian Call to Action by J. Matthew Sleeth

This is especially recommended for being upbeat, interesting, fairly short, quite easy to follow, and with good discussion questions. Thoroughly evangelical, compelling, offering a lot of inspiring ideas.

Green Revolution: Coming Together to Care for Creation by Ben Lowe

This is the best book on this topic I've read all year—engaging, serious, enjoyable, and full of great testimonies from folks (especially in evangelical colleges) who are doing so very much on this issue. A cool foreword by Shane Claiborne illustrates its progressively evangelical vibe. I can't say enough about this energetic new voice and this excellent introduction to creation care, local activism, stuff that can be done, and projects that cry out to be done.

Tending to Eden: Environmental Stewardship for God's People by Scott Sabin

There are a number of reasons why this fine work might be the best choice for a starter study; it really does have a fresh voice, and provides good attention to global concerns, showing the connections between poverty and ecology. I like the "step aside with" sections, which are nice introductions to people you should know, inspiring vignettes about Robert Linthicum, Matthew Sleeth, Calvin DeWitt, JoAnne Lyon, Leroy Barbar, Rusty Pritchard, *et al.*

For the Beauty of the Earth: A Christian Vision for Creation Care by Steven Bouma-Prediger

In recent years I am quick to say this is my favorite book on the subject; perhaps I should say the best semi-scholarly book. It is truly a masterpiece—meaty, thoughtful, Biblically-wise and very, very important, for being both solid and reliable and, at times, a bit creative and fresh. Perhaps a bit more than a typical book club or Sunday school class might want, but a "must-read" for leaders and anyone truly serious about the topic. Bouma-Prediger is a science professor at Hope College and has written several other important books, though *For the Beauty* is truly his life's work, and is a must for those wanting to be well-read on the topic.

Christianity, Climate Change and Sustainable Living by Nick Spencer, Robert White, and Virginia Vroblesky

Wow, what a book! Spencer is a thoughtful and reliable theologian who runs a think tank on public theology (in the UK) while White is an esteemed science professor at Cambridge University—not too shabby, eh? Ms. Vroblesky is the former National Coordinator of the esteemed evangelical creation care group A Rocha, a group we love, with a faith-based, activist bent. Good, good, stuff! This is timely, balanced, helpful, and enjoyable, although not what I'd call introductory or simple. A rave endorsement from Steven Bouma-Prediger illustrates that this is a book of much, much substance. One of the best.

Walking Gently on the Earth: Making Faithful Choices about Food, Energy, Shelter and More by Lisa Graham McMinn and Megan Anna Neff

Please, please give this wonderful book a chance— it is hopeful and interesting and mature and wise. And captivating. It deserves a large readership, should be a best seller. Let me tell you why: it is honest, real, beautifully written, theologically clear and yet poetically inspiring, and it is hopeful. It has few easy answers, invites deeper conversation, is broad and profound and practical in the very best sense. It is more than a field guide for faithful living (although in many ways it is one) and it is more than tirade against pesticides and sweatshops. It looks nicely and thoughtfully at alternative energy sources and wonders about how we should arrange our families, our lifestyles, our neighborhoods as we walk through an unjust world. Very provocative and much to ponder. Ben Lowe says of *Walking Gently on the Earth:* "By challenging how we see the world, [McMinn and Neff] help us understand, in practical ways, that balance is a thing of beauty, and that celebration and stewardship go hand in hand."

It is my hunch that we will rarely care much about stuff we take little delight in. We must pray that God shapes our desires and that we come to appreciate creation—it is God's handiwork, after all, and we dare not be cavalier about the things He made, sustains, and says is good. Gee, you've read the end of Job, haven't you? Or the long zoological Psalm 104? So get a few of these nice books to help yourself to enjoy the awesome wonder of this world and to remember our calling to blessed creation care.

Adapted from Learning to Love What God Loves: Creation Care and Christian Discipleship, *a much longer* BookNotes *review posted on April 26, 2011.*

Creative Nonfiction
Gregory Wolfe

CREATIVE NONFICTION AS A LITERARY GENRE is a little like a trending Hollywood star: it's basking in the glow of enormous popularity but inwardly it's wracked by doubts about its true identity.

It's been that way from the beginning. I mean, think about it: literature starts with poetry and drama—you know, Homer, Aeschylus, and Co.? Then in the eighteenth century the novel makes its debut and becomes everybody's darling: from Dickens to Dostoevsky and from Fielding to Flannery O'Connor, the novel is touted as the great civilizational achievement—the narrative art that simultaneously encapsulates the world and provides us with profound insights into it.

Where does creative nonfiction fit into this tale? The name of the genre is already unprepossessing. Nonfiction defines itself not by what it is but by what it's not. With such a shaky start, adding the word "creative" feels like putting a teacher's gold star on a C- test score.

What had nonfiction meant for a couple thousand years? Generally speaking, it meant prose about things that were not made up. That would include works of history and biography, the fundamental records of national and cultural legacies. These were modes of human thought that valued truth, facts, and reason. What really happened at the battle of Themopylae? What did Caesar say when he crossed the Rubicon?

This sort of record-keeping had great dignity, of course, but as early as Aristotle's *Poetics*, poetry and drama were given a higher place in the literary pantheon. In that work, Aristotle famously said of history and poetry: "But they differ in this, that the one speaks of things which have happened, and the other of such as might have happened. Hence, poetry is more philosophic, and more deserving of attention, than history. For poetry speaks more of universals, but history of particulars."

Poor particulars. They seem so humdrum compared to the free-ranging speculations of philosophy and poetry that can skip and leap up into the empyrean realm of universal truths. Thus, nonfiction from the early days has come with the baggage of the mundane and the whiff of mere utility.

But with all due respect to the titanic brain of Aristotle, the fact is that his distinction has done much to obscure our understanding of how great writing works. We've always known, for example, that history and biography employ narrative, just like epic poetry and drama. Narrative is anchored in concrete particulars, revels in deep structures that may not be immediately visible to the casual reader, and requires a mastery of description and dialogue, not to mention rendering convincing characters who live and breathe on the page. And what about the beauty of finely crafted sentences? Back in the olden days when we started Latin in public middle schools, we read Caesar's *Gallic Wars* in part because of the elegant simplicity of his syntax.

In short, the greatest works of nonfiction use an almost identical toolset to that found in fiction. That means they've always been "creative."

I SPY: POINT OF VIEW

Well and good. But now I have to step back and admit that there is a plausible argument for considering creative nonfiction to be a more recent—and more amorphous—genre than either fiction or poetry.

At the heart of much of what's commonly meant by creative nonfiction is the "I"—that is, the presence of the authorial perspective, not only in terms of point of view but also in the sense of the emotional urgency of the author and her particular predicaments.

And that's a phenomenon that's relatively modern. With the Renaissance and Reformation era came a new emphasis on the individual as protagonist of his own story. Prior to this time period, nonfiction that included a personal dimension was rare, the major example being Augustine's *Confessions*. That book, perhaps the first true memoir, was written in the form of a prayer, and yet even though it is addressed to God it remains deeply revealing about Augustine's personality.

The *Confessions* was not like Caesar's *Gallic Wars*: it did not recount the external deeds of a powerful public figure. Rather, it related the intimate details of a private individual who was born and raised on the fringes of the Roman

Empire. Augustine writes about stealing the fruit from a pear tree as a boy, but he treats it with the same *gravitas* as Caesar's crossing the Rubicon.

It isn't until the sixteenth century, with the advent of Michel de Montaigne, that nonfiction with an intimately personal voice and perspective makes an appearance. Montaigne's particular form, the essay, derives from a word meaning "at attempt." That is a characteristic note with Montaigne and his ilk moving forward. Writing here is thought of not as the setting down of previously considered and settled ideas but as fundamentally exploratory in nature. The contemporary memoir writer, Patricia Hampl, has said: "I don't write about what I know: I write in order to find out what I know."

Montaigne wrote about everything from cannibalism to his most intimate bodily functions. While his essays cover a wide variety of subjects, he said that in the last analysis "I am myself the matter of my book." Hampl again provides an elegant gloss on this idea: "Memoirists, unlike fiction writers, do not really want to 'tell a story.' They want to tell it all—the all of personal experience, of consciousness itself. That includes a story, but also the whole expanding universe of sensation and thought ... Memoirists wish to tell their mind. Not their story."

Memoir, of course, is only a subset of creative nonfiction, but it is a central one. Even writing that focuses more on the external subject—as much travel and nature writing do, for example—still has an element of subjectivity. So it is fair to say that writing memoir is at least a part of every great personal essay.

But it's precisely here—in the emphasis on subjectivity and the alleged importance of an individual's private experience—that memoir and creative nonfiction in general have come in for heavy criticism. In the past two decades, as memoirs have become more and more revealing of scandal, trauma, and indiscretion—everything from incest to drug use to gang membership has been on display in recent books—a reaction has set in. One of the *New Yorker's* chief critics published an essay a few years ago entitled "But Enough About Me," which included these words:

> Unseemly self-exposures, unpalatable betrayals, unavoidable mendacity, a soupçon of meretriciousness: memoir, for much of its modern history, has been the black sheep of the literary family. Like a drunken guest at a wedding, it is constantly mortifying its soberer relatives (philosophy, history, literary fiction)—spilling family secrets, embarrassing old friends—motivated, it would seem, by an overpowering need to be the center of attention.

There is more than enough fuel for this particular fire, obviously, but there's some evidence that the high-water mark of self-indulgent memoirs may have been reached. The debate will be with us always, because the personal dimension of creative nonfiction, while it offers fabulous rewards for the reader, will continue to dance on the precipice of vanity and self-involvement.

Conversion Stories

For readers of the Christian faith, it might seem that memoir is dangerous territory at best. After all, we have been counseled to lose our lives in order for them to be saved. How can writing about oneself not fall afoul of that admonition?

There's truth to that way of thinking, but there are also surprising twists to be found in this discussion. Let's recall that one of the first great works of creative nonfiction was none other than Augustine's *Confessions*. What made that work so groundbreaking was precisely the conviction underlying it that an ordinary life—any ordinary life—was as precious and dramatic as that of emperors, generals, and bishops. In Augustine's theology, Christ's salvific work means that each of us is eternally important—unique, unrepeatable, and infinitely valuable. Our redemption in Christ means that every human journey can bear witness to the grace and mercy of God—and that the very individuality of each witness adds up to a magnificent symphony of praise and thanksgiving.

Moreover, the *Confessions* contained an intuition that would prove to be central to all later creative nonfiction, whether written by religious believers or not. Augustine's story wasn't self-puffery; it was all about what we in the creative nonfiction business call "self-incrimination." That is, at the heart of all great memoir is the ability of the author to perceive his mistakes, limitations, and faulty judgments. It is this frank admission of one's contingency that helps to form a bond with the reader. We admire the searing honesty of great memoirs because we want to know the truth. We also want a narrator with whom we can identify, because we, too, are contingent beings on a journey toward self-improvement, and we cannot grow without admitting our faults.

It may have taken centuries for writers of faith to follow in Augustine's footsteps, but in due course they did. The historians have reminded us how important spiritual journals were to the early Puritans, for example. Then there are the classic works that have become a part of the literary canon. One such book is *Grace Abounding to the Chief of Sinners,* subtitled *The Brief Relation of the*

Exceeding Mercy of God in Christ to His Poor Servant John Bunyan. Though he was more famous as the author of *Pilgrim's Progress,* Bunyan's *Grace Abounding* was a milestone work in the emerging tradition of Protestant conversion narratives. In the nineteenth century, another landmark book came out of the Roman Catholic experience in the form of John Henry Cardinal Newman's spiritual autobiography, *Apologia Pro Vita Sua,* which recounts his own conversion to the Church of Rome.

In the twentieth century, this form of creative nonfiction reemerged in new and startling ways. Here are a few thoughts about four groundbreaking works in this genre.

The Seven Storey Mountain by Thomas Merton

Just three years after the end of World War II, a young Trappist monk published a memoir entitled *The Seven Storey Mountain.* Within a year, over 100,000 copies of the book were in print. This was hardly an outcome that anyone could have predicted.

The conventional wisdom had it that after the privations of the war Americans wanted nothing more than to enjoy some worldly pleasures. So why did a book about a man's conversion not only to the Roman Catholic Church but to one of the most austere monastic orders suddenly become all the rage? What was this book about and why did it appeal so strongly to readers?

Part of the answer has to be that the conventional wisdom about the postwar period is just plain wrong. Sure, people wanted a respite from rationing, but they were also horrified by the Holocaust and the devastation wrought by the war, and hungry for meaning in the shadow of Hiroshima. Along comes a passionate young man, a graduate of Columbia University and someone at home in the world of literary and intellectual pursuits, who chooses to give up all his privileges and seek a radically different way to live. Someone who could embrace paradox and convey the sense that paradox might contain the richness of divine mystery—that God's voice could best be heard in contemplative silence. Someone who could write of his entry into the Abbey of Gethsemani in Kentucky: "Brother Matthew locked the gate behind me, and I was enclosed in the four walls of my new freedom."

Later in his life, Merton would look back at *The Seven Storey Mountain* and wince at the pietistic and philosophical tone that he saw in it. He was, after all, only twenty-nine when he began writing the book, and it is suffused with the zeal of the convert.

But it is also true to say that the book has an earnestness and passion that continue to speak to readers seventy years later. "I was not sure where I was going, and I could not see what I would do when I got [there]. But you saw further and clearer than I, and you opened the seas before my ship, whose track led me across the waters to a place I had never dreamed of, and which you were even then preparing to be my rescue and my shelter and my home."

In lines like these it is clear that Merton is a true son of his distant forebear, Augustine. The same capacity for fusing rhetoric and spiritual longing is present in the modern monk, as in his ancient father in faith.

Pilgrim at Tinker Creek by Annie Dillard

In 1974, another book by an extremely young writer took off in a way that no one could have imagined. *Pilgrim at Tinker Creek* won its author, Annie Dillard, a Pulitzer Prize at the ripe old age of twenty-six.

If there is a book that puts the "creative" in "creative nonfiction," this is it. Like all great books, it is both unique and original and yet organically tied to a literary tradition. One might say that the book owes a great deal to two great canonical American writers, Ralph Waldo Emerson and Henry David Thoreau. Its most obvious antecedent would be Thoreau's *Walden*, because *Pilgrim* is also a book about the experience of someone living for a year close to nature in what appears to be deep solitude. Like *Walden*, *Pilgrim* embraces not only the minutely observed details of the created order but also the larger philosophical and theological questions that creation poses for us.

Perhaps the crudest term to define *Pilgrim* would be to call it "nature writing," but it is so much more than that. There are readers of Dillard's work who tend to sentimentalize her *oeuvre* a bit, focusing on some of the ecstatic epiphanies the author has in the midst of mountains, streams, and forest groves. But *Pilgrim* is not a book for sentimentalists. The world of nature it reveals is often terrifying, depressing, and almost wholly alien from human sensibilities. In this book shocking, violent, and grotesque things happen by the creek on a daily basis. For example, a frog gets its innards sucked out by a demonic insect. And that's just on page 5.

But it's not all horror. There are epiphanies here and they are shot through with lyric ecstasy. For example: "I had been my whole life a bell, and never knew it until at that moment I was lifted and struck." Or: "Our life is a faint tracing on the surface of mystery, like the idle curved tunnels of leaf miners on the face of a leaf. We must somehow take a wider view, look at the whole landscape, really see it, and describe what's going on here. Then we can at least wail the right question into the swaddling band of darkness, or, if it comes to that, choir the proper praise."

It is worth noting that *Pilgrim* is not an easy book to read and not just because of the rough stuff. It's dense with language and reflection. But that's what makes it a classic: there is a richness of thought in this book that I'm convinced has never been fully appreciated. The biblical allusions and theological ruminations are a mother lode of insight into God, nature, and the human condition. For those who might want to work their way up to *Pilgrim* I would recommend starting with her slim volume, *Holy the Firm*, and the essay collection, *Teaching a Stone to Talk*.

Dakota: A Spiritual Geography by Kathleen Norris

Kathleen Norris these days is best known for her book *The Cloister Walk*, which, like the works of Thomas Merton, is centered around the wisdom and practices of the monastic life. But the book that made her name, and paved the way for dozens of other works of creative nonfiction after it, was *Dakota: A Spiritual Geography*. Taking a page from Dillard, Norris uses the austere landscape of the Dakota plains as her central metaphor and theological touchstone.

Unlike Dillard, who tends to register her impressions but not tell the reader anything significant about her personal life, Norris writes true memoir, in which her story remains the heart of the book. This, too, is a conversion narrative, a tale of faith abandoned in youth and rediscovered in middle age. Norris, like Merton before her, makes a name for herself in the literary circles of the northeast and in particular New York City. And like the Trappist monk before her she finds that world ultimately shallow and self-centered. For Norris is also an Augustinian, feeling the pull of memory—in this case the world of her ancestors, who lived hard lives, guided by faith, in the often harsh and unforgiving environment of the American flatlands.

The key formal aspect of *Dakota* is the way it is structured in short essays, varying in length from a page to a dozen pages. Norris was hardly the first writer to work in the style of the "braided essay," in which a number of interrelated themes are woven through a longer narrative, but she became one of its most distinguished practitioners. Her primary tropes are the landscape, the monastic practices of the Benedictine monks she comes to know and love, and poetry itself as a form of moral and spiritual practice.

In a typical passage, Norris writes: "Maybe the desert wisdom of the Dakotas can teach us to love anyway, to love what is dying, in the face of death, and not pretend that things are other than they are. The irony and wonder of all of this is that it is the desert's grimness, its stillness and isolation, that brings us back to love." Seeing the plains as a desert enables her to connect to the Desert Fathers, those solitary monastics of the early church who withdrew from the hustle and bustle of the city to discover the spiritual riches of silence and contemplation.

Hunger of Memory: The Education of Richard Rodriguez by Richard Rodriguez

Hunger of Memory: The Education of Richard Rodriguez was published in 1982 by the small, independent publisher David R. Godine. While Godine had a long track record of putting out first-rate literary works, its books rarely sold in large numbers. *Hunger of Memory* broke the mold, becoming a book that was both widely admired and politically controversial. It told the story of a first-generation Mexican-American who grew up in the sun-drenched, middle-class world of Sacramento, California. From one perspective, *Hunger* is preoccupied with those categories that have been so important in contemporary discourse: race, class, gender, and ethnicity. But close readers of the book could instantly tell that the tale Rodriguez had to tell steadfastly refused political reductionism.

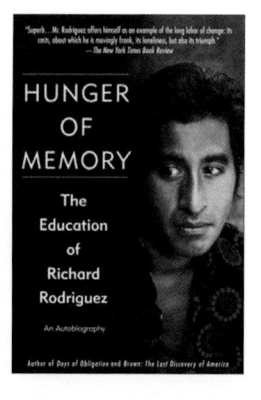

The debate sparked by this book centered around the issues of bilingual education and affirmative action (from which Rodriguez benefited as a college

student). For many in the early 1980s, bilingual education was a political cause, a way of fighting for the right of disadvantaged populations—most prominently, the Hispanic population—to be able to retain the language in which they lived and moved and had their being. But Rodriguez felt that such an approach was both sentimental and counterproductive. He wrote: "Dangerously, [the bilingualists] romanticize public separateness and they trivialize the dilemma of the socially disadvantaged."

But the heart of *Hunger of Memory* was not political; it focused on the glories, ironies, and tragedies of American culture as it faced the fraught and complex task of assimilating populations from other parts of the world. Rodriguez sees both the opportunities that American society offers and the restrictions and hierarchies that impede true freedom. He reserves much of his criticism of American culture for its sentimentality and individualism. He believes the Mexican culture of his parents offers balancing virtues, grounded as they are in community and a worldview that is willing to face the tragic dimensions of a fallen world.

To invoke the concept of a fallen world is not to arbitrarily impose a religious category on Rodriguez's text, for another aspect of the book is the way it affirms the Roman Catholic faith in which he was raised. Rodriguez, like Merton and Norris, demonstrated that he was willing to ruffle the feathers of the cultural elites among whom he traveled by confessing his Christian faith. Here is an example of how he treats religion in the book: "Of all the institutions in their lives, only the Catholic Church has seemed aware of the fact that my mother and father are thinkers—persons aware of the experience of their lives. Other institutions—the nation's political parties, the industries of mass entertainment and communications, the companies that employed them—have all treated my parents with condescension."

In his later books, Rodriguez would come out as a gay man, but throughout his career he has held firmly to his Catholic faith and identity. He does not disguise his anger and frustration with his Church's teachings, but, true to his own vision, he has proven willing to live within a tragic tension rather than do what most of his contemporary intellectuals have done: walk away from, and dismiss, the faith of his youth. Richard Rodriguez may not be the most popular public intellectual in America, but he is certainly one of the most admired. His contributions to creative nonfiction will be recognized for a long time to come.

THE FOURTH GENRE IS HERE TO STAY

Creative nonfiction was for a long time known as the "fourth genre"—the Johnny-come-lately after the grand old literary forms of fiction, drama, and poetry. While individuals may have a personal preference for one literary genre over another, there are few that will dispute that the fourth genre is no longer a second-class citizen (so to speak). Its time has come. It's here to stay.

At a time when "alternative facts" plague our politics and media, writing that attempts to do justice to the complexity and wonder of the world will have an increasingly important role to play. Creative nonfiction may center around the author's "I," but that does not doom it to narcissism. Indeed, writing honestly from our limited, subjective point of view may be the most spiritual way to acknowledge our place in the world as created, fallen, and redeemed. The greatest nonfiction has a way of limning the outlines of our human brokenness while finding new and inventive modes to choir the proper praise.

What more could you want from a book?

education

G. Tyler Fischer

what is education?

The school board meeting was coming an end . . . or so they thought. A sweaty but determined man stepped up to the microphone in the aisle of the humid high school auditorium. The meeting had gone routinely up this point, and a couple of board members were even checking their watches and thinking about getting home early. There was only one more thing on the agenda: questions to the board from the audience. Only a few hardy souls sat through the dreary meeting and only one was standing by the microphone waiting. The respectable board members sat around a grand mahogany semicircular table that whispered, "we know, but we deign to listen." The whole thing smelled like authority: well dressed, urbane, and a little smug. The board chairman spoke with his mouth too near his own microphone. His voice boomed, "Now, for questions," and the hall was filled with the scraping sound of reverberation. Everyone—including the board chair—winced. He motioned to the man in the aisle. The man stepped up to the microphone, cleared his throat, and said:

"What is education?"

This is my weird fantasy. I want to ask that question of a group of people who should know the answer... but don't.

Our culture spends billions of dollars to provide K–12 and collegiate education to just about anyone who will receive it. Culturally, we invest zealously in education and prisons.[1] We unquestioningly believe as a culture that more education is better. That, however, is why I want to ask that question to the room full of experts; because I am afraid that our culture cannot even answer the most basic definition question: "What is education?"

I worry that the answers of the best and brightest in our culture would be something like *education is*

- job training;
- the best way to get ahead in life, how to make money, acquire a beautiful spouse, have a happy life, have children who can get an education so that they can get ahead in life... (etc., etc., etc.,)[2]
- a means to set oneself above the rest of humanity—i.e., to acquire power, wealth, or status.

While our educational leaders might have better sense than to say these things out loud, it seems that our educational system is aching to achieve exactly what we won't say.

Really, this should not shock us. People have been thinking about education this way for a long, long time. In Ancient Greece, Socrates (a man seemingly intent on bothering everyone he met) had many opponents who fought against his teaching. They eventually had him arrested, charged (ironically) with corrupting the youth (by the actual corruptors), which finally led Socrates to commit suicide. These opponents were called Sophists. The root meaning of their name comes from the Greek word for wisdom, but they did not seek wisdom for the same reason as Socrates. They taught pupils techniques that would enable them to acquire power. Today, educationally, we have become children of the Sophists more than of Socrates. For us, education has become a means to an end, typically wealth, power, or "happiness."

But why did Socrates educate and why did he learn? For this answer we need look no further than the dialogues of his disciple, Plato. In *The Republic*, Socrates tells us that the philosopher must drag people from the cave that they are in, out into the sunlight of truth so that they can see the world as it really is. In the cave, men are tied up, lying on the ground, watching shadows on the wall, believing that these shadows are reality. So, men are trapped and they are ignorant. All the philosopher has to do is to get them out into the sunlight.[3]

Plato's view of man (trapped in a cave and full of ignorance) might seem grim, but the Bible paints an even bleaker picture. John's Gospel tells us that "this is the judgment: the light has come into the world, and people loved the darkness rather than the light because their works were evil" (3:19). If a philosopher came to help the tied up people get out of the cave, the Scriptures warn that these men, once freed, might turn against their liberator and kill him so that they may stay in the darkness. The crucifixion of Jesus proves this (as does the fate of Socrates!).

So, if men hate wisdom, why do we spend so much time trying to impart it and what hope should we have that any of our efforts will have an impact?

What Education Books You Should Read & Why

And, by the way, *what is education?*

Before we go further, let me share my working definition of education in hopes that this definition can help us consider the question of why we should try to impart it to others.

> Education is the process of imparting the knowledge and skills needed to live as a full and loving member of a community.

Education is a *process*. It is not an event. Education takes time and effort over time. Some of those efforts happen in classrooms with teachers. Education also involves how we walk in the halls, how we talk with our parents, and other character-forming habits that we practice.

It is a process of *imparting* knowledge and skills. *Imparting* implies a teacher. While there are some that are autodidacts, people who learn without the aid of a teacher, they must find their teachers in the pages of books. Thus, everyone has a teacher, whether it is a physical teacher, a book, or the lyrics of their favorite band's music.

Also, it imparts both *knowledge* and *skills*. Knowledge should not be limited to just factual data, but also stories, principles, and patterns of living. Imparting skills is essential to our education. The Greeks are our instructors in this. Education in the Greek city-states was radically different from one to the other. An education in Athens meant knowing philosophy, being able to speak persuasively, and (probably) knowing how to row a trireme, an Athenian ramming war boat. In Sparta, it meant knowing how to fight as an infantry soldier. In his wonderful book *The Greeks*, H.D.F. Kitto, reflecting on the words of Pericles, notes that the Greek city-state, the *polis*, was an educational institution: "The Greeks thought of the *polis* as an active, formative thing, training the minds and the character of the citizens . . . '*Polis*' then, originally 'citadel' may mean as much as 'the whole communal life of the people, political, cultural, moral—even economic . . .'"[4] So, an education included the stories, instructions in the moral commitments of the community, as well as skills needed for flourishing in the community.

The Scriptures echo this integrated and holistic approach to education. Deuteronomy 6 includes the *Shema*, the great confession of faith in the Old Testament, which speaks substantively about education:

> Hear, O Israel: The Lord our God, the Lord is one. You shall love the Lord your God with all your heart and with all your soul and with all your might. *And these words that I command you today shall be on your heart. You shall teach them diligently to your children, and shall talk of them*

when you sit in your house, and when you walk by the way, and when you lie down, and when you rise. You shall bind them as a sign on your hand, and they shall be as frontlets between your eyes. You shall write them on the doorposts of your house and on your gates. (emphasis added)[5]

Parents were required to diligently teach the law of God to the young at all times. The commitment to worship the Lord was at the core of the conversation between fathers and sons and mothers and daughters. Education then is at the core of a worshipping community.

Education, good education, should enable full and loving *membership* in the community. Similarly, Irenaeus, an early church leader, said, "The glory of God is a man fully alive." Education should prepare young men and women to bear responsibility in the community and through the pain, suffering, and joy of bearing that responsibility, the young should be fitted to bear leadership in the community and the weight of glory. Education, then, should train young people to love the stories of and the faith of the community. It should give them a vision for what maturity in the community looks like. This maturity should be their longing as they grow up. It should be the harbor that they seek for their lives. This is the discipleship that they enter into and the tradition that they have to live up to.

As one reflects on the current state of education in the West, it is easy to see why it is crashing and burning. Our schools are failing and our young people are listless because we have destroyed our own stories and have rejected the paths of our forefathers. We have burned our own house and then said to each other, "Be warm and fed." Tragic and ridiculous! Thus, most education has slouched into self-reflective sophistry offering wealth, power, and status divorced from any deeper meaning in life.[6]

Finally, education is work aimed at the *community*. By this, we don't mean that it has to be done by a community. Biblically, parents are consistently at the center of the education of their children. Whether one attends a school or chooses to teach children at home, the parents are at the center and should have the deepest interest in providing their children with a sound education. The parents provide the education, but the education prepares the child for participation in the community. A well-educated young man or woman is prepared to step into a role of responsibility in their own family, to engage in work and worship as a community, and to educate their own children. Thus, the stories, mores, and prosperity of the community is preserved from one generation to the next.

CHRISTIAN EDUCATION

This view of education (which has been the view of education through all history up to our modern era) is a religious view of education and can be seen in each faithful generation. Religious commitments drove parents and communities to invest in education. In the Scriptures we see sons continuing the work of the fathers. Solomon builds the Temple to complete the work of his father, David. In classical literature, we see Telemachus becoming a man by searching for and supporting the homecoming of his father, Odysseus. (Some paganism, then, actually agrees with Christianity on the normal hopeful outcome of education: a cultural heritage along with its values, practices, and worship will pass from one generation to the next.[7])

For modern Western culture it is an imperative that we return to the roots of our cultural education and embrace Christianity. Without faith, without a commitment to the God of the Bible, His laws, His stories, and His Gospel, our education will flounder toward job training, sophistry, and power obsessions.

THE CLASSICAL TRADITION

When one reflects on education being the transmission of a cultural heritage, it is easy to see why the classical tradition must be renewed if education in the West is to be revitalized. Modern society rejects the pattern of education passing a cultural heritage from one generation to the next. All of the deep commitments in the West to liberty, freedom, individual rights (inalienable ones), and all the core values of the Republic stem from the marriage of the classical tradition and the biblical view of man, both as glorious creation made in the image of God and broken, sinful rebel who must not be trusted with power. To summarize, the classical and Christian tradition is the cultural heritage of the West that we should strive to reinstate today.[8]

THE CLASSICAL CHRISTIAN EDUCATION IMPERATIVE

Thus, we have begun to see writers from all branches of the church calling out for a return to something called classical Christian education.[9] One could just as easily call it traditional Western education because it is the kind of education that was practiced in most communities in the West up until the industrial revolution.

This classical Christian education provides a cultural heritage to normalize education, one needed for full and loving participation in culture and community. It looks to the cultural heritage of the Bible and the classical tradition.

This, of course, has not kept students from rebelling against this tradition. The largest failures of this education are not those who reject the tradition like Nietzsche and Marx, but those who claim the tradition but fall short of the truth, beauty, and goodness to which the tradition is committed.

Classical and Christian education is not just a set of stories or a list of mores and commitments, but a cultural heritage supported by the skills necessary to build up, criticize, or correct that very heritage. Classical education focuses on the Seven Great Liberals Arts. Many schools and homeschoolers involved in classical education now focus on the skills of the Trivium—the first three of the Seven Liberal Arts: grammar, logic, and rhetoric—during K–12 education.[10] While there can be robust debate about the exact meaning of these skills the nature of the debate focuses us on some key insights.[11] Classical education focuses its effort on teaching students basic skills like reading and mathematics as they learn grammar and facts. It helps students to think clearly and critically about ideas and arguments as they learn to think logically and construct arguments. It focuses on skills of communication and persuasion as they learn the skills of rhetoric.

Interestingly, these skills are actually the skills needed to criticize or correct the classical and Christian tradition. This is most clear in the imparting of logic and rhetoric. With logic and rhetoric arguments are made and people are convinced and led.[12] It is easy to see, then, why state run schools are not best at providing classical education. The state often has interests that don't match the interests of a classical Christian education. States are the status quo and want to protect the status quo. The classical Christian form of education provides students with eternal truths, moving stories, and the skills to oppose the status quo and, if necessary, overturn it. Classical Christian education as it clings to both the Christian faith and the classical tradition should be, at its best, a self-policing tradition.

War Training

Finally, we are foolish if we fail to see the connection between education and cultural dominion. The old adage says, "The hand that rocks the cradle rules the world." When we look at the confusion of our current crop of educational cradle rockers, we should expect nothing but mush in our culture's future.

Education, true education, however, can be the beginning of a reassessment of things and a starting point for cultural renewal. Here are a few readings that can help your family and community become part of fostering this needed renewal:

"The Lost Tools of Learning," an essay by Dorothy Sayers

First presented at Oxford in 1947, this essay called for a renewal of the classical tradition in education. It is a must-read if for no other reason than the sheer joy of reading it. It presents a compelling argument in a persuasive manner.

In it the mystery writer Dorothy Sayers lays out the basic structure of a classical education in its first three parts: Grammar, Logic, and Rhetoric. She also points out how these liberal arts actually fit with the way the mind develops. Young children learn through memory. Middle schoolers love to argue. High school students enjoy fitting in with adults and being able to speak and communicate winsomely. (Her essay can be found online and in an appendix in the following book.)

Recovering the Lost Tools of Learning:
An Approach to Distinctively Christian Education
by Douglas Wilson

Dorothy Sayers tossed a rock down from a high hill, but in her day this challenging essay did not cause a movement or reform in education. Little could Sayers have known, however, that her stone would hit its mark some thirty years after her death. Her essay advocating classical education fell into the hands of a pastor in Moscow, Idaho named Douglas Wilson. This pastor had made a fateful promise to his wife, Nancy, saying that if there were no schools in town to which they felt comfortable sending their daughter Rebecca, then he would start a school. Rebecca was nearing school age and Douglas Wilson was reading essays on education for inspiration on how to start a school.

In Wilson, Sayers found a courageous soul who was willing to swim against the current. Wilson and a few friends started the Logos School in Moscow, Idaho in 1980. This school was the beginning of the renewal of self-consciously classical and Christian schooling.

After producing some incredible results at the Logos School, Wilson wrote his book *Recovering the Lost Tools of Learning.* This book built on Sayers, essay and gave people the motivation and blueprint for starting a classical Christian school. The publication of this book was the beginning of an avalanche. It eventually triggered the creation of the Association of Classical Christian Schools

(ACCS). This group has grown now to represent about 275 schools around the world. It also inspired thousands of homeschool families to execute Wilson's educational ideas at home.

This book is an easy read, but the ideas in it are presented in ways that force the reader to think about education, and whether Christian families can go with the flow of education in our culture.

All Christians thinking about education should read Douglas Wilson's *Recovering the Lost Tools of Learning*.

"The Work of Local Culture"
an essay by Wendell Berry

Berry is a feisty farmer/philosopher/poet from rural Kentucky. His essays, books of fiction, and poetry run the gamut from the lighthearted to the hopeless. This essay, "The Work of Local Culture," is his most powerful essay on education and community. It is an essay on the life of a healthy community, so education is front and center. He looks both at the classical and Christian traditions of education. He also views what the modern world has done to education and to the local community. It does not present a pretty picture.

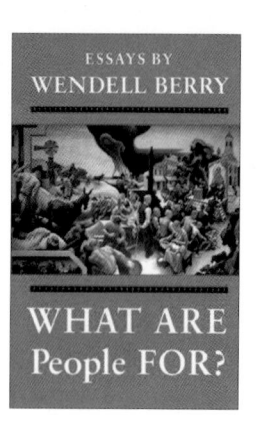

Berry's work in some ways is preparatory for all other reading on this list. He causes his reader to burn the ships and abandon hope that educational reform is coming from the state, the corporations, or the universities. He destroys false hope, but in that destruction he provides a glimmer of true hope. If hope is coming, it must come from the local communities themselves. A community, to be a true community, must take back control of education as a first step toward flourishing—culturally and economically.

This essay can be found in numerous places. In print, you can find it in his book *What are People For?*[13] My favorite way to experience this essay is the audio version read by Ken Myers of Mars Hill Audio in his *Anthology #3: Place, Community, and Memory*.[14]

The Abolition of Man by C. S. Lewis

This book strikes at the heart of modern, secular education, revealing that modern education is not really education at all. It ends up destroying the end goal of true education. True education aims to produce men and women who are fully and lovingly engaged in the worship and work of a community. Modern education produces "men without chests" as Lewis famously said. This work is a must-read for those considering being about the task of education in the modern world.

Norms and Nobility: A Treatise on Education
by David Hicks

This book is a fascinating examination of education from a classical viewpoint. It is bite-sized; you won't be able to put it down. It looks at the purpose of education but gets down into very practical advice on how to talk about deep ideas with children. It is a gem.

The Classical Liberal Arts Tradition: A Philosophy of Christian Classical Education by Ravi Jain and Kevin Clark

This wonderful new book is a historical exploration of the roots of Western Christian education. Jain and Clark, are both teachers at the Geneva School of Orlando, Florida (a charter member of the ACCS). They have done an excellent job fleshing out classical education historically. This book will help you think through what was happening in a classical education historically, and will cause you to consider how what you are doing today should be questioned or altered. It is an exceptional book.

Endnotes

1 At the time of the publication of this essay these shocking findings can be found online at https://www2.ed.gov/rschstat/eval/other/expenditures-corrections-education/brief.pdf. Interestingly, this study claims that schools have received short shrift *because* government spending on education has only doubled while spending on corrections has quadrupled over the last 30 years. This, of course, only tells a sliver of the story. Education spending went from $258 billon to $534 billon, while corrections increased from $17 billion to $71 billion. For more on this, see: https://www.ed.gov/news/press-releases/report-increases-spending-corrections-far-outpace-education.

2   There is a delightful, modern-day, reimagined Socratic dialogue between the Gadfly of Athens and a college student in Peter Kreeft's book *The Best Things in Life* (Downer's Grove, IL: InterVarsity Press, reprint 1984).
3   Interestingly, Greek education is attractive to the modern age because it is thought to be more secular than most forms of education in Western history. Socrates, however, was trying to make contact with the permanent world of the forms, with a world beyond all material manifestations. His task was against the stories of the Olympian gods, but it is not anti-theological. It is really an attempt to see the world as God sees it.
4   H.D.F. Kitto, *The Greeks* (New York: Penguin, 1951), 75.
5   Deuteronomy 6:4–9, ESV (Emphasis mine).
6   We wonder why the young are cynical today! Never have young people had to live with the pressure to construct "meaning" to make life tolerable. The young are smart enough to recognize that if life has no meaning then power, wealth, and status are just as meaningless.
7   Wendell Berry's essay, "The Work of Local Culture," mentioned below, has an excellent description of this pattern.
8   The West is thankfully not a tribe. It is not ethnocentric or racist. It welcomes all comers. Its cornerstones are laid by Africans like Augustine along with slaveholders like Jefferson and descendants of slaves like Martin Luther King, Jr., who used the words of Jefferson to call America to live up to its Western ideals.
9   Notably, Douglas Wilson amongst the Protestant branch of the church with strong support from conservative Lutherans like Gene Edward Veith, but also Rod Dreher's strong assertions that all Christians should be providing their children with a classical Christian education in his chapter on education in *The Benedict Option*, from an Eastern Orthodox position. These have been joined recently by strong Roman Catholic advocates like Anthony Esolen's recent *Out of the Ashes: Rebuilding American Culture*, where he advocates classical Christian education.
10 It is doubtless true that classical education does not limit itself to the Trivium skills alone in K-12. The mathematical and musical arts are in the Quadrivium, the last four of the Seven Great Liberal Arts, and no school that I know of holds off math until college. For further discussion of this, see Evans and Littlejohn's *Wisdom and Eloquence*.
11 This robust debate should not be viewed as a weakness of classical Christian education, but as one of its great strengths. Wilson's seminal work, *Recovering the Lost Tools of Learning*, affirmed "Sayers' Insight," which is that grammar, logic, and rhetoric actually fit with the way a student's mind develops. More recently, Chuck Evans and Robert Littlejohn, in their book *Wisdom and Eloquence*, criticized Sayers and proposed that these three arts are subjects. Both insights actually support each other, in my experience as an educator, and classical education benefits from these and even more recent insights like those of Jain and Clark.
12 Sayers' lines in "The Lost Tools of Learning" on training students in logic are some of my favorites. She notes: "It will, doubtless, be objected that to encourage young persons at the Pert age to browbeat, correct, and argue with their elders will render them perfectly intolerable. My answer is that children of that age are intolerable anyhow; and that their natural argumentativeness may just as well be canalized to good purpose as allowed to run away into the sands."
13 Wendell Berry, *What are People For?* (Berkeley, CA: Counterpoint Press, 2nd ed. Reprint, 2010), 153ff.
14 At the time of the publication of this chapter, a reading of this essay could be downloaded for a nominal fee at: https://marshillaudio.org/catalog/place-community-and-memory.

ETHICS
David P. Gushee

YOU HAVE TO FIND A REALLY GOOD BOOKSTORE TO LOCATE any books on Christian ethics. This does not contribute to warm feelings on the part of Christian ethicists towards the bookstore industry. It is part of a broader neglect and misunderstanding of our field that its practitioners feel very keenly. This essay is going to need to do some spadework related to Christian ethics before venturing to recommend what particular books you should read, and why.

At one level, Christian ethics is a task, the task of Christians thinking about morality from within the framework of Christian faith. This task is ineluctable. Every Christian with a pulse undertakes it. Every time a Christian asks, "What does Jesus require of me?" she is doing Christian ethics. You don't have to have an advanced degree to do Christian ethics. Sometimes you're better off not having one.

At another level, Christian ethics is an academic discipline, like psychology, art, or criminology. Unlike these disciplines, however, Christian ethics is often treated as standing under some broader disciplinary umbrella.

So, for example, Christian ethics is often understood to be nestled under the broad umbrella of Christian theology, when "theology" is understood to mean thinking theologically about Christian belief and practice. Christian ethics sometimes huddles under the umbrella of biblical studies, when biblical studies is understood to mean reading Scripture to direct and reflect upon Christian belief and practice. Sometimes Christian ethics is nestled under philosophy, especially when the "Christian" part weakens and the ethics part is disentangled from faith. In secular universities, most often ethics is treated as a branch of philosophy.

Christian ethicists don't really want our discipline to have to huddle under someone else's umbrella, because a) sometimes umbrella-holders decide they don't care if we get wet, and b) we think our discipline is its own thing and should be recognized as such.

I happen to be a very strong partisan of this perspective. I believe that Christian ethics is a stand-alone discipline that has as much significance for academia or the church as any other discipline. I am going to tell you a bit about how I understand the history and contours of my beloved discipline, and as I map the field I will tell you about a few books you absolutely must read.

Ancient Ecclesial-Formational Christian Ethics

Christian Ethics: A Historicial Introduction
by J. Phillip Wogaman

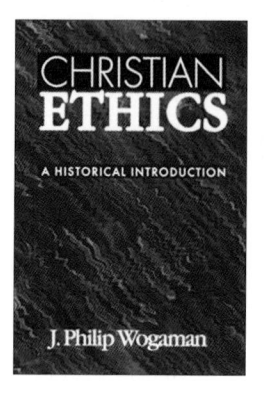

I have already suggested that a thing called "Christian ethics" began two millennia ago, in continuity with the Jewish tradition(s) out of which Christianity emerged. This is Christian ethics as moral formation of professed followers of Jesus, in Christian community, usually involving some authoritative role for Christian leaders.

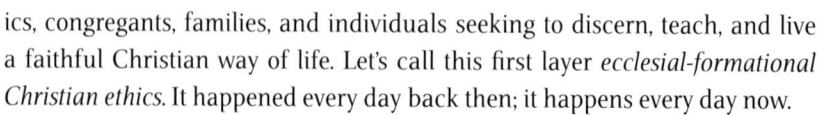

Long before there was an academic discipline that became known as "Christian ethics," there were clerics, congregants, families, and individuals seeking to discern, teach, and live a faithful Christian way of life. Let's call this first layer *ecclesial-formational Christian ethics*. It happened every day back then; it happens every day now.

The type of literature within the field of Christian ethics relevant to this ur-layer is sometimes called "history of Christian ethics." Its primary sources are the surviving texts of ancient, medieval, and early modern Christianity. Moral instruction back in the day was rarely separated out as "ethics" over against "theology," so anyone digging around in the Church Fathers will find "Christian ethics" along with other types of teaching materials. Read in Augustine, Aquinas, Luther, Calvin, Wesley, or any other classic Christian figure, and you will find some Christian ethics.

A good place to get an overview of historical Christian ethics is in Philip Wogaman, *Christian Ethics: A Historical Introduction*, and the companion volume *Readings in Christian Ethics: A Historical Sourcebook* (both with Westminster John Knox Press, now in second editions). I have used these as course textbooks at the undergraduate level and found them a highly effective pair. There you have it, my first recommendation of what you should read in Christian ethics.

THE BIRTH OF "CHRISTIAN SOCIAL ETHICS"
Christianity and the Social Crisis
by Walter Rauschenbusch

Christian ethics as a modern, self-identified, independent academic discipline was born late, which is one reason why it has struggled to maintain its foothold in treacherous academic terrain. This new discipline arose in explicit reaction against most prevailing versions of ecclesial-formational Christian ethics, and in explicit commitment to a different kind of project. I propose that we date the birth of the modern discipline of Christian ethics, especially in America, to 1880 or so, when the first classes and professorships in "Christian sociology," "applied Christianity," and "Christian ethics" began to appear.

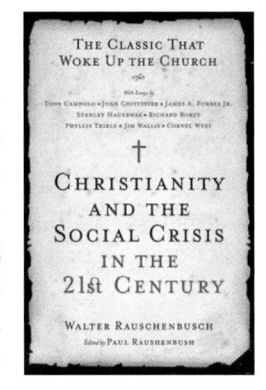

The timing is not coincidental. The modern discipline of Christian ethics was born to bring to bear the resources of Christian faith on the urgent social evils attendant on the rise of modern industrial capitalism. Eventually, this work became known as *Christian social ethics*. It emerged all over the Western industrialized world, addressing similar concerns in different contexts, in both Protestant and Catholic versions. It competed with and was informed by Marxist and socialist treatments of the same urgent problems.

Though he had important predecessors, I believe that Baptist pastor, church historian, and Social Gospeler Walter Rauschenbusch qualifies as the primary founder of American Christian social ethics, establishing a paradigm for doing Christian ethics that remains with us today.

Rauschenbusch first offered his ethic at length in 1907 in the blockbuster *Christianity and the Social Crisis* (still in print with Westminster John Knox), arguably the founding text of modern Christian social ethics, and my second recommendation as to what you must read in our field. That book set the tone for Christian ethics as a modern discipline. It offered a takedown of the great majority of Western Christian history and called for a recovery of Jesus' own message and ministry of the reign of God. This then generated social reform proposals that tracked quite closely along the lines of then-contemporary progressive politics.

Rauschenbusch's portfolio of policy proposals was not generally very radical, and many of the policy ideas eventually became law. They mainly involved advancing worker's rights, social insurance, health care, consumer protection, and urban living conditions. The broader project was challenging self-interested economic ideologies that grind up human beings and go unchallenged in the name of liberty.

Rauschenbusch was sure that these political and economic reforms were fundamentally moral issues. He believed that the right stance to take on these issues was clear from a fair-minded reading of the prophets and Jesus. He did not need to create a new religion to address "the social problem." The religion was already there. It just needed to be recovered and mobilized.

AFTER RAUSCHENBUSCH
Basic Christian Ethics by Paul Ramsey

It is fair to say that the Rauschenbusch tradition of Christian social ethics came to dominate the new discipline, and often continues to do so over one hundred years later. Christian ethics is Christian social ethics, undertaken mainly by white American Protestant Christian scholar-churchmen, aiming to address one or more social issues from the vantage point of Christian ethical principles, such principles almost always interpreted as having public policy implications that would fall to the left of the political spectrum. I could recommend three hundred books that would exemplify the pattern, but that would be boring.

So let's continue our narrative.

After World War I, and especially after the Depression, and really characterizing the entire period from about 1928 to about 1968, mainline American Protestant Christian social ethics embraced a new spirit reflective of the distressingly apocalyptic era in which it was produced. (The apocalyptic spirit hit earlier in Europe, more deeply affected by the trauma of World War I, which helps to explain the emergence of the early Karl Barth.) But it arrived in full force here only with the rise in labor strife in the 1920s, the stock market crash of 1929, the Great Depression, the rise of fascism, World War II, and then the Cold War.

Ethicists writing during this period generally lost the immanent-reign-of-God optimism characteristic of Rauschenbusch at his most buoyant. They still desired to apply Christian theological and ethical principles to American and global problems, but the problems seemed more intractable and more dangerous than ever before.

The theologian-ethicist whose work dominated this era was of course Reinhold Niebuhr of Union Seminary in New York. Here I recommend two main works: first, his 1928 *Leaves from the Notebook of a Tamed Cynic*, written while he was pastoring in Detroit. This was a new kind of voice for a Protestant cleric, much more realistic about power politics, social conflict, and the limits of moral suasion and human good will. Niebuhr's cynicism was not really tamed.

These themes were only heightened in his classic *Moral Man and Immoral Society*, which he himself said would have been better titled *Immoral Man and Even More Immoral Society*. This classic Niebuhrian text offers stark pessimism/realism about the human condition, claiming that sinful human self-interest runs so deep that only the exercise of power can force people to do what is right. The book is breathtakingly insightful about dominant forms of structural sin.

Humanity kept on going. The Cold War did not result in the obliteration of the human species in an all-out nuclear war, as so many feared. In the 1960s, ethicists like Paul Ramsey of Princeton tried to bring Christian ethics to bear on new developments in American warfare and in biomedicine, in particular. His *Basic Christian Ethics* remains a signature text of our discipline (also still in print with Westminster John Knox Press). Many of our discipline's progressives found him too accommodating to American power and too confident of American virtue, attitudes which did not survive the Vietnam era in which Ramsey was at his height.

Progressive Catholic Social Ethics
Compendium of the Social Doctrine of the Church
by Pontifical Council for Justice and Peace

The times, they were a-changing. The new professional guild of Christian ethicists, ultimately called the Society of Christian Ethics, was founded in 1959. Its all-male, all-white, all-Protestant ranks were broadened in the 1960s, one step at a time.

American Catholic social ethics emerged. Most of the earliest American Catholic social ethicists pursued a project like that of their mainline Protestant friends. They often focused on American public life and social problems, worked within the parameters of American liberal democracy, pursued recognizably progressive ends, and were white men. Key figures included Charles Curran,[1] Richard McCormick,[2] David Hollenbach,[3] Daniel Maguire,[4] and James Keenan.[5] Their work still bears reading, and they all remain active today.

Of course, being Catholic did (and does) make a recognizable difference. Liberal Catholic social ethics is fed by historic Catholic traditions of moral theology and is informed by the teachings of the Roman Catholic magisterium. Liberal Catholic social ethics also has been demonstrably aided by the Catholic Social Teaching tradition and by the opening of the Church during Vatican II. The global nature of the Catholic Church also has made liberal Catholic social ethics less parochially American than Protestant ethics has tended to be.

My pick for primary texts in early Catholic social ethics might surprise you. I was most shaped by encountering primers on Catholic Social Teaching and then collections of the ethics-focused texts of Vatican II. Therefore, my recommendations here include *Vatican Council II: Constitutions, Decrees, Declarations* (Costello, 1996), and *Compendium of the Social Doctrine of the Church* (U.S. Catholic Conference, 2005). But I could also point you to abundant works over three generations of Catholic scholarship.

LIBERATIONIST ETHICS & ETHICS BY PEOPLE OF COLOR

Jesus and the Disinherited
by Howard Thurman

The 1960s saw the birth of a new kind of Christian ethics altogether—ethics written by people who were not white, not male, not American, not European. Ethics written by people of color, by women, by voices from the Global South, by people who had heretofore been on the margins of recognized academic theological production.

Of course, "Christian ethics" had always been produced by such populations. Some of it had been published, some of it had been sung, much of it had been preached. But the exclusion of everyone other than white men from leadership in the recognized mainstream academy and white churches meant that the ethics produced in these communities had been hidden "behind the veil," blocked from the white male gaze.

It remains the case that much of the most important writing about what it means to be moral under conditions of oppression, marginalization, and disempowerment was not and still is not produced by people with doctorates in Christian ethics.

In the African-American community, for example, rich traditions of ethical reflection are everywhere, in spirituals, sermons, pamphlets, novels, and so on. But systematic written reflections on these traditions that began to be taken seriously by white people date mainly from the 1960s—though here I insert the next of my favorite books in Christian ethics, Howard Thurman's *Jesus and the Disinherited* (1948, still widely read and in print). To Thurman, of course, we can add the seminal contributions of Martin Luther King, Jr., who earned a doctorate in theology but whose on-the-fly writings from 1955 to 1968 remain significant in Christian ethics. My preference remains his "Letter from a Birmingham Jail," more like a tract than a book but a signature text in any proper review of Christian ethics.

Since the 1960s and 1970s, as women and people of color, women who are people of color, Native Americans, LGBTQ Christians, and so many other diverse persons have emerged within the discipline of Christian ethics, our field has evolved considerably.

The works produced by these new voices among us vary. Some aim to elucidate received moral wisdom from within particular social locations and to articulate it in writing. Some work at ecclesial-moral formation for persons, and faith communities, of color. Some seek liberal-progressive social reform, joining the broader conversation that has long occurred in the majority Christian social ethics tradition. Some identify particular social-ethical problems, or dimensions of social-ethical problems, especially relevant in communities of color, and to focus sustained analytical and advocacy attention on those problems. And some follow up on W.E.B. DuBois' famous 1903 claim in *The Souls of Black Folk* that "the problem of the twentieth century is the problem of the color line," and analyze aspects of that color line problem: the social construction of race, the history of racism, the effects of racism on people of color and on those defined as white, and so on.

Liberation ethics remains a good overall name for every type of Christian ethical approach that names systemic oppression based on nationality, race, ethnicity, citizenship status, gender, and now also gender identity and sexual orientation, as among the world's gravest moral evils that must be redressed through liberative efforts on the part of Christians, churches, and all people of conscience.[6]

While many voices have contributed to the Christian liberationist ethics of the last generation, I would here like to pay tribute to my esteemed friend and colleague Miguel de la Torre for his particularly distinguished contribution. The extent, depth, and quality of his work over the last three decades is remarkable. I only hope that his recent turn to *Embracing Hopelessness* (Fortress, October 2017) does not mean what I fear that it means—that de la Torre has given up hope either in God's deliverance or in his fellow Christians. To start in the de la Torre corpus, I recommend his *Doing Christian Ethics from the Margins* (Orbis, 2nd edition, 2014).

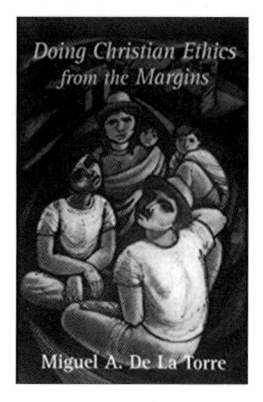

THE HAUERWAS REVOLUTION
The Peaceable Kingdom: A Primer in Christian Ethics
by Stanley Hauerwas

Finally, no review of must-read books in Christian ethics can miss the contribution of another esteemed friend and colleague, Stanley Hauerwas. He offers a sustained and powerful critique of the dominant Christian social ethics tradition and has created, and created space for, multiple alternative visions of Christian ethics.[7]

Hauerwas has claimed that for American Christian ethics from the Social Gospel until the emergence of Anabaptist ethicist John Howard Yoder (don't miss his *Politics of Jesus*), "the subject of Christian ethics in America was always America," and that this was a grave mistake.[8] He has argued that the primary agenda of Christian ethics should be forming a faithful Church and focusing on the character and practices of Christian disciples. This agenda can be viewed as a retrieval of the ecclesial-formational Christian ethics with which I opened this reflection, and therefore a challenge to the entire American Christian social ethics tradition since Walter Rauschenbusch. This is a theme of many of his books, including his early *A Community of Character* (Notre Dame, 1981). One of his earliest and best overall constructive statements is in *The Peaceable Kingdom: A Primer in Christian Ethics* (Notre Dame, 1983). The early Hauerwas is my favorite Hauerwas.

Hauerwas' challenge to liberal American Christian social ethics has been comprehensive. He has challenged the confidence of much Christian ethics and the meaningfulness of a reformist-progressive agenda within American liberal democracy. He has questioned how much Christians should support liberal democracy and its ideals, triggering constant arguments related to how U.S. Christians should in fact relate to the ubiquitous, unquestioned democratic political order.[9] He has revalorized much Christian tradition, helped open space for the recovery of a focus on major historic thinkers like Aquinas and Augustine,[10] and participated in projects aimed at mining the ethical implications of biblical, sacramental, and liturgical theology. All these are precisely the kinds of projects Rauschenbusch would not have undertaken.[11] He has resisted self-identification as an ethicist and instead prefers to be described as a theologian, which is itself another break from the dominant tradition[12]—as is his repudiation of any particularly Protestant dimension to his own thought.[13]

All these moves have opened space for more theologically inclined and traditional Catholics,[14] Eastern Orthodox,[15] mainliners,[16] Europeans,[17] and evangelical Protestants[18] to find points of connection with Hauerwas (whether as his students, or his admirers) and to find a home in the discipline of Christian ethics even if they are not liberal democratic social reformers. Partly due to his impact—though surely a variety of other factors have been at work—our discipline no longer resembles that of the 1959 American Society of Christian Social Ethics, at least not monolithically. Christian ethics research today demonstrates far more points of connection with Church, tradition, historic figures,[19] discipleship, character, and liturgy—in general, with the ecclesial-formational tradition of Christian ethics, a tradition to which I find myself more deeply connected than ever now that I am pastoring a church.[20]

WHAT ELSE TO READ?

Christian ethics as a discipline now has multiple layers, lineages, and traditions. There is no consensus, and no imaginable recovery of such. We have among us ecclesial-formational ethicists, mainline Protestant social ethicists in various lineages, progressive and more conservative evangelical ethicists, all kinds of Catholic ethicists, some but not enough Eastern Orthodox ethicists, post-Christian religious ethicists, comparative ethicists, ethnographers, specialists in figures, strands, and traditions, and all kinds of cross-cutting work emerging from younger scholars especially. Our discipline continues to attract extremely thoughtful people, who over the next forty years will produce a new canon of works in Christian ethics that every well-informed Christian will need to discover. But feel free to begin with the dozen or so books that I have recommended in this essay. I am grateful to the Borgers for providing space for works like this to be sold, and savored.

ENDNOTES

1 Charles E. Curran, *The Development of Moral Theology: Five Strands* (Washington: Georgetown University Press, 2013). Earlier: *The Catholic Moral Tradition Today: A Synthesis* (Washington: Georgetown University Press, 1999).
2 Richard A. McCormick, S.J., *Corrective Vision: Explorations in Moral Theology* (Kansas City: Sheed & Ward, 1994).
3 David Hollenbach, S.J. *The Global Face of Public Faith: Politics, Human Rights, and Christian Ethics* (Washington: Georgetown University Press, 2003).
4 Daniel Maguire, *The Moral Revolution, The Moral Core of Judaism and Christianity: Reclaiming the Revolution* (Minneapolis: Fortress Press, 1993).
5 James F. Keenan, *A History of Catholic Moral Theology in the Twentieth Century: From Confessing Sins to Liberating Consciences* (London: Continuum, 2010).
6 One helpful survey is Charles L. Kammer III, *Ethics and Liberation: An Introduction* (Maryknoll, NY: Orbis Books, 1988). Orbis, a Catholic house, has for decades been the unchallenged publishing headquarters for liberation theology and ethics.
7 Author of over twenty-five books in Christian ethics, the publishing career of Stanley Hauerwas began in the early 1980s and continues in his retirement today.
8 Hauerwas regularly repeated this claim. One place to see it in print is here: https://peacetheology.net/anabaptist-convictions/hauerwas-on-jhy/.
9 See his *A Better Hope: Resources for a Church Confronting Capitalism, Democracy, & Postmodernity* (Grand Rapids: Brazos, 2000).
10 Hauerwas opens the door to the continuously surging recovery and reconsideration of Thomas Aquinas and Augustine. On the latter: Eric Gregory, *Politics & the Order of Love: An Augustinian Ethic of Democratic Citizenship* (Chicago/London: University of Chicago Press, 2008); see also Paul J. Griffiths, *Lying: An Augustinian Theology of Duplicity* (Grand Rapids: Brazos, 2004).

11 Hauerwas was the co-editor of a massive Blackwell Christian ethics reader organized entirely on liturgical lines: Stanley Hauerwas and Samuel Wells, *The Blackwell Companion to Christian Ethics* (Oxford: Blackwell Publishing, 2004). In this line see Brian Brock, *Singing the Ethos of God: On the Place of Christian Ethics in Scripture* (Grand Rapids: Eerdmans, 2007).

12 For a recent discussion of this point, see his *The Work of Theology* (Grand Rapids: Eerdmans, 2015), ch. 1.

13 On his very weak attachment to Protestantism, and Protestant ethics, see Hauerwas, *Work of Theology*, ch. 3.

14 This is the best place to note that most well-known conservative Roman Catholic ethicists do not participate in the mainstream Christian ethics guild. Consider John Finnis or German Grisez. Hauerwas has, however, contributed to opening up space for that kind of Catholic to do work other than liberal/progressive reformist ethics.

15 Some top figures: Vigen Guroian, *Incarnate Love: Essays in Orthodox Ethics* (Notre Dame: University of Notre Dame Press, 1987); Joseph Woodill, *The Fellowship of Life: Virtue Ethics and Orthodox Christianity* (Washington: Georgetown University Press, 1998), Stanley Samuel Harakas, *Living the Faith: The Praxis of Eastern Orthodox Ethics* (Minneapolis: Light & Life Publishing, 1992); Christos Yannaras, *The Freedom of Morality* (Crestwood, NY: St. Vladimir's Seminary Press), 1984. Eastern Orthodox ethics offers a great example of a Christian ethical tradition that long predated mainline liberal Christian social ethics and through its many centuries preserved its distinctive character, rooted in Scripture and tradition, as understood by Eastern Orthodoxy.

16 For conservative-leaning mainliners, see Lutheran ethicist Gilbert C. Meilaender, *The Theory and Practice of Virtue* (Notre Dame: University of Notre Dame Press, 1984); D. Stephen Long, *The Goodness of God: Theology, the Church, and Social Order* (Grand Rapids: Brazos, 2001).

17 Among others, Michael Banner, *Christian Ethics and Contemporary Moral Problems* (Cambridge: Cambridge University Press, 1999), a resolutely theological treatment of social-ethical problems.

18 Even though Stanley Hauerwas is not an evangelical, many evangelicals (conservative, moderate, and liberal) have been influenced by Hauerwas, perhaps more than by any other single Christian ethicist in this last generation. Conservative example: J. Daryl Charles, *The Unformed Conscience of Evangelicalism* (Downers Grove, IL: InterVarsity Press), 2002. Moderate example: Jonathan R. Wilson, *Gospel Virtues: Practicing Faith, Hope, & Love in Uncertain Times* (Downers Grove, IL: InterVarsity Press), 1998. A Hauerwas evangelical who picked up philosophical interests of the polymath master is Brad Kallenberg. See his *Ethics as Grammar: Changing the Postmodern Subject* (Notre Dame: Notre Dame University Press, 2001). Two profound, holistic progressive ethical thinkers affected by and somewhat parallel to Hauerwas died too young: James Wm. McClendon, Jr., *Systematic Theology: Ethics* (Nashville: Abingdon Press, 1986), and Stanley J. Grenz, *The Moral Quest: Foundations of Christian Ethics* (Downers Grove, IL: Intervarsity Press, 1997). See also Wyndy Corbin Reuschling, *Reviving Evangelical Ethics: The Promises and Pitfalls of Classic Models of Morality* (Grand Rapids: Brazos, 2008).

19 All kinds of historical figures are being retrieved for consideration in dissertations and monographs. For example, William J. Danaher, Jr., *The Trinitarian Ethics of Jonathan Edwards* (Louisville: Westminster John Knox Press, 2004). It is most unlikely that a new Christian ethicist in 1974 would have written such a text.

20 Most introductions to Christian ethics now emphasize Christian character, community, virtue, and other Hauerwasian themes rather than just focusing on contested social problems.

See Russell B. Connors, Jr. and Patrick T. McCormick, *Character, Choices & Community: The Three Faces of Christian Ethics* (New York: Paulist Press, 1998); Victor Lee Austin, *Christian Ethics: A Guide for the Perplexed* (London: Bloomsbury, 2012); Timothy F. Sedgwick, *The Christian Moral Life: Practices of Piety* (Grand Rapids: Eerdmans, 1999).

Fantasy

Matthew Dickerson

ON JULY 16, 2011, BYRON BORGER BEGAN HIS *BOOKNOTES* with the following anecdote and comment.

> Someone perhaps unaware of the ongoing conversation said tentatively to a friend recently that it seems like there are some Christian symbols and Biblical allusions in *Harry Potter*. Could that be, she wondered. It's a good insight and she may be surprised to know that there is a virtual cottage industry of recent writing, reflecting on the deeper meaning of the wonderfully-crafted fantasy books.

Borger's reference to the deeper meaning and the wonderful crafting of one particular work of fantasy literature suggests the heart of this chapter. Before we get there, however, I should acknowledge one sense in which this chapter is unnecessary, or at least less necessary than it might have been say, fifty or twenty or even ten years ago—the time frame to which Borger was referring. In the same *BookNotes*, Borger himself goes on to note, "As our own local newspaper's religion writer observed, not too many years ago conservative Christians accused Rowling of witchcraft and Satanism, but that is changing. (We lost more than one customer and even a friend a decade ago over our display of that first *HP*.) Oh, how times have changed." Yes, times have changed. And the willingness of a bookstore to carry an important book even when it means losing some customers is one reason for the change.

Another reason for the change is likely this: there is a good answer to the question suggested in this chapter's title, and it has been well articulated. Regarding why one *ought* to read books in the great tradition of mythopoeic literature and the literature of Faerie, I think immediately of J.R.R. Tolkien's insightful essay "On Fairy-Stories." Tolkien does an excellent job laying out a compelling answer, and I have returned to that answer often. If nothing else, his coining of the term *eucatastrophe* makes it a worthwhile read. The final three paragraphs and the connection between fairy tales and the Gospel are beautiful. I could repeat some of his reasons now, but you would be better off simply picking up the essay and reading it yourself. (When you finish, then read Tolkien's short stories "Leaf by Niggle" and "Smith of Wootton Major," which get at some of the same ideas through the imagery and narrative of story—and fairy-stories, at that—rather than through essay. The essay "On Fairy-Stories" along with the autobiographical allegorical fairy tale "Leaf by Niggle" can be found together in a single collection titled *Tree and Leaf.*)

If there are nuances and angles Tolkien missed, many are captured in a shorter (and more accessible) essay by C.S. Lewis, in which the title itself is part of the answer: "Sometimes Fairy-Tales Say Best What Is To Be Said." Despite these excellent answers, I and my friend David O'Hara still managed to publish a book on the topic: *From Homer to Harry Potter: A Handbook of Myth and Fantasy*. I suppose that book, and a few others I have written or co-written about J.R.R. Tolkien and C.S. Lewis, make me a part of that "virtual cottage industry" of which Borger spoke.

So is there *still* more to be said? Well, yes. In a way. I suppose one way to address the topic is to say that you should read fantasy because you should read. Yes, you should read fantasy. You should also read poetry, creative nonfiction, theological writing, art, history, and science. I could go on. (But I won't because you have the rest of the chapters of this collection to make that case.) And while some of the reasons for—which is to say, some of the benefits of—reading fantasy literature may be especially particular to that mode of literature, many of the reasons are the same as the reasons for reading poetry, literature, or creative non-fiction. To put this slightly differently, I could argue that there are many reasons you should read fantasy, but I would also have to acknowledge many reasons to do a hundred other things with the same precious slice of your finite time. Certainly reading of any good literature should be high on that list. (But so should eating dinner with a friend, child, spouse, or even an enemy.)

I read fantasy literature from time to time, particularly when it comes with the recommendation of somebody whose literary opinion I trust. I also read poetry. I read essays. (I'm especially fond of Wendell Berry.) I read recent novels. (Wendell Berry is a beautiful novelist as well as essayist and poet, and I'm glad I didn't dismiss his novels as genre fiction since they fit in the category of *agrarian* novels.) I sometimes rediscover older works of fiction that I missed. (I only discovered Wallace Stegner when I was fifty-three years old, and I became an immediate fan.) I read short stories, and also works of theology, and books about science. Two of my favorite recent books are nonfiction narratives written by scientists, one about rivers and one about trees. The genre of one of my favorite recent authors is sometimes described as magical realism; her stories are certainly surreal at times, but wouldn't be described as fantasy. So fantasy literature is an important part of my bookshelf and reading, and it offers something that the other the genres of literature I read don't offer to the same extent—but it is still only a part.

We'll come back to this. First, a diversion, brought up by the previous two paragraphs. I often laugh—though as an author of a three-volume fantasy novel as well as several books about fantasy literature, I sometimes want to cry—at the use of the phrase "genre literature" to describe fantasy, often in a deprecatory tone. Yes, fantasy is a genre in a sense. For the most part, readers don't need labels on a bookstore shelf to know when they are reading a work of fantasy. (Tolkien, in the essay I mentioned earlier, also gets at what this literature *is*, before he addresses why it is important and worthwhile.) There are a few disagreements, of course. Both the *Star Wars* movies and C.S. Lewis' Ransom Trilogy (also called his Space Trilogy) are often referred to as science fiction, but I think both are more rightly identified as fantasy. The fact that I can make that argument (whether you agree with it or not) indicates that there are indeed conventions which make the label meaningful to a degree. Then again, Madeleine L'Engle's Time Quartet is hard to fit in either place and so labels only go so far.

My own contention is that either all literature is genre literature, or no literature is. Some speak or write as though a modern novel set in a well-known present-day setting is somehow *not* a genre. They refer dismissively to other forms of literature—say historical fiction, or mystery, or science fiction—as genres, but their own preferred style of literature as somehow not being a genre. My favorite local independent bookstore in Vermont actually has a section labeled "genre fiction" (without specifying any particular genre) next to a section labeled "fiction," as though some fiction is "genre fiction" and some is not. That's a bit like somebody from Boston speaking of somebody from eastern Tennessee as having an accent, or somebody from New Jersey thinking of Texans as having accents without acknowledging their own. (Being from Vermont, I know that everybody outside of Vermont speaks with an accent.) It's like an atheist thinking that somehow theism requires faith, while atheism doesn't.

Historically speaking, the "modern" novel is a relatively recent art form with a set of conventions of its own. The modern novel is a genre, every bit as much as fantasy literature is a genre, or science fiction is a genre, or detective stories are a genre. If the modern novel didn't have a clear set of conventions, it would be impossible to point to fantasy literature as *not* following those conventions. Either all literature is genre literature, or no literature is.

This may all seem like a digression, but it gets to my answer. Should you read fantasy literature? The reality is that there are more books published in a few weeks in a single language than most people could read in a lifetime. A quick Wikipedia search tells me there were over 300,000 books published in the United States in 2013. I'd need to read 6,000 books per year, which is more than sixteen books per day, every day for half a century to get through the books published in one country in that one year. There aren't as many genres as there are books, of course, but just to read, say, three books each from every differently labeled shelf in Hearts & Minds Books would be a great undertaking.

Should you read fantasy literature? One answer is yes, if you read some of it and like it. But I think the same answer might be given for many other genres or modes of writing, including some I have either never read or have read but don't go back to. I have many reasons to believe that Shakespearean drama is worth reading, but I haven't read one of Shakespeare's plays since I was in college. I read little science fiction, though I know there are numerous works in that genre well worth reading. I can say the same about the nineteenth-century American novel, and also about works of history about any period (with the exception of medieval history, which I have read as much for the sake of research for my historical novels as for particular enjoyment). When somebody tells me they have tried to read fantasy, but they don't enjoy it or "couldn't get into it," I feel no desire to compel them to keep reading it—unless I find out that the selections of fantasy they have read are examples of the poorer kind. Which leads me to my next answer.

Should you read fantasy? Yes. Which is to say, you should read *good* literature, and if you want to read fantasy literature then you should read *good* fantasy literature, the kind that—to use Borger's words—has "deeper meaning" and is "wonderfully-crafted." There is plenty of poorly written fantasy literature (including some that is quite popular), and also some fantasy with well-crafted prose yet which lacks what I (and Borger) might call depth. Not surprisingly, lots of sex and violence has often been rewarded with financial success in fantasy literature just as it has in the film industry. Fortunately, there are also works of fantasy literature full of beautiful prose, compelling characters, and with narratives full of significance (and which don't glorify violence or sell sex). Tolkien's own writing falls in that category. There are several other twentieth- and twenty-first-century authors whose works of fantasy I would also add to this list, and I'll get to that at the end of this chapter. My life would be shallower and poorer without the works of these authors. (But then, it would probably be richer in a different way I'm sure if I read more Shakespeare.)

Here also is a guilty confession. I have read other works of fantasy in which only two of the three descriptions fit: they offer characters I care about, and narratives where it matters what happens—where something important is at stake—but with prose that in and of itself is uninspiring. I would rather read these works than another work of literature that offers beautiful prose—i.e. beautiful, well-crafted sentences—but where nothing matters, where I don't particularly care what happens, and the characters and their situations do not move me.

And now I've come finally to reasons why I still read fantasy literature despite all of the other worthwhile genres—including the genre of modern novel—calling for my attention. At the heart of fantasy literature, especially that subcategory often referred to as *epic fantasy* or *high fantasy*, is the presence of some sort of cosmic struggle. I might even say it is one of the characteristics that defines the genre. There is something at stake. There is a battle. And this, I believe, is a true reflection of the nature of the universe in which we live, evident from Genesis 3 to the end of the Revelation. It's easy to forget this struggle in the day-to-day of our living. Or, worse, it's easy to think that somehow our battle is against other humans. Epic fantasy reminds me of the truth of this cosmic struggle. And ironically, the best fantasy literature reminds me that the way this struggle is won involves precisely the day-to-day of our living and habits and virtues: showing mercy to a poor and miserable *Gollum* creature even though it would be safer and also just to slay him, and even when we have no idea how that act to show mercy will change the tides of the world in a few decades.

For the next two reasons, I turn to the writings of Eugene Peterson for hints. In his book *Tell It Slant*, Peterson makes an interesting comment about the parables Jesus tells as part of his travel narratives.

> The parable is a form of speech that has a style all its own. It is a way of saying something that requires the imaginative participation of the listener. Inconspicuously, even surreptitiously, a parable *involves* the

hearer. The brief, commonplace, unpretentious story is thrown into a conversation and lands at our feet, compelling notice.... And then we begin seeing connections.... Before we know it, we are involved....

Most parables have another significant feature. The subject matter is usually without apparent religious significance. They are stories about farmers and judges and victims, about coins and sheep and prodigal sons, about wedding banquets, building barns and towers and going to war, a friend who wakes you up in the middle of the night to ask for a loaf of bread, the courtesies of hospitality, crooks and beggars, fig trees and manure.

Spiritual masters are particularly fond of parables, for there is nothing more common than for people who want to talk about God to lose interest in the people they are talking to. Religious talk is depersonalized into godtalk. Godtalk is used to organize people in causes that no longer involve us, to carry out commands that no longer command us . . . Just then, the master drops a parable into the conversation. We stumble over it, no longer able to cruise along in the familiar word ruts. The parable forces attention, participation, involvement.

What Peterson says about this strange genre known as *parable* is perhaps even more true of the fairy tale or work of fantasy. Indeed, think how many parables sound strangely like what we would now call fairy tales. "Once upon a time there was a king." Fairy tales are rooted in the day-to-day. (It is possible for modern readers to lose touch with this because we have lost touch with the cottage in the woods, and so what was day-to-day in medieval Germany is strange and novel to us.) Likewise, fantasy literature—a close cousin of the fairy tale—engages in these profound questions, but without religious talk or Godtalk. Fairy tales and fantasy stories are full of farmers (*The Lord of the Rings* has Farmer Maggot and Farmer Cotton as bookends of the tale), judges (just judges as well as unjust ones), victims, coins, sheep (and dragons that eat sheep), prodigal sons, and weddings. Of course they have lots of towers (despite the title of the second book of *The Lord of the Rings*, there are actually far more than only two) and going to war. I'm not sure I've read any books more about the courtesies of hospitality than the stories set in Narnia and Middle-earth. They have crooks (and sometimes burglars) and beggars (who may be wizards in disguise), and how we treat them is vitally important. Yes, we live in the midst of a cosmic war, and yet it is better to show mercy to a prisoner and gentleness to a potential enemy than to win a battle by becoming people who are unmerciful and abandoning the virtue of gentleness. How desperately that idea needs

What Fantasy Books You Should Read & Why 95

to fill our imagination today! J.R.R. Tolkien, in part by working hard to remove from his writings all traces of religion as we know it in our primary world, actually made his books even more deeply moral and theological.

Then there is the imagination. If we are to understand the Bible we need to train our imaginations to understand story, imagery, and myth—some of the most important literary forms of the Bible itself. Fantasy engages the imagination as well as—and I think better than—any other genre. (I could make a similar argument about poetry, which also develops the imagination, though in a different way.) This trained imagination not only is vital to the reading of Scripture, but it is vital to empathy: the ability to see the world through the eyes of somebody else who is very different. There are good arguments that reason itself, often seen in contrast to imagination, actually goes hand in hand with the imagination as a means of knowledge. The great philosophers and apologists all seem to turn to metaphors to communicate their most important points. Plato wrote myths.

And, of course, imagination may be the most important way that our moral character is developed. We act heroically (or not) because our imaginations have been shaped by the heroes we choose, far more than by any abstract principles. Fantasy literature provides these imaginary heroes. What would Frodo do? Or Bilbo? Or Faramir? They would choose to show gentleness and mercy even at the cost of their own lives.

But finally, there is this. As scholar Tom Shippey and others have argued, fantasy literature is the dominant literary mode of our day. In order to both understand the culture of Athens, and to communicate the Gospel to and within that culture, Paul had to become familiar with the important myths of Athens in his day. The ancient Athenian story of the Unknown God became the connection point for Paul to the people of Athens. I think a comparable point could be made about anybody who wants to understand and communicate with a culture in which the Harry Potter stories are one of the most widely read and widely loved books of our day. Every fall I hold several dinners at my house, each for twelve to fifteen first-year college students. At every meal I ask the students present to share a work of art that has influenced their lives. Almost without fail, at every meal, the Harry Potter stories get mentioned by at least one student as that work. As Borger said in those *BookNotes*—and it gave the old bookseller a "bit of hope" to say it—"Harry Potter is here to stay."

So, to end, here are a few other works of post-Tolkien fantasy I think are here to stay—or ought to be. This list will bring you from shortly after I was born up to the current decade. Though I'm not interested in arguing which are the best works of fantasy ever, I can certainly claim that each of these is both wonderfully-crafted and deeply meaningful. Not all of these authors share my worldview or faith. Yet all of these works have had an important impact on my life and imagination, and I have found them worth not only reading, but rereading. Collectively, in spanning half a century, they also show both a continuum and a trend.

The Chronicles of Prydain by Lloyd Alexander

From 1965 to 1968, Lloyd Alexander published a series of five books, starting with *The Book of Three* and ending with the Newbery Award-winning *The High King*. Collectively the series is known as *The Chronicles of Prydain*. Like the better-known Narnia stories of C.S. Lewis, Alexander's works can be read and appreciated by children. I first read them in middle school or high school. I also returned and read them again as an adult, and then again to my own children. Inspired by Welsh legend, yet also original in the telling, they are beautifully written coming-of-age stories that present heroism and love and self-sacrifice not as abstractions or principles, but as flesh and blood.

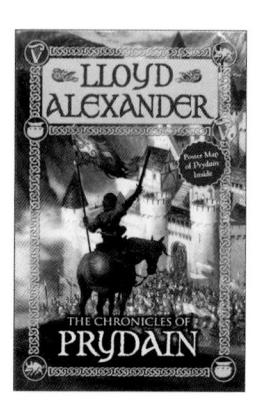

The Earthsea Trilogy by Ursula K. Le Guin

From 1968 to 1973 Ursula K. Le Guin published her well-known series: *A Wizard of Earthsea*, *The Tombs of Atuan*, and *The Farthest Shore*. (Two and three decades later, she would add two more books to the trilogy, turning it into a cycle.) Le Guin's "answers" to some of life's biggest questions, especially around the meaning of death, were markedly different from those of J.R.R. Tolkien. Yet her stories are beautifully told and never didactic, and through the growth and change of the hero Ged, who learns to become a wizard, readers see the costs of hubris, and the virtue and reward of humility and sacrifice. The books—despite the importance of wizards and dragons—are creative, and not at all derivative of the writings of

Tolkien. At the core of the wizard's power is the importance of names and naming. Long before J.K. Rowling came along, Le Guin also introduced readers to a school for young wizards—with all the angst associated with that age.

The Riddle Master Trilogy by Patricia McKillip

The late 1970s and the 1980s was my own personal golden age for reading fantasy literature. The market for that genre had not yet been saturated with formulaic writing. Some great authors were contributing. As a young adult, moving from high school to college to graduate school to newly married life, my own imagination clung to and was influenced by the best of these works. Not only did J.R.R. Tolkien's long-awaited masterpiece *The Silmarillion* finally come posthumously into print in 1978, but from 1976 to 1979 Patricia McKillip also managed to produce an imaginative, captivating three-volume work that remains among my all-time favorites: *The Riddle-Master of Hed, Heir of Sea and Fire,* and *Harpist in the Wind.*

The Book of the Dun Cow by Walter Wangerin, Jr.

In 1978, Walter Wangerin Jr. published his American Book Award-winning novel *The Book of the Dun Cow,* which straddles the worlds between fairy tale, epic fantasy, and myth, drawing equally on *The Canterbury Tales,* old Norse myth, and his own experience as a pastor. The books provide a powerful portrayal of evil, not just in the vast, powerful, demonic Wyrm, but in the petty bickering, jealousy, and pride of common everyday barn creatures. I have been drawn back to reread *The Book of the Dun Cow* perhaps more than any other book not written by C.S. Lewis or J.R.R. Tolkien. Wangerin followed that in 1985 with the haunting and deeply moving sequel *The Book of Sorrow* (1985) which has perhaps the most powerful portrayal of forgiveness I have ever read outside the Gospel story itself.

The Pendragon Cycle by Stephen Lawhead

About that time, Stephen Lawhead entered the scene. After a debut fantasy series for young adults, he crafted a beautiful Arthurian trilogy published from 1987 to 1989: *Taliesin*, *Merlin*, and *Arthur*. Though set (loosely and with a few liberties, but also carefully and with great texture) in the real historical England of the fourth and fifth century, they also weave in the myth of lost Atlantis to create a work of fantasy set in our world. I recommend these works more than any other versions of the Arthurian legend, and *Taliesin* especially remains among my all-time favorites. Like Ursula Le Guin, Lawhead followed that up several years later with three new books in the Pendragon Cycle published in the late 1990s, while also going on to write more fantasy and a wonderful trilogy retelling the Robin Hood tales.

The Auralia Thread Quartet by Jeffrey Overstreet

And that brings me to this millennium, where I end with a relatively new author of fantasy literature, Jeffrey Overstreet, who crafted one of the most unique and original fantasy worlds and fantasy series: *Auralia's Colors* (2007), *Cyndere's Midnight* (2008), *Raven's Ladder* (2010), and *The Ale Boy's Feast* (2011). The heroes are compelling, and the moral vision is powerful as it brings readers through many surprising turns, forcing us to pit traditional expectations of fantasy heroes, villains, and monsters with notions of mercy, compassion, and humility. These books epitomize the ability of fantasy literature to take our eyes off of this present world, onto a world of enchantment and magical creatures and fantastic landscapes, and yet somehow to end up able to see *this* world—our own "real" world—with greater clarity than we have ever seen it before.

FILM

Denis Haack

THE FIRST TIME I MET BYRON BORGER he was standing beside a huge table. It was piled so high with all sorts of books that the idea struck me that if I hung around a bit I might witness it collapse under the sheer weight of all those stacks. It didn't, but what did happen was even more fascinating.

The book table was in the lobby of a hotel in Pittsburgh where a student conference, Jubilee, was underway. The conference is designed around a simple yet profound idea: because Christianity is true it speaks intelligently and creatively to every part of life and reality. I was there as a speaker; Byron was there to offer books that would help students think Christianly about whatever they were studying, whatever they were pursuing as a vocation. As I waited for the table to collapse, a student walked up and told Byron what he was studying. I don't remember what the subject was except that it was a field so obscure and rarified that when I was a student I found the course descriptions in that department to be incomprehensible. Could Byron, the student asked, recommend any books that would help him pursue his coursework from a Christian perspective? Absolutely, Byron replied, and began rummaging through the stacks of books until he found what he was looking for. The student walked away with an armful of books, delighted.

After the student walked away with his purchase, I told Byron I was looking for something new to read that would stretch me. I have just the thing, Byron said with obvious delight, walked to the other end of the table, rummaged in one of the piles, pulled out a slim book, and handed it to me. It was a book on architecture by an atheist, he told me, and was must reading. Beautifully written, nicely illustrated, and full of insight. So I bought it, read it, and he was right on all counts. *The Architecture of Happiness* by Alain de Botton is one of the most delightful books I have ever read. It showed me how the design, form, utility, and beauty—or ugliness—of buildings actually affects my life, my feelings, even my beliefs. I may be unconscious of how they affect me, but affect me they do. *The Architecture of Happiness* also showed me that learning to thoughtfully and carefully observe things so common I usually overlook them opens a door to live more abundantly.

Byron's reputation had preceded that meeting, but our interaction in that hotel lobby told me several things. Byron loves books. He loves Christ. And he believes that there is not a single square inch of created reality over which Christ does not proclaim, "I am Lord."

On the other hand, most people I know who know Byron wonder how he is able to read and review so many books while hosting so many book tables in so many places and running Hearts & Minds Bookstore. My conclusion is that it's divine unfairness in how God distributes gifts. I try not to think about it very much. But believe me, it is a gift.

Speaking of the bookstore, I'm really not qualified to be included in this book because I've never once visited Hearts & Minds where Beth and Byron fit books to people. I got close one time but that's it. They send me books through the mail, which is wonderful—the staff is amazingly efficient—but this lacks the lovely intensity of being handed a book by someone who loves books and is surrounded by books. Where most people see shelves of books I see rows of portals, openings into new worlds where new ideas, new people, new stories wait to be entered and embraced. A good bookstore like Hearts & Minds, so rare today, is an enchanted place.

Over the years I have been drawn to, and needed, books on film. I love good movies because I love stories and the way the cinema sweeps us up and away into them. Human beings can't live without stories, and today that means we can't live without the movies. Even if we don't watch them ourselves their stories and themes weave their way through our modern world in social media, conversations, advertising, sermons. We were created for story, placed into an unfolding story of reality and history, and make sense of life through stories. I believe all human stories are an echo of The Story revealed in Scripture.

I was raised in a fundamentalist family and didn't see a movie until I got to college. Hollywood, we were taught, was decadent, and going to the movies was worldliness that would corrupt our morals and destroy our testimony. But I had fallen in love with good stories and was delighted when I could lose myself in some adventure of the imagination. By the time I was in senior high I had begun to question what I had been taught, and to doubt the veracity of the Christianity in which I had been raised.

And then I discovered a newly published book, *The God Who is There* (1968), by a strange little man in knickers, Francis Schaeffer. It wasn't a book on film, but addressed film with sensitivity as it showed how the Gospel had something powerful to say about all of life, culture, and history. I learned that Schaeffer had a colleague named Donald Drew who wrote what is to me the first book on movies from a distinctly Christian perspective. And it changed my life.

Images of Man: A Critique of the Contemporary Cinema by Donald Drew

It's out of print now, and dated (1974), since the world of popular culture never slows, never pauses, and has since moved on. Still, *Images* holds a special place in my heart and imagination. Reading it showed me how to think and live with greater clarity and faithfulness as a follower of Christ in the modern world. "The cinema is a weathervane," Drew said, "pointing to the postulates and lifestyles which surround and subsume us all, even though most of us most of the time are oblivious to them."[1] Movies are not merely entertainment, though they are entertaining, but as the stories of our world embody the deepest fears, questions, hopes, and yearnings of our world. If you can find a copy, *Images* is still worth reading because of Drew's deep commitment to personal holiness, to Scripture and to the arts.

Drew (and Schaeffer) helped me see that the cinema, like all good art, touches on the things that matter most. It's the function of stories to do so. It's not that storytellers manipulate what they are doing to address big issues—when that happens they produce not art but propaganda. Rather, in calling us into existence God places us to live out the story of our life within a greater story, the story of reality as it unfolds in history. And that is why our stories—including the stories told in movies—implicitly, and sometimes explicitly, raise the perennial questions of existence.

"Storytelling of all kinds, cinematic and otherwise," Roy Anker says, "stimulates people with the vital questions of what the world is like, what is likely to happen next, and why what happens does happen."

From its very beginnings, not much more than a hundred years ago, one of cinema's great appeals has been its regular, and often compelling, attempt to throw some light on those "big questions" about the way the world is...

In short, despite its reputation as a mindless, soul-less diversion, even cinema regularly wrestles with the central deep mysteries about origins, meaning, purpose, intimacy, destiny, morality, and the possibility of God—those domains of human inquiry to which philosophy, theology, and the arts have traditionally devoted themselves.[2]

Catching Light: Looking for God in the Movies
by Roy Anker

Roy Anker has written so helpfully on film that whenever he publishes a book I simply order a copy. In *Catching Light* Anker reflects on a series of classic films divided into four great themes. You've probably seen them, and if you haven't you should—they're the kind of movies that stand up well over time. In the first section he covers movies (*The Godfather, Chinatown, The Deer Hunter*) that help us comprehend the darkness of our fallen world. We all know of the brokenness, of course, but these films allow us insight into how that brokenness brings alienation and suffering into every corner of human existence. In the second he reviews four films (*Tender Mercies, Places in the Heart, The Mission, Babette's Feast*) that depict a distinctly Christian view of the light that has shone into our dark world. Then Anker has us consider a series of films that are fables (*Star Wars, Superman, Close Encounters of the Third Kind*), stories that propose solutions that are both fantastic and attractive to broken people. And finally he turns his attention to three films (*Grand Canyon, American Beauty, Blue*) in which protagonists are surprised by truth, by a glimmer of light, by a sudden hopefulness that is more than their secularism suggests possible. By the time we reach the final page, we want to watch the films again because Anker has taught us how to sit in a darkened theater and watch with our eyes open, our minds engaged, and our imaginations aflame.

Of Pilgrims and Fire: When God Shows Up at the Movies by Roy Anker

Dr. Anker, besides teaching literature and film at Calvin College, has published numerous movie reviews in various publications. He collects twenty in *Of Pilgrims*, adding discussion questions, what to look for as you watch the films, and suggestions for further viewing. "The best collection of seriously Christian film reviews in years," Byron says. "Illuminating for the insight about particular movies, and an education on how to engage culture Christianly, this is masterful, luminous, provocative, and thrilling. A must for any film buff." I agree totally, except that I'd suggest that Christians who aren't film buffs and only watch a movie occasionally would also be wise to read this book. It's like watching movies with a trusted and godly mentor who loves and knows movies because he loves and knows Jesus.

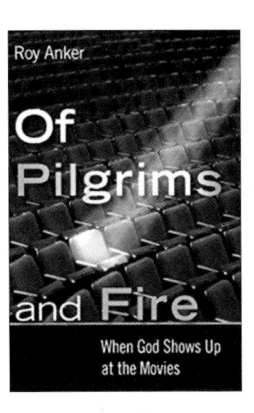

Movies are an exquisite art form, the primary storytelling medium in our modern world. As such, the cinema helps to both reflect and shape our culture, helping to form our social imaginary by inviting us into stories shown in splintered light. We are welcomed into new worlds, revealed in image, sound, and word, that spawn reflection and an ongoing conversation about the things that matter most.

"There is a conversation going on in popular culture that the church is not engaged in and is often unaware of," Craig Detweiler and Barry Taylor assert.

> Ideas are exchanged in the marketplace. The dramas of life, lived between the wedding song and the funeral march, are played out in the marketplace. It is where humans face the challenges of living and dying, in ways not adequately addressed by stock, religious propositions. The belly of messy culture is also the place where questions of ultimate existence and realities are posed in naked, stripped-down fashion, devoid of the religious language of etiquette and propriety.[3]

If more Christians are engaged in that cultural conversation today it is partly the result of Hearts & Minds Bookstore and the books on film they've recommended and distributed.

Eyes Wide Open: Looking for God in Popular Culture, revised and expanded, by William Romanowski

If you only read one book on a Christian perspective on film, make it this one. Romanowski provides not merely the biblical and theological grounding for watching movies Christianly, but he provides helpful tools we can use to develop skill in cultural discernment. "Few books are as accessible and insightful, as serious and as playful, as balanced and wise, as *Eyes Wide Open*," Byron says. "And few books are as foundational, essential... Bill's book is solid, helpful, interesting, and important." *Eyes Wide Open* grows out of a biblical understanding of life and culture, and is written with a deep passion for Christian faithfulness in a pluralistic and post-Christian world. And it is written, thankfully, by a man who writes well, who has done his homework, and who walks along with us to help us engage the movies through the spectacles of Scripture instead of just telling us what to do. He includes a series of thoughtful questions we can use to reflect on and discuss the films we watch—it's worth the price of the book.

Reel Spirituality: Theology and Film in Dialogue by Robert K. Johnston

As the cinema grew since its development in the final decade of the nineteenth century, Christians have had a varied response to the movies. So did the educated elite who tended to dismiss popular culture as lowbrow entertainment, and to prefer high art that was morally uplifting and tasteful. Johnston, who teaches theology and culture at Fuller Seminary, places those responses on a continuum so we can think through our own response in light of Scripture. He wants us all to become film critics, not in a professional sense but so that we engage with film as believers rather than just passively allowing the movies to wash over us. "It is a fact," he says. "Movies function as a primary source of power and meaning for people throughout the world. Along with the church, the synagogue, the mosque, and the temple, they often provide people stories through which they can understand their lives." This is an art form that is far too powerful for passive viewing, and a cultural force too significant not to reflect on it theologically. "Although there are several more basic books on the topic," Byron writes, "this is a serious and thoroughly Christian work on film studies. Very well done."

The books on film I've listed here are only the proverbial tip of the iceberg. There are others I could list that are worth listing because they are worth reading. Still, these represent the basics, a place to begin, a short list that should be in every church library and every Christian home. Start here and you'll find your way to the rest easily. But do start with these because they equip us to understand, appreciate, and thoughtfully engage with one of the most powerful and influential art forms ever imagined in history. By the time young adults reach high school they need to have the skills of discernment that these authors describe and demonstrate. And we need to have them if we want our conversations about movies—at work or with neighbors—to be seasoned creatively with the greater Story of the gospel.

Hearts & Minds Bookstore lists all these books, and much more, on their website. Beth and Bryan Borger and their delightful Hearts & Minds enterprise are like a beacon of light in a dark night. They don't just sell books, but offer us a chance to become wise. I esteem them highly for having blessed me so often with so many good books, recommended with warmth, unfailing good cheer, and a deep, passionate love for the Gospel.

Endnotes

1. Donald J. Drew, *Images of Man: A Critique of Contemporary Cinema* (Downers Grove, IL: InterVarsity PRess, 1974), 9.
2. Roy M. Anker, *Catching Light: Looking for God in the Movies* (Grand Rapids, MI: Eerdmans, 2004), 4-5.
3. Craig Detweiler and Barry Taylor, *A Matrix of Meanings: Finding God in Pop Culture* (Grand Rapids, MI: Baker Academic, 2003), 23, 27.

HISTORY
Daniel Spanjer

HISTORY IS THE QUEEN OF THE HUMANITIES; so said the great Donald Kagan, Yale professor and historian of Ancient Greece (author of one of the great histories of Ancient Greece, *The Peloponnesian War*. Since Herodotus and Thucydides, history has been the starting point of humanity's investigations into itself. The linear relationship between the past and the present contains trends, continuities, and inconsistencies that reveal the character of people and societies. While people and societies are the subjects of many other disciplines, history uniquely seeks to learn the lessons that only narratives can tell. It is the stories linking person to person, society to society, and age to age that shed light on peoples' actions, ways of thinking, and behaviors. Great history is great storytelling about people and events in the past, thus history stands alone as a reading and writing discipline.

History has fallen out of favor in contemporary intellectual culture as the humanities have lost their territories to a rival kingdom ruled by the social sciences. History now reigns over an area too small to be considered a kingdom. Since World War II the social sciences have set out to do what the humanities, such as history, were never intended to accomplish—solve humanity's problems. Social scientists seek to understand people by studying quantitative statistics, while history utilizes the fluidity and connectivity of narratives. Stories may connect people to the past but do little to address modern-day difficulties. In a pragmatic culture, history has failed to deliver clear answers to humanity's problems and so has too often been relegated to general studies requirements in colleges. Worse than that, social science writers have simply accommodated historical events and situations as so many data points in their quest and thus have, in a way, diluted what was once the starting point for appreciating the nuances of human experience.

As a young history major during undergraduate studies, my department debated whether the college should consider the history degree a science or an art. As a budding academic I thought I would storm the Acropolis and force the college muckety-mucks to modernize the department by making history a science. You see, I believed history was part of the scholar's mission to seek the truth through verification. Whereas art communicates emotion and aesthetic experience, science seeks reality. Both the department and the college rebuffed my advances, which frustrated me then. After completing my PhD in history, I now agree with my *alma mater*. History is not a science at all, it is an art. Should it be reduced to a science, it would finally die the death that contemporary scholars have been unfairly reporting.

History is not an effort to validate truth by using the past because its subject is humanity, not human bodies. While biology, economics, and sociology can define their subject, historians realize that their subject is far too complex for quantitative measures. The social sciences can measure power, interest, and advantage, but history explores human character, an effort equivalent to capturing a starry night on a cotton canvas. Like any other art, history does not seek to register facts but rather to show symmetry and meaning in a holistic way. The historian interprets the dissonance and complexity of events to reveal something rational yet beautiful. An artist practices the skill of synthesis in order to reify qualities too complex for statistics or economic models. At its best, therefore, writing history is an act of creativity but not *ex nihilo* creation, for the historian can avoid neither medium nor audience. History is real by its very existential subject and its discerning object, the reader, whose learning constitutes its end. Yet only through an act of creation can the historian draw from the mass of facts a picture exhibiting the beauty in unity, meaning, and plot that we all recognize as an actual part of human life. A well-written piece of history is not a scientific analysis or a quantifiable study of causes and effects. It is a beautiful story told by a scholar who must communicate meaning with all the complication and asymmetry that real life entails.

So, the historian is the artist, trained in his medium to animate flat facts into a living story. The nature of the discipline fosters tremendous variety because the sheer diversity of forces that connect past events to each other and to the present render any story of the past fractional at best. Thus, historians must choose which forces moved the narrative of history along, and which events and people played the most significant roles in that story. In other words, historians must choose a story line which presents the past as a coherent plot despite its seemingly incoherent mass of facts. The variety of plots ensures that history always changes, despite what so many of my colleagues mean when they offer the jibe, "I guess teaching history gets boring because it never changes." Well, the facts may not change but the story of how they related and intertwined is something that no one will ever completely know.

History is the art of evaluating the past and organizing its parts to explain why it happened as it did, not registering the fact that something happened. Chronology is an easy thing to construct, for most of human history, but distinguishing between causal and coincidental events is a Herculean task. The historian must interpret the data of past events to paint a story that is true to the facts while being realistic to the human experience. Why would a soldier run across a battlefield to certain death or a family brave oceans to find a new home or a worker endure grueling hours for little pay? The artist must divine a plot, the telling of which will help the reader understand what he or she will never experience.

In order to see the unique task that falls to the historian, consider a past event such as the American Revolution. Many contemporary scholars study the Revolution as the source of all the nation's social ills or the promise of the nation's future. Increasingly the narrative of history is falling victim to what William James once called the "cash value" of ideas—the worth of any historical event for the world today. But history is more plot than instrument. It is the story of why people did the things they did and how those decisions impacted other people, times, places, and events. For the historian, the American Revolution, and any other past event, is an eminently human story that was driven by the awesome complexity of human knowledge, interest, and passion. So, any history of this event must consider the mind of the actors, the spirit of their age, and the forces of their lives. The historiography of the American Revolution is the schematic for the variety of interpretations used by the historians who attempted to tell the story of this significant event. Without space to describe the wide variety of historical interpretations of why the Americans fought and won their independence from Great Britain, consider these two.

Some historians have argued that the Americans fought their eighteenth-century revolution because it made economic sense. Merchants saw the fiscal benefits of trading without the costs of British regulation. Charles and Mary Beard championed this story of the Revolution at the turn of the twentieth century. It is arguable, but the height of what is now called the Progressive approach to the American Revolution was most aptly presented by Forrest

McDonald, in *We the People: The Economic Origins of the Constitution* (1958). Some historians believed that the Progressive model erred by giving too much weight to financial interest and the lemming-like support of laboring populations, not to mention the agrarian sectors. In 1968, Bernard Bailyn countered the Progressives by arguing that the American patriots fought the Revolution, not for money, but because they believed in ideas like liberty and virtue. In *Ideological Origins of the American Revolution*, Bailyn reintroduced a nineteenth-century interpretation of American independence that inspired a new generation of historians to look again at the familiar facts to divine a new story with a well-known ending. These are just two of many schools of history on the American Revolution which show the role of the historian—to organize the overwhelming complexity of past events into a story that makes the best sense of the human experience.

The Glorious Cause: The American Revolution, 1763-1789 by Robert Middlekauf

While historians must have a scholar's grasp of past events, they are defined by how well they can tell the story of the human experience. This enterprise unleashes the artistic creativity of a wide variety of thinkers, each contributing one plot to the vast mural of human history. For the sake of simplification, all histories can be distinguished by two measures: the plot which drives their stories (which we looked at briefly) and the scope of those stories. While some write monographs on single events, others attempt to pull decades of the past into a single narrative. Robert Middlekauf is the latter type of intrepid historian, who tells the tale of the American Revolution from 1765 to the penning of the Constitution. While addressing so many of the forces that contributed to this complicated event, Middlekauf organizes his narrative around an idea. He argues that a vision materialized in colonists minds, out of the swirling events of the 1760s and 70s, to create a republic in a world governed only by monarchies. He tells his story by skillfully analyzing battles in some places while adeptly sculpting biographical vignettes in others. *The Glorious Cause* sets out to show the genius of the Revolution despite its messiness and heralds George Washington as its hero even with his flaws. Middlekauf's story is as fluid as a novel and as informed as an encyclopedia.

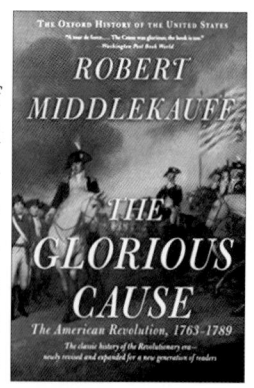

Postwar: History of Europe Since 1945 by Tony Judt

Tony Judt tells a story as big but about a subject far less focused. In *Postwar* Judt's writing strains to make European events after World War II, from France to Poland, fit a single plot. He concedes to the scope of his subject but tells a history nonetheless. He begins his story by finding Europe stuck between the two victors of World War II, the U.S., and Russia. From the repatriation of Hitler's victims and the judgements rendered by local populations against Nazi sympathizers to the failures of Brezhnev's economic expansion, Judt shows the birth and growth of modern Europe. What makes Judt's work so impressive is that he tells the smaller stories that make up his book in such a way that the reader often forgets that they belong to a large narrative. The scope of Judt's work is grand but his writing is not grandiose. Like any beautiful work of art, one can get lost in the details but will only truly enjoy the work by standing back. *Postwar* exudes an informed realism while it also lays out the hope that Europe can yet strike a *tertium quid* between fading Cold War powers that may yet redeem the worst of the twentieth century.

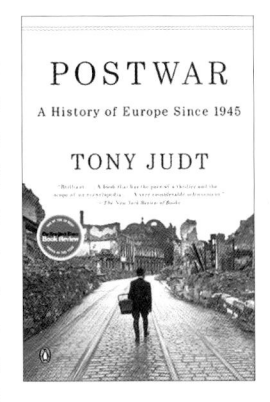

I find Middlekauf's and Judt's work so valuable because they seek continuities in impossibly complex subjects like societies and nations. With tremendous skill and effort, they effectively organize overwhelming amounts of information into stories that show the meaning in eras and the identities of people. While I enjoy the amazing work of large-scale histories, my favorite works are monographs that tell the stories of how ideas inspired individuals. Despite the economic and social pressures that nudge people to think in certain ways humans have the amazing capacity to explain the swirling currents of life by using clear ideas. Unlike animals, which respond to impulses, people navigate through life. They do not just see the world that is, they imagine what it could be. Some histories revel in this supremely human quality and then develop plots directed by how agents used ideas to fix their headings despite the pain it engendered.

The Rise and Fall of the American Left
by John Patrick Diggins

Of the many intellectual historians, I enjoy John Patrick Diggins. Diggins had the ability to show how people remained loyal to ideas almost regardless of the dissonances between those ideas and the realities of life. In *The Rise and Fall of the American Left* he gives voice to the irony of clear ideas. With precision and flourish, Diggins analyzes the way in which American leftists insisted that life should fit the precise categories of their ideas but could not grasp the fact that it does not. He deftly assesses the influence that Hegelian rationalism and industrial social evils had on the political theorists, socialist scholars, and activists who leveraged Marx to predict the future of America. Diggins charts the variant trajectories of various Leftist movements which, while opposing one another, still remined loyal to a single ambition—to repair the damage that industrialization unleashed on U.S. society by replacing its free market foundation. While disappointments never dimmed the Left's hopes, they did introduce stresses that led its adherents to develop creative solutions that all revolved around the same goal.

Progressivism by Arthur Link
and Richard L. McCormick

Diggins' approach to the American Left reveals the usefulness of the history of an idea. Historians have long abandoned the History of Ideas as a genomic experiment which, at the turn of the twentieth century, promised to show the lineage of all modern thought. But Diggins is a marvelous example of a historian willing to see the usefulness and persuasiveness of an idea over time. For some strange reason, people desire to make sense of the seeming chaos of their experiences. Sometimes a single and very general idea has an indelible power to attract thinkers across cultures and through time. Arthur Link and Richard L. McCormick do something very similar in their succinct history titled *Progressivism*. There is no Marxian desire to trace the expanse of humanity's past in the hopes of singling out a Reason for human progress. Rather, Link and McCormick show the power of an idea to inspire and rally bureaucrats, scholars, and intellectuals, who all faced the burdens of industrialization at the end of the nineteenth century. Whereas so many today are trying to find out if they are on the "right side of history," Link and McCormick are satisfied simply to show a single side of history. The modesty and clarity of their ambition gives the work a gravitas not proportional to its page count.

Link and McCormick claim that "Progressivism was the only reform movement ever experienced by the whole American nation." If one reads the Great Awakening as purely theological, one might agree with this statement, but the artistic ambition of the statement captures the imagination. Their story only investigates a small fraction of American life while the plot engages an entire country. This is the art of the story—to synthesize from a very real, complex set of events a perceivable plot. A narrative like this must exude a certain modesty because any claims to understand something as vast as American society would sound like dime novel fiction. But Link and McCormick draw the broadest possible outline around their subject—Americans feared the power of depression and economic panic to destroy the hope of economic prosperity.

Progressivism builds on a negative explanation of one of America's most dynamic movements. Inspired by the idea of minimizing the negative effects of economic evils, Progressives converted moral problems into statistical errors. Thus, science, education, and bureaucratization held out the promise of saving humanity from itself. While Link and McCormick appreciate the overconfidence of such a hope, they recognize that it laid the groundwork for twentieth-century politics, military, and economics. In their effort to defend the poor against different economic threats, Progressives developed scientific, bureaucratic, and administrative measures which would manage the consumer revolution, win a world war, and help rebuild an entire war-torn continent.

Edwards on the Will: A Century of American Theological Debate by Allen C. Guelzo

Progressivism and *The American Left* are just two examples of histories that trace the intellectual patterns that tie together people who may be hardly related in time and space. George Marsden accomplishes the same task in his marvelous history of American Fundamentalism, titled *Fundamentalism and American Culture*. Marsden deftly outlines the sinews that link Evangelical movements of the early nineteenth century with the Fundamentalist responses to modernism in the early twentieth. Allen Guelzo reveals the continuities among Edwardseans who may have lived in different centuries yet remained faithful to an idea. *Edwards on the Will* is an exercise in meticulous cartographical narration. Having armed himself with a scholastic grasp of the facts, Guelzo maps out the life of Edwards' theology across more than a hundred and fifty years.

For those who may not be as moved as I am by the power ideas exert on people looking to organize their lives, some histories seek even narrower subjects. Biographies represent one of the most popular of historical genres. It is not to say that broader histories have no use to common readers but these ofttimes require the reader to be familiar with less well-known movements, historiographical contexts, and events. Biographies, on the other hand, reduce their contexts to the life of a single individual, which allows the historian to engage their subject's time period in a way more natural to a reader. The story of a single life has a natural flow. Yet, synthesizing a person's identity and character by analyzing a lifetime of decisions and thoughts is a very difficult task to do well. As with any other genre of historical writing, I can only recommend a few of the great artworks available to you. Given limitations of space, I will recommend two.

Here I Stand: A Life of Martin Luther
by Roland Bainton

The first has become a timeless piece of historical writing as its author takes the complicated character of German history in the sixteenth-century and makes it accessible to nearly any reader. Yet, at the same time, he brings his reader into a relationship with his complicated subject. Roland Bainton's *Here I Stand* is a model biography because it not only tells the life of Martin Luther but through the telling connects the reader to one of the most significant moments in Western history. This makes Bainton's work a brilliant piece of history because it beautifully weaves one person's micro narrative into a much larger story so that the two somehow become intertwined. He brings the crises of sixteenth-century Germany and the Roman Catholic Church into focus through the lens of a single monk, yet without aggrandizing his subject. Bainton introduces his readers to Luther the man while allowing them to experience the social, philosophical, and political intricacies of the European Reformation.

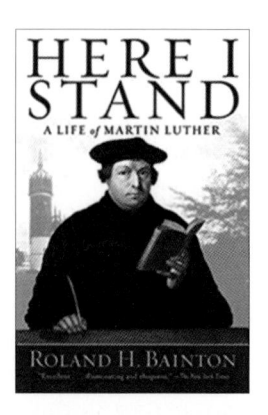

Augustine of Hippo: A Biography by Peter Brown

Like Bainton, Peter Brown tells the story of a single individual's life as a window into one of history's most complex and important moments. *Augustine of Hippo* is a majestic biography which combines the intimate analysis of Augustine's personality with the seismic shifts happening during the fall of the Roman Empire. Like Luther, Brown shows that Augustine is a liminal figure who flourishes in the gap between two worlds. Augustine's life captures the nuance of late Roman Neo-Platonism and the bureaucratic architecture of a nascent Europe. Brown's artful writing reveals a real person who, while against the canvas of history is a towering figure, upon close inspection becomes a life-sized person. Augustine could be petty and rancorous as much as he also set the course of Western Christianity. While Brown may, at times, make too much of too little, the reader who finishes the book will be rewarded with a better understanding of a critical man and a critical moment in time.

Biographies such as those written by Bainton and Brown allow readers to engage their subjects at an intimate level. This is difficult to do well, since these writers were separated from their subjects by huge gaps of time, space, and culture. The skill with which these authors tell their stories gives the impression that such writing is easy, but informed readers of history know differently. No matter how skillful the historian, facts remain stubborn bedrock stones which must be excavated, measured, and positioned carefully so that the story built on them is sound history, not merely colorful fiction. At the same time, the edifice must be beautiful. You will know a good history book because after reading it you will walk away from it with the same conflicted feelings and heady thoughts that remain once you have walked away from a Van Gogh, Rembrandt, or Renoir. As you close the cover you sense that you have learned more about yourself and have come to appreciate the world and its God more than you did before you turned past the dedication page.

So history is not social science, although the two are often confused for one another. As they both take people for their subjects, they tend to look very similar, but in their purpose and constitution, they have very little in common. George Santayana has been repeated far too often to be thought of as profound so I will not bore you with the quote. Reading history teaches us how to repeat the things we prize and avoid the pitfalls we fear, but only incidentally.

The more that scholars write history as a means of identifying pitfalls to avoid the less like history it becomes. History is not a catalog of human experiences but a metaphor or picture of human life to which readers connect. It inspires readers and opens up horizons which science cannot reveal. Do yourself a favor, read a good history book and it will move you. Enlightenment, which every reader prizes, is not a scientific experiment, it is a human experience that imparts wonder, not answers to problems.

Reading Law
Mike Schutt

In the old days, "reading law" was synonymous with "legal education"—aspiring attorneys and barristers "read the law" to become a lawyer, almost always "reading" as an apprentice to a practicing lawyer. Before law schools, one was able to truly "profess" law only through apprenticeship. This "reading the law' model is an apt metaphor for Christian discipleship—apprenticeship to Christ. Disciples—apprentices—are learners. We are first to be hearers of the Word, of course, but we are also called as novice learners, apprentices of the Master's teaching, learning to build culture as we join Him as co-laborers in His redemptive work in the world. Written instruction for this labor in the world is essential to our task.

The bookstore section on law reveals a wide array of such instruction. From "true crime" to legal textbooks, political commentary, biography, jurisprudence, and history. Why should one wade into this swamp of theory, story, and history?

For law students and lawyers, one answer to this question is addressed by Steven Garber in this volume.[2] Our vocation as lawyers drives us to think faithfully about the substance of our calling to the law and our work of loving our neighbors through our legal gifts. Books like Joseph Allegretti's *The Lawyer's Calling*[3] and my own book on Christian calling and the legal profession[4] are directed to this vocational task. In addition, several shorter volumes of devotional direction help the lawyer and law student think vocationally.[5] In fact, knowledge about the content and history of one's profession is one of the very things that professionals *profess*:

> There is an obligation to know the truth about one's profession. . . . It is hard to imagine any endeavor that may be called "professional" that does not involve this learned or cognitive dimension. In the traditionally recognized professions of theology, law, and medicine, a premium was placed on learning.[6]

Reading law is not just for the legal professional, however. The "law section" of the bookstore has broad appeal. God is a God of justice, and His great act of demonstrating that justice worked to free us from the bonds of sin and slavery and paved the way for our transfer from the kingdom of darkness into the kingdom of His marvelous light. The very character of God draws us to think also about human justice, rooted as it is in the *imago Dei*. We long for justice, and our hearts are broken by injustice. We also know that we and our neighbors flourish best under human institutions that seek to live up to the challenge of serving as ministers of God's law, despite our fallen nature.

In addition, we in the West live in societies where legal and political systems developed in tandem with the spread of the Christian faith. The growth of the bedrock concept of "the rule of law" as preferable to the rule of man, for example, owes much to Christianity:

> The rule of law, then, has religious roots. One would expect, therefore, that the flourishing of the rule of law in the Anglo-American tradition has something to do with Christianity, the dominant religion of the culture that developed the common law. [In a very important sense], Christianity is part of the common law. The common law is the fundamental law of the Anglo-American legal system. It has been developed by judges since the middle ages, and continues to be developed by judges today. It is the law that other elements of our legal system presuppose.[7]

In short, particularly in the Anglo-American system, biblical Christianity provided "an especially rich soil for the growth of the rule of law," and "the flourishing of the rule of law in the common law tradition owes much to the Christian faith."[8] So reading authors in the Christian tradition gives us a particular perspective on the cultural mandate[9] that is already abundantly evident in the American legal system.

Finally, we read law because law matters in the world and in America. Our quality of life, our freedom, our social interactions, are all profoundly shaped by law and legal theory. To pick up a book in the "Law" section of the bookstore is to engage current events, to understand popular culture, and to equip oneself to live wisely and love one's neighbors well.

What Law Books You Should Read & Why 119

For centuries, scholars, kings, and lawmakers have assumed, discovered, and rediscovered this deep, fruitful entanglement of Christianity and law. From the Code of Justinian,[10] to the laws of Alfred the Great,[11] to contemporary commentary on American justice,[12] the writing is vast. It is impossible to narrow the choices to even two dozen central books that will do justice to the history of that relationship. In service to the cause of honoring the important work of Hearts and Minds, however, I will suggest three broad areas for readers to mine in law: 1) theological foundations, 2) the work of legal historians Harold Berman and John Witte, and 3) anthologies, compilations, and collections, highlighting throughout examples from the amazing fruit of the love of the Borgers for justice—and even for Christian lawyers,[13] embodied so often through their tireless service to the Christian Legal Society.[14]

THEOLOGICAL FOUNDATIONS

Russell Kirk opens *The Roots of American Order* with a simple truth: "This, then, is the high contribution of Israel to the modern social order: the understanding that all true law comes from God, and that God is the source of order and justice."[15]

In short, we see the foundation of Western law in the picture God paints for us around Mount Sinai: God rescues His people, gathers them in community, and shows them how to live for Him and with one another, through law given from on high. True law comes from God, and He is the source of justice. Human law begins with God's law.

So reading law begins with the Old Testament, moves to the New, works through a handful of the Church Fathers, on to Augustine's *City of God*, then Aquinas' *Treatise on Law*, and finally to the works of Luther, Melancthon, and Calvin on human law and the Gospel, Richard Hooker's *Laws of Ecclesiastical Polity*, William Blackstone's *Commentaries*, the development of Catholic social teaching, especially Pope Leo XIII's *Rerum Novarum*, the work of Herman Dooyeweerd and Abraham Kuyper, and finally to the proliferation of Evangelical, Roman Catholic, and Orthodox scholarship built on this rich tradition.[16]

Where to begin reading on the vast topic of theological foundations of law? Let's start with natural law.

The Treatise on Law: Summa Theologica Questions 90-97 by Thomas Aquinas

> St. Thomas's treatment of law is found in the second part of his *Summa Theologica*. Since the *Summa* is noted for its architectural order—it is regularly compared with a medieval cathedral—the way in which Thomas locates law in his wide discussion of morality and the precise place he gives it provide a show-and-tell aspect of his view.
>
> . . .
>
> Thomas . . . speaks of eternal law, natural law, human law, divine law, and the law of sin—and in that order. What he means by eternal law is divine providence, the way in which God has fashioned and orders his creation. Natural law is said to be a peculiarly human participation in eternal law. And then there is human law. . . .
>
> In order to understand why providence is called "law," we have to refer it to human law as being both like and unlike it.[17]

Seven centuries after Thomas wrote his *Summa*, a Baptist preacher found himself in jail for encouraging civil disobedience against the injustice of racial segregation. Finding time to pen a philosophical defense as he sits in his jail cell, Martin Luther King, Jr. writes:

> How does one determine when a law is just or unjust? A just law is a man-made code that squares with the moral law or the law of God. An unjust law is a code that is out of harmony with the moral law. To put it in terms of Saint Thomas Aquinas, an unjust law is a human law that is not rooted in eternal and natural law.[18]

Citing Martin Buber, Augustine, and the story of Shadrach, Meshach, and Abednego in the Bible, King creates a concise treatise on civil disobedience and the role of the Church. He closes on a prophetic note: "If the church of today does not recapture the sacrificial spirit of the early church, it will lose its authentic ring, forfeit the loyalty of millions, and be dismissed as an irrelevant social club with no meaning for the twentieth century."[19]

Byron Borger's *BookNotes* for August, 2013 (the 50th anniversary of King's March on Washington)[20] includes a selection of 19 books on Martin Luther King, the Civil Rights Movement, and the March on Washington. Byron reviews Jonathan Rieder, *The Gospel of Freedom: Martin Luther King Jr.'s Letter from a Birmingham Jail and the Struggle That Changed the Nation*:

You probably know that the famous "Letter from a Birmingham Jail" has been put into dozens (if not hundreds) of anthologies and readers, and is considered one of the great pieces of literature and social ethics ever penned. Reading this wonderful book would be a great honor to the great Dr. King, and will help you realize some of what was "in the air" in the years right before the famous March on Washington. In fact, one can hardly understand the "I Have a Dream" speech without knowing about Birmingham.[21]

Rediscovering the Natural Law in Reformed Theological Ethics by Stephen J. Grabill

A nice reading bridge between Aquinas and the nineteenth-century Reformed tradition is Grabill's book, which notes the historic distrust of natural law theory in Protestant theology, traces some of it to Karl Barth, and then notes a "renewed interest in natural law among Protestants." Beginning with Barth's "displacement" of natural theory from contemporary theology, he works through the history of the Reformation, walking out his thesis that "the older magisterial Protestant tradition (Lutheran and Reformed) not only inherited but also passed on the doctrines of *lex naturalis* and *cognitio Dei naturalis*, especially the idea of an implanted knowledge of morality, as noncontroversial legacies of patristic and scholastic thought."[22]

His detailed chapters on Calvin, Vermigli, Johannes Althusius, and Francis Turretin shed helpful light on law and theology in the early reformation era.

Reading in the Reformed tradition of law and culture, particularly Abraham Kuyper's theory of "sphere-sovereignty," adds essential perspective to one's understanding of theological foundations of law, particularly because these are Byron and Beth Borger's people:

> I could almost write a book—and over the years, nearly have—about... why my own faith journey was enhanced when I discovered the work and witness of Abraham Kuyper, the larger than life Dutch pastor, theologian, scholar, activist, and Prime Minister of Holland who lived from the end of the 1800s into the early 1900s. It may have been Kuyper who introduced the phrase "worldview" to contemporary evangelicals (see the hefty one-of-kind-book on the history of the phrase in *Worldview: The History of a Concept* by David Naugle for the real scoop on that.) Kuyper's dense set of lectures given at Princeton in 1898 are

still in print from Eerdmans, entitled *Lectures on Calvinism*, although it could easily be marketed as "Serious Lectures on a Christian Worldview." It was Kuyper who gave us that memorable line about the ascended Christ claiming "every square inch" of creation— "Mine!"— a colorful call to missional action on every front of social and cultural life.[23]

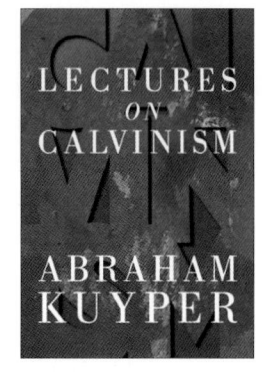

Lectures on Calvinism by Abraham Kuyper

Kuyper's third lecture, "Calvinism and Politics," expounds his "sphere theory" of jurisdiction as it relates to the State and to other social institutions such as the church, business, and the family. Due to its clarity and brevity, it will be useful as an introduction to even the non-expert in legal philosophy:

> In [Calvinism and Politics] Kuyper seeks to explain from a Christian perspective the origin of governmental power as well as necessary limitations on that power. The lecture's title

reflects Kuyper's commitment to reformed theology and occasionally puts off potential readers from different theological traditions. To ignore the lecture on this basis, however, would be a mistake; the lecture actually resonates with readers across denominational lines.... The "Calvinistic" doctrine that serves as the foundation of his piece is simply the "Sovereignty of the Triune God over the whole Cosmos."[24]

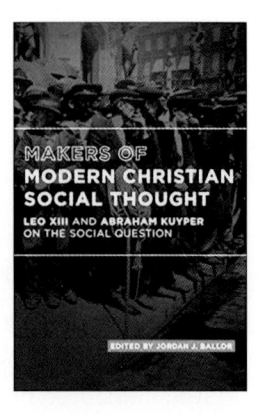

Makers of Modern Christian Social Thought: Leo XIII and Abraham Kuyper on the Social Question edited by Jordan J. Ballor

This recent volume from the Acton Institute highlights Kuyper's theology on "the social question" and contrasts it to that of his Roman Catholic contemporary, Pope Leo XIII. Jordan Ballor's introduction is brief and insightful, highlighting similarities and differences in these influential pastor-theologians. It might also serve as a nice introduction for evangelicals to the Roman Catholic doctrine of subsidiarity and the historical context of socialism to which much of Catholic social doctrine was responding.[25]

Le Fondemont theologique du droit
by Jacques Ellul[26]

I admit that I have just recently read this for the first time, and I am still processing its scope. I include it, in part, because my friend Eric Enlow, Dean of Handong International Law School, believes it to be one of the books "most helpful to the project of cultivating Christian legal thought."[27] From Dean Enlow:

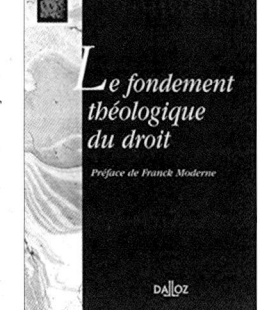

> Ellul . . . warns Christians not to be captivated by traditional legal philosophies. They depend on man's understanding of the world's natural principles. Their wisdom is foolishness because Jesus, having made a spectacle of worldly powers, is now the foundation of all rule and authority. Whether the proposed foundation is the nature of man (Aristotelian natural law), the state (positivism), or the world (naturalism), Christians reject any hollowed out jurisprudence that deceptively displaces Jesus. Ellul affirms, however, natural law's value and historical role in the development of all legal systems.[28]

Ellul's historically generous and insightful critique of both natural law and modern philosophy is a helpful tool in orientating anyone hoping to see Christ in His justice-related work in the world.

The Work of Berman & Witte

> In almost every profession, to be steeped in its history is to possess a vantage point. One cannot claim status as an economist without having read Adam Smith.[29]

Harold Berman (1918–2007) was one of the founders of the modern law and religion movement.[30] A longtime professor at Harvard Law before moving to finish his teaching career at Emory, Berman wrote widely on the intersection of law and religion, helping to found Emory's Center for the Study of Law and Religion.

John Witte, Jr. was a student of Professor Berman's at Harvard Law School and a close colleague at Emory. He is now the director of the Center for the Study of Law and Religion at Emory, and he has continued Berman's work in the field of law and religion. A prolific and respected scholar, Witte is an expert on law and religion, marriage law, and legal history.

Between them, Witte and Berman have published more than fifty books, written upwards of six hundred articles and essays, and delivered lectures on the intersection of law and religion around the world.

I want to highlight three of their books.

Law and Revolution: The Formation of the Western Legal Tradition by Harold J. Berman

Dr. Witte describes the "grand narrative" that Berman sketches in his books on historical Christian legal thought:

> There is a distinct Western legal tradition, Berman argues, a set of legal ideas and institutions that has evolved by accretion and adaptation over the centuries. The exact shape of these legal ideas and institutions at any given time is determined, in part, by the underlying belief systems of the people ruling and being ruled.[31]

Along the way, Berman's incisive historical analysis "methodically (and repeatedly) takes aim at the prevailing dogmas and idols of ... conventional scholarship of every trendy ideological stripe ...."[32] Indeed, Berman's sharp observations on "the crisis" in modern law are invaluable.

> The crisis of the Western legal tradition is not merely a crisis in legal philosophy but also a crisis in law itself. Legal philosophers have always debated, and presumably always will debate, whether law is founded in reason and morality or whether it is only the will of the political ruler. It is not necessary to resolve that debate in order to conclude that as a matter of historical fact the legal systems of all the nations that are heirs to the Western legal tradition have been rooted in certain beliefs or postulates: that is, the legal systems themselves have presupposed the validity of those beliefs. Today those beliefs or postulates—such as the structural integrity of law, its ongoingness, its religious roots, its transcendent qualities—are rapidly disappearing, not only from the minds of the philosophers, not only from the minds of lawmakers, judges, lawyers, law teachers, and other members of the legal profession, but from the consciousness of the vast majority of citizens, the people as a whole; and more than that, they are disappearing from the law itself. ... Thus the historical soil of the Western legal tradition is being washed away in the twentieth century, and the tradition itself is threatened with collapse.[33]

The forty-five page introduction to *Law and Revolution* could stand on its own as an impressive and insightful book, and it is worth the price of the volume.

Professor Berman closes this masterpiece of legal history by reinforcing its broad theme:

> Tradition is more than historical continuity. A tradition is a blend of conscious and unconscious elements. In Octavio Paz's words, "It is a society's visible side—institutions, monuments, works, things—but it is especially its submerged, invisible side: beliefs, desires, fears, repressions, dreams." Law is usually associated with the visible side, with works; but a study of the history of Western law, and especially its origins, reveals its rootedness in the deepest beliefs and emotions of a people. Without the fear of purgatory and the hope of the Last Judgment, the Western Legal tradition could not have come into being.[34]

At 558 pages, *Law and Revolution* is challenging, but it is an important book, well worth the effort for anyone interested in thinking faithfully about the history of Western law and its relationship to Christianity.

Faith and Order: The Reconciliation of Law and Religion by Harold J. Berman

This volume is a collection of Berman's speeches and articles across a wide variety of topics. Professor David Caudill describes *Faith and Order* as "a 'greatest hits' collection by one of the best law-and-religion scholars of the late twentieth century."[35]

The book is divided into four parts: Historical Themes (many of which are covered in Law and Revolution), Sociological and Philosophical Themes (including a critique of Max Weber's sociology of law[36]), Theological, Prophetic and Educational Themes (more on these below), and Russian and Soviet Themes (Berman was also an expert in Soviet Law).

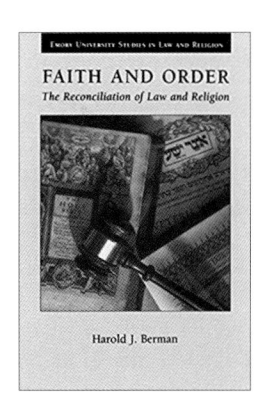

Part Three includes two articles (chapters 17 and 18), that are worth highlighting for their focus on legal education.

Chapter 17, "The Crisis of Legal Education in America," discusses Berman's view that "[l]aw teachers and law students ... are more one-sided, and more mistaken, in their view of the nature of law than were their predecessors in any other period of American History." He continues, "We have been overwhelmed by the belief that law is politics... not in the sense that Aristotle meant when he said law is politics, but more in the sense that Max Weber and V.I. Lenin meant when they said that 'law is politics, namely, domination.' We have forgotten that 'law is also morality' and 'history.'"[37]

Berman attributes this shift to "[t]he triumph of the positivist theory of law—that law is the will of the lawmaker." This has led to "a deep cynicism about the law."[38] To counteract this shift, Berman recommends that we recognize the importance of "the ancient Judaic and Christian foundations of our legal tradition." And "we must restore the integrity of our jurisprudential heritage" by joining together again the separate strands of positivism, natural law theory, and historical jurisprudence.

Chapter 18, "Is There Such a Thing—Can There Be Such a Thing—as a Christian Law School?" explores the idea of a Christian law school by examining Notre Dame's history and distinctiveness. Berman's description of the "prophetic" and "priestly" aspects of being a Christian lawyer are worth considering.[39]

God's Joust, God's Justice: Law and Religion in the Western Tradition by John Witte

Here Witte presses the same thesis that threads its way through Berman's *Law and Revolution*: "Law and religion have always been intertwined in the Western tradition and ... the continued health of this tradition suggests that they should continue to be so."[40]

The first two sections of the book lay out a framework on the relationship of law and religion in the Western tradition, like Berman, generally, but with the added bonus of application to the American system and some attention to the question of religious freedom. The final section is a *tour de force* on family law and its interaction with religion.

I recommend this book here because it is a good example of the practical value of Christian scholarship. Witte brings careful history and biblical truth to bear on timely topics—human rights and American liberties. He also demonstrates that it is possible for real legal scholarship rooted in the Christian tradition to make a difference in ordinary law practice, as his work on historical and religious foundations of family law and marriage has done.

ANTHOLOGIES, COMPILATIONS, AND COLLECTIONS
A Covenant to Keep: Meditations on the Biblical Theme of Justice by James Skillen

This is included here first because it is a favorite of Byron Borger, who says so in his *BookNotes* review:

> [James Skillen] is an old friend of the Coalition for Christian Outreach, one of the world's leading scholars on Abraham Kuyper's reformational worldview and a gem of a political theorist. He is a guy you can trust as civic-minded, truly nonpartisan, concerned with orthodox biblical doctrine and responsible social involvement. Not one to overstate a case or get caught up in flamboyant rhetoric... Jim's work at the Center for Public Justice is one of the nation's best-kept secrets, and one of the CCO's most under-utilized allies.
>
> Recently, he compiled what may be 25 years of his Bible studies and devotions inspired by the view of the Scriptures that we call "historical redemptive" and which is best seen in the Promise & Deliverance commentaries. Not moralistic, nor stretching to force the Scriptures to "address" contemporary issues, Covenant to Keep opens up the grand sweep of the Scriptures and shows that public justice and social righteousness is integral to the redemptive work of God in history.... This is one of the best Bible studies/devotionals I have ever seen....
>
> The book includes excellent and provocative discussion questions, several really choice case studies of folk who are working hard for justice in particular places, and it is laid out in an orderly, thematic fashion. It is truly a useful handbook to the Bible and a great example of how to read the Bible faithfully, allowing it to illumine our lives, current events and our need for restorative justice.[41]

Christian Perspectives on Legal Thought edited by Michael McConnell, Robert Cochran, and Angela Carmella

This collection highlights how scholars from various Christian traditions, including the Catholic, Calvinist, Anabaptist, and Lutheran, see law and justice, and provides a Christian critique of legal theory and various legal subjects.

Part One describes "Christian Perspectives on Schools of Legal Thought," those schools being

various forms of enlightenment liberalism, Legal Realism, the Critical Legal Studies movement, Feminism, Law and Economics, and Critical Race Theory. Part Two takes Niebuhr's "Christ and Culture" model and applies it through the lens of various traditions: those who "reconcile Christ and law," those that see "Christ transforming law," the separatists—those that see "Christ against the law," and those that see "Christ and law in tension." There are several wonderful essays in this section, and the collection highlights quite starkly how differently diverse disciples of Jesus see their roles in the world.

The volume closes with "Christian Perspectives on Substantive Areas of the Law," featuring, among others, John Witte on marriage law, Joseph Allegretti on legal ethics, and Notre Dame's John Nagle on environmental law.

A Higher Law: Readings on the Influence of Christian Thought in Anglo-American Law
edited by Jeffrey A. Brauch

This book had its genesis as teaching materials for Professor Brauch's introductory course in the Christian foundations of law. A collection like this is invaluable. It is self-consciously "Christian"—it is designed as a textbook for Christian law students, after all—yet it addresses most of the important topics in a more typical jurisprudence course. In addition, and this is the book's big strength, it can afford to take the time to highlight the important issues facing Christian students embarking on a career in law. For example, it closes with questions on whether "higher law thinking" has any relevance to human law today. More particularly, what about all of the Christians who believe that higher law is important to human law, even in today's legal system, but who disagree on how it might apply? Rarely are we given the opportunity to compare arguments from sources discussing the role and applicability of Old Testament law in creating contemporary legal rules, for example.

In addition, this text introduces readers to some of the most important thinking from conservative Christian scholars seeking to self-consciously apply Scripture and tradition to modern legal theory. For example, Craig A. Stern's landmark essay "The Common Law and the Religious Foundations of the Rule of Law before *Casey*"[42] lays out four Christian doctrines—the doctrine of God, the doctrine of man, the fall, and the atonement—and explains each, describing how the common law reflects—and follows—these doctrines. This is Christian legal theory at its finest. At the same time, it is an instructive and edifying model for students of the law on how to think as disciples of Jesus.

Likewise, the debate that Brauch presents between Professor Jeffrey C. Tuomala and Judge Richard Nygaard on the value of criminal punishment (primarily over the efficacy of retribution) is a gold mine for students who desire to learn how to work with theological doctrines in the context of practical, current legal theory. Tuomala argues, for example, that one's view of Christ's atonement will drive one's view of criminal punishment.

A Higher Law assumes that law and legal theory in the West were based on a particular view of law—a view that there is a higher law and that it matters to how we "do" human law. It traces the shift in thinking away from higher law, highlighting legal philosophy over the centuries. In the opening section, we hear from Harold Berman, Aquinas, Blackstone, Kuyper, and others, all excerpted in their own words. Part B focuses on clashes in legal philosophy that work themselves out in specific areas of contemporary law: criminal justice, punishment, procedure, contracts, constitutional law, and civil rights. Part C addresses whether higher law matters and what options are available in making it "work" in today's world.

A Higher Law is well worth exploring. After all, exploring these big questions surrounding law, faith, and legal theory is one great reason that we ought to "read law" together in the first place.

Endnotes

[1] Associate Professor, Regent University School of Law; Director, Law Student Ministries and the Institute for Christian Legal Studies, Christian Legal Society. JD, University of Texas School of Law.

[2] See Steven Garber, *Vocation*.

[3] Joseph Allegretti, *The Lawyer's Calling: Christian Faith and Legal Practice* (Mahwah, NJ: Paulist Press, 1996).

[4] Michael P. Schutt, *Redeeming Law: Christian Calling and the Legal Profession* (Downer's Grove, IL: InterVarsity Press, 2007).

[5] Thomas E. Baker and Timothy W. Floyd, eds., *Can a Good Christian Be a Good Lawyer?* (South Bend, IN: University of Notre Dame Press, 1997); Eric Mounts, *In His Chambers: A Ninety-One Day Devotional Experience for Lawyers* (Bloomington, IN: Westbow Press); Lynn R. Buzzard, ed., *What Does the Lord Require of You? Devotional Readings for Lawyers* (Beaver Falls, PA: Geneva School of Law, 1997).

[6] Jude P. Dougherty, *Western Creed, Western Identity: Essays in Legal and Social Philosophy* (Washington, DC: Catholic University Press, 2000), 185.

[7] *Ibid*, p. 504 (footnotes omitted).

8   Craig A. Stern, "The Common Law and the Religious Foundations of the Rule of Law Before Casey," *University of San Francisco Law Review* 38, no. 3 (Spring 2004): 505. Also available online: http://repository.usfca.edu/usflawreview/vol38/iss3/4
9   And God blessed them. And God said to them, "Be fruitful and multiply and fill the earth and subdue it, and have dominion over the fish of the sea and over the birds of the heavens and over every living thing that moves on the earth." And God said, "Behold, I have given you every plant yielding seed that is on the face of all the earth, and every tree with seed in its fruit. You shall have them for food. And to every beast of the earth and to every bird of the heavens and to everything that creeps on the earth, everything that has the breath of life, I have given every green plant for food." And it was so. *Genesis* 1:28-30 (ESV).
10 See, for example, Craig A. Stern, "Justinian: Lieutenant of Christ, Legislator for Christendom," *Regent University Law Review* 11, no. 1 (1998-99).
11 See, for example, Stephen C. Perks, *Christianity and Law* (Kuyper Foundation, 1993), a concise overview of the importance of and influence of the Law Code of Alfred the Great (871-899).
12 There are easily more than one hundred thoughtful books, published since 2000, that fit this category. For example, Nicholas Wolterstorff, *Justice: Rights and Wrongs* (Princeton, NJ: Princeton University Press, 2010); Bryan Stevenson, *Just Mercy: A Story of Justice and Redemption* (New York: Spiegel and Grau, 2014); Robert Cochran and David VanDrunen, eds., *Law and the Bible: Justice, Mercy and Legal Institutions* (Downer's Grove, IL: InterVarsity Press, 2013); Michelle Alexander, *The New Jim Crow: Mass Incarceration in the Age of Colorblindness* (New York: The New Press, 2012); Jonathan Burnside, *God, Justice, and Society: Aspects of Law and Legality in the Bible* (Oxford, UK: Oxford University Press, 2010).
13 The feeling is mutual: Christian Legal Society attorneys and their families are big fans of Byron and Beth Borger and Hearts and Minds Bookstore.
14 For nearly fifteen years, Byron and Beth have set up the conference bookstore at the CLS National Conference. They serve lawyers and attendees so well that many CLS members have threatened to skip the national conference if the Borgers are not there.
15 Russell Kirk, *The Roots of American Order* (Wilmington, DE: Intercollegiate Studies Institute, 4th edition, 2003), 20.
16 Some readers are already miffed that I left out the medieval scholastics, Johannes Althusius, and John Owen and the Puritans. As I said, the entanglement of law and religion is deep, fundamental, and rooted in the character of God Himself.
17 Ralph McInerny, "Introduction," to Thomas Aquinas, *Treatise on Law* (Washington, DC: Regnery Gateway, 1998), v, ix-x.
18 Martin Luther King, Jr., "Letter from a Birmingham Jail" (1963), 4, http://www.moodychurch.org/static/uploads/globaladmin/mlk_letterbirminghamjail.pdf.
19 *Ibid.*, 9.
20 Byron Borger, "*BookNotes:* Great Books about Martin Luther King, the Civil Rights Movement, and the March on Washington, (August 24, 2013)," Hearts and Minds Books, https://heartsandmindsbooks.com/2013/08/great_books_about_martin_luthe/.
21 *Ibid.*
22 Stephen J. Grabill, *Rediscovering the Natural Law in Reformed Theological Ethics* (Grand Rapids, MI: Eerdmans, 2006), 1.
23 Byron Borger, "*BookNotes:* Richard J. Mouw, Abraham Kuyper: A Short and Personal Introduction," (June 28, 2011), https://heartsandmindsbooks.com/2011/06/a_long_personal_review_of_a_sh/.

What Law Books You Should Read & Why 131

24 Jeffrey A. Brauch, "Abraham Kuyper's 'Calvinism and Politics,'" *Journal of Christian Legal Thought* 1, no. 1, (Spring 2011): 10.
25 See also, Michael A. Scaperlanda and Teresa Stanton Collett, eds., *Recovering Self-Evident Truths: Catholic Perspectives on American Law* (Washington, DC: Catholic University of America, 2007).
26 Marguerite Wieser, trans., Jacques Ellul, *The Theological Foundation of Law* (New York: Seabury Press, 1969).
27 See Volume 1 of the *Journal of Christian Legal Thought*, collecting essays from a variety of law professors on a book or article they believed to be "helpful to the project of cultivating legal thought." Dean Enlow wrote on Ellul. Professors also suggested works by Pope John Paul II, Robert Cover, Joseph Vining, Abraham Kuyper, John Calvin, John Milbank, Jacques Maritain, John Ryan, Thomas Shaffer, Joseph Allegretti, Jeff Tuomala, Josef Pieper, Harold Berman, and Amy Uelman, among others. See *Journal of Christian Legal Thought*, 1, no. 1 (Spring 2011).
28 Eric G. Enlow, "Jacques Ellul, The Theological Foundation of Law," *Journal of Christian Legal Thought*, 1, no. 1 (Spring 2011): 12.
29 Dougherty, *Western Creed*, 186.
30 John Witte, Jr., "Harold J. Berman (1918-2007): Law, Religion, and Revolution," *Journal of Christian Legal Thought*, 1, no. 1 (Spring 2011): 26.
31 Ibid., 26.
32 Ellis Sandoz, "Law and Revolution: The Formation of the Western Legal Tradition, by Harold J. Berman" (Book Review), *Louisiana Law Review* 45, no. 5 (1985): 1111.
33 Berman, *Law and Revolution*, 39.
34 Berman, *Law and Revolution*, 558.
35 David Caudill, "Faith and Order: The Reconciliation of Law and Religion, by Harold J. Beman (Book Review)," *Journal of Law and Religion* 16, no. 2 (2001): 713-17.
36 "One reason for the acceptance of Weber's legal sociology is that few people have carefully reviewed his historical and legal scholarship but instead have merely assumed that since it is so immense it must be sound." Harold J. Berman, *Faith and Order: The Reconciliation of Law and Religion* (Atlanta, GA: Scholars Press, 1993), 240.
37 Ibid., 334-35.
38 Ibid., 335-36.
39 Ibid., 349-51.
40 Brett T. Wilmot and John Witte, Jr., "Scholarly Exchange on John Witte, Jr., *God's Joust, God's Justice: Law and Religion in the Western Tradition*, Grand Rapids, Mich: Eerdmans, 2006," *Conversations in Religion and Theology* 5 (2007): 226-239 (November, 2007).
41 Byron Borger, *Booknotes*, "Postmodern Pilgrims."
42 Craig A. Stern, "The Common Law and the Religious Foundations of the Rule of Law Before Casey," *University of San Francisco Law Review* 38, no. 3 (Spring 2004): 505.

Literature
Karen Swallow Prior

MY FINGERS SLID ACROSS SMOOTH BOOK SPINES, skimming the familiar titles lined up on the shelf, firmly and tightly, like little soldiers standing at attention. Soon I spotted the name of an old friend: *King of the Wind* by Marguerite Henry. It had been many, many years since I'd read this book—the tale of a royal Arabian horse and the adventures he shared around the world with a Moroccan stable boy named Agba—and countless other horse stories by Henry. It had been nearly as many years, too, since I'd stood in this space, a nearly sacred place, the library of my childhood. Maybe it really was sacred, the reliquary of my soul.

The relics, these books on the shelves in this quiet alcove, brought me here, a small-town public library nestled in the corner of a building not unlike a cathedral. The power of these books brought me, not only back to this physical space, but also to this place in my life, for on this trip I was returning to my hometown and to the library of my youth as a doctoral candidate in English literature, a life centered professionally on books. But my relationship with books was much more than professional; it was—is—personal. Deeply personal. Books have formed the soul of me.

I know that spiritual formation is of God, but I also know—mainly because I learned it from books—that there are other kinds of formation, too, everyday gifts, and that God uses the things of this earth to teach us and shape us, and to help us find truth. One such gift is that my soul was entrusted to two good parents, one a mother who loves books and who read consistently to her children as we were growing up. Just as weekly attendance at church and Sunday school was part of what it meant to belong to my family, so too was my mother reading to each of us, my two older brothers and me, every night at bedtime. These rituals were part of our lives well past the age when most of my friends were no longer tucked into bed, or read to, or made to go to church by their parents. Even into my brothers' teen years our mother made the rounds to each separate bedroom, reading a section nightly from books of our choosing.

I'm not sure when we felt we had outgrown the bedtime stories, but I do know that my brothers and I each came to feel we had outgrown church. The bedtime stories, however, ceased long before compulsory church attendance did. Even friends or cousins who slept over on Saturday night knew they would be attending church with our family come Sunday morning. For most of them, this was the only time they ever went to church, so naturally, I was apologetic. And embarrassed. We New Englanders may derive from Puritan stock, but the stoic independence more than the religious piety has survived into the current age. I made up to my friends by entertaining them during the service: snickering at the drops of spittle that seeped from one corner of the pastor's mouth while he preached, making naughty puns on the names of the parishioners, and singing the hymns in a high, quavering old lady voice only the friend next to me could hear. Anyone needing evidence of the human soul's need for formation need look no further than a sneering child seated on a church pew on a Sunday morn.

Although being raised by God-loving parents is no guarantee that one will love God oneself, it certainly helps. I did love God, even if it didn't always show, but for much of my life, I loved books more than God, never discovering for a long, long time that a God who spoke the world into existence with words is, in fact, the source of meaning of all words. My journey toward that discovery is the story of this book. I thought my love of books was taking me away from God, but as it turns out, books were the backwoods path back to God, bramble-filled and broken, yes, but full of truth and wonder.

Books and the reading of books fill the memories of my early childhood as much as anything else. My childhood rituals of reading encompassed a complicated set of ceremonies, rules, and traditions not unlike those of the church.

I learned to read on my own with Dr. Seuss' *The Foot Book*, in my room, using a finger to trace each word as I sounded it out. An older playmate nearby, engrossed silently in another book, gave me an exasperated "Shhhh!" as I pronounced every word. Indignant at being shushed while carrying out such a significant task as reading by myself, I soldiered on, whispering,

In the house,
and on the street,
how many, many
feet you meet.

I remember the titles, pictures, and words of so many favorite books: the colorful chaos of *Richard Scarry's Busy, Busy World*; the tale of Ralph, the rodent with the helmet made of half a ping-pong ball in *The Mouse and the Motorcycle*; the adventures of the mutt every child wishes were her own, *Clifford the Big Red Dog*; *Casey The Utterly Impossible Horse*, which contradicts every girl's horse fantasy; the story of the inimitable and enviable antihero *Harriet the Spy*; that tomboy of tomboys, *Ramona the Brave*; the smart and sassy Nancy Drew series; the delightful and whimsical *Charlie and the Chocolate Factory*; *Where the Red Fern Grows*, which left me weeping inconsolably the night I finished it, alone, lying in the top bunk of my bedroom; my favorite horse book ever, *The Black Stallion*; and *Pippi Longstocking*. I secretly liked that my dad's special nickname for me was "Pippi" because of my own freckles and pigtails. I didn't even point out to my father that my pigtails didn't stick straight out like Pippi's did. I remember *The Lion, The Witch, and The Wardrobe*. Ever since, I have loved wardrobes so much that my own home is furnished with as many as I can reasonably fit.

Some of these titles were among those I scanned all those years later in the library at Cumston Hall. By now many new titles by more recent authors I'd never heard of overwhelmed the old, familiar titles. I smiled to think of young readers who loved these new books and who would be eager to spread their love of the stories to others, as I had done with my beloved books as a child.

One summer, when I was about seven, I was inspired to share my love of reading and my own books with everyone I could. Everyone at the time consisted of the twins next door and a few other kids on the neighboring blocks. I made my own lending library out of the basement of our little Cape Cod bungalow in the suburbs of Buffalo, where we lived for a few years when my father was transferred from his office in Maine. I borrowed a rickety little bookcase, one constructed of particleboard my mother had covered with a contact paper made to look like real wood, except that it was gray, not brown. I organized my books on the shelves according to reading level and author, designed homemade library cards, and invited all my friends over to traipse down the basement stairs and crowd around that bookcase to make their selections. How vividly I remember that day! Glowing, I checked out each book and bestowed upon my friends what I knew to be the source of one of the greatest joys in the world.

I have little memory of the succeeding days of my library, short-lived as they surely were. Although my friends humored me for a spell, I don't think they were nearly as excited about my library as I was. I'm not even sure whether I ever got all my books back.

Church stifled me. But books made my world feel bigger and made me feel freer. Some of these books took me to places most people would say a young girl shouldn't go, but my parents never restricted my reading, unlike many parents today who seem to spend a lot of time fretting over what to allow their kids to read or not to read.

It seems to me to be an entirely negative, not to mention ineffective, strategy to shield children from reality rather than actively expose them to the sort of truth that emerges organically from the give-and-take of weighing and reckoning competing ideas against one another. Discovering truth is a process that occurs over time, more fully with each idea or book that gets added to the equation. Sure, many of the books I read in my youth filled my head with silly notions and downright lies that I mistook for truth, but only until I read something else that exposed the lie for what it was.

Books meet with disapproval because of their objectionable content. Wisdom, however, considers not only what a book says (its content), but how it says it (its form). Just as important as—or perhaps more important than— whether a book contains questionable themes like sex or violence or drugs or witchcraft or candy is how those topics are portrayed. Are they presented truthfully in terms of their context and their consequences? Are dangerous actions, characters, or ideas glamorized in a way that makes them enticing? Are the bad guys presented with so much sympathy that the reader tends to identify with them? Are the good guys so insipid that you couldn't imagine having lunch with one of them, let alone having one as your friend? Discerning judgments of literature consider form as much as content, just as with any other art.

Not long ago, in my present life as a college administrator and English professor, the parent of a freshman came to me to complain about a story being taught in his daughter's literature class. The story was "Rape Fantasies" by Margaret Atwood. It's a humorous story about a serious topic, and the gist of it is that in coping with the ever-present possibility of rape in our lives, women think about what they would do or how they would handle such a threat if it arose. The fact that the characters don't think about rape in very realistic terms only emphasizes just how unthinkable such a thing is.

Well, this father was having none of it. He feared the story might lead male students to think women want to be raped and that it was traumatic for female students (namely, his daughter) to read. He would not allow her to read it, and he thought the professors in my department shouldn't be assigning it to students. He had read it because, he explained to me, he read all of his daughter's assignments before she did and blacked out with a marker anything he thought she shouldn't read. He thought this entire story needed to be blacked out; I wish I were making this up.

"But rape is a very real threat that women have to live with and think about," I tried to explain.

"Not my wife or daughter," he shot back. "They don't have to think about it."

I could see that the conversation was going nowhere.

This man needed a reality check. "Well, I fantasize about rape every day," I said.

He squirmed in his chair and looked down. "I don't need to know about that," he muttered.

"Why, yes, you do," I answered, my voice growing firm.

"You see, I'm a runner, and I live out in the country where I have to decide every day whether or not I want to run on the main road, trafficked by logging trucks, or on a quiet, deserted dirt road.

"Most days, I choose the dirt road. And on the rare occasion when a vehicle comes down that road, I pay attention. I know all the regulars by heart, and if an unfamiliar one approaches, I think about which way I'll head through the woods if I need to, and I keep my phone at the ready. That's what I fantasize about every day."

He was quiet for a moment, but a very short one. "Well, my daughter doesn't need to worry about that."

"But someday when she's out walking on the street at night, alone, she will," I insisted. What would this man think, I wondered, if he knew that when I was seventeen and came home from school one day and told my parents that my health teacher had been propositioning me—in class—my parents didn't intervene. They expected me to take care of the matter on my own and that if I couldn't, only then would I come back to them for help.

I took care of it myself.

"No, she won't. Because she will never be out walking the street at night alone," he said, shaking his head. "I'll never let her do that."

And to that there was nothing I could really say.

This is why books should be "promiscuously read."

These are the words of John Milton in his famous 1644 anti-censorship tract, *Areopagitica*. In the midst of the English Civil Wars, when the price for a wrongheaded idea might well be one's head, Milton argued passionately in this treatise that the best way to counteract falsehood is not by suppressing it, but by countering it with truth. The essence of Milton's argument is that truth is stronger than falsehood; falsehood prevails through the suppression of countering ideas, but truth triumphs in a free and open exchange that allows truth to shine. This was, I think, the essence of my parents' approach to their children's reading, though they didn't express it this way. My parents hadn't ever read Milton, but they had good instincts and a good dose of common sense.

While Milton wrote *Areopagitica* in a context far removed both chronologically and politically from the U.S. Constitution, his argument against the licensing orders of the seventeenth-century English government was instrumental in the thinking that shaped the First Amendment. Milton's stance is even more significant when one considers that he was arguing against the policies of his own Puritan faction. Milton demonstrated the universal power of truth not only in the content of his treatise, but also in the very act of countering his fellow Christians: by standing for truth even against his own party, Milton embodied the very power of truth. Milton thus exemplifies the person of integrity whose allegiance is to truth rather than comfort, to doctrine rather than political or social expediency.

Even outside of Milton's context as a seventeenth-century Puritan, his argument for promiscuous reading is instructive, because such an approach is still both the means and the mark of the intellectually and spiritually mature person. If only that father who brandished the black marker against his daughter's college textbooks had read—and received—Milton's wisdom.

Today the word promiscuous is usually associated with sexual behavior, but this is a more recent usage, one that comes from the word's actual meaning—indiscriminate mixing. It's easy to see the sexual application of the word from this definition but instructive to think about in the context of reading. It's surprising, I think, to realize that pious and scholarly Milton is actually arguing for indiscriminate, disorderly reading. And lots of it. In Milton's day people had more fears surrounding promiscuous reading than promiscuous sex (the latter being rarer), so Milton had quite the challenge ahead of him.

In making his argument, as a churchman speaking to fellow churchmen, Milton cites the biblical examples of Moses, Daniel, and Paul, who were all steeped in the writings of their surrounding pagan cultures. Milton also invokes a leader of the third-century church who asserted that God commanded him in a vision, "Read any books whatever come into your hands, for you are sufficient both to judge aright and to examine each matter." Such advice mirrors the Pauline suggestion to "test all things and hold fast to that which is good." Milton puts it most profoundly when he says,

> Well knows he who uses to consider, that our faith and knowledge thrives by exercise, as well as our limbs and complexion. Truth is compared in Scripture to a streaming fountain; if her waters flow not in a perpetual progression, they sicken into a muddy pool of conformity and tradition. A man may be a heretic in the truth; and if he believe things only because his pastor says so, or the Assembly so determines, without knowing other reason, though his belief be true, yet the very truth he holds becomes his heresy.

In other words, the power of truth lies not in abstract propositions but in the understanding and willful application of truth by living, breathing persons which can occur only in the context of liberty.

Indeed, for Milton, this necessary freedom is seen in the character of God. For God is not, Milton argues, one to "captivate" His children "under a perpetual childhood of prescription," but rather, God expects us to exercise reason, wisdom, and virtue. "What wisdom can there be to choose... without knowledge of evil?" asks Milton. What praise for "a fugitive and cloistered virtue, unexercised and unbreathed, that never sallies out and sees his adversary, but slinks out of the race where that immortal garland is to be run for, not without dust and heat." Those "who imagine to remove sin by removing the matter of sin" have a poor understanding of human nature and the human condition, argues Milton. What would Milton have said to my youth leader who burned his rock music?

And what of books, my beloved books? The "best books," Milton argues, "to a naughty mind are not unappliable to occasions of evil." On the other hand, "bad books," Milton continues, "to a discreet and judicious reader serve in many respects to discover, to confute, to forewarn, to illustrate." How aptly an analogy might be drawn between the way Milton depicts God demanding of His children the exercise of reason, wisdom, and virtue and parents who might draw out the same in their children through liberal reading and testing of ideas through books.

But beyond the practical uses of truth in exercising virtue and cultivating maturity, Milton waxes most eloquent when he describes the very nature of truth itself:

> For who knows not that Truth is strong, next to the Almighty? She needs no policies, nor stratagems, nor licensings to make her victorious; those are the shifts and the defences that error uses against her power. Give her but room, and do not bind her when she sleeps... And though all the winds of doctrine were let loose to play upon the earth, so Truth be in the field, we do injuriously, by licensing and prohibiting, to misdoubt her strength.
>
> Let her and Falsehood grapple; who ever knew Truth put to the worse, in a free and open encounter? Her confuting is the best and surest suppressing.

I know that we live in an age in which many no longer believe in "Truth-with-a-capital-T," but I happen to be one who, despite being familiar with the arguments that there might not be such a thing, still believes in truth and its power. There is perhaps no better evidence to me of the power of Truth than what I read one day in a note to me from the professor who had introduced me to Milton's *Areopagitica*. He'd long left my university and his wife, and gone with a new wife to a new university in New York City. The brief message said he wasn't quite sure how it had happened—but that he had come to believe in the God of Milton's *Areopagitica*—and my God.

So this was my introduction to *Areopagitica* and, more importantly, the idea that the God I had been raised to believe in was not a God of record burning and book blotting, but a God of freedom. "You will know the truth, and the truth will set you free." I had heard this my whole life. Now I saw it to be so.

And I felt utterly liberated.

I was beginning, finally, to understand that the antagonism I had always felt between the life of the church and the life of the mind was false. Why had this truth been obscured from me for so long? Why had it seemed hidden from me by the church, only to be uncovered by an unbelieving professor? I'm not clear about where the perception of this antagonism came from—from culture, from politics, from bad preaching, or from all of the above. But the fact was that there was no essential conflict between the tenets of my faith and freedom of the mind. The oppression I had felt in the church was of human origin, not divine.

So it was a newly-imparted lesson from John Milton that drew me, so many years later, back to that place, one important stop on my journey with books.

Standing there, surrounded by the smell of polished wood and musty books, I slipped my index finger into the cradle formed atop the bound pages of the book and deftly pulled *King of the Wind* from the shelf. Instinctively, I opened the inside back cover. By this time, computers had long since replaced the old-fashioned means of checking out books—signing the card, stamping a due date, and filing the card away until the book's return—so I didn't really expect to see the small sheet of lined cardstock nestled within a paper sleeve glued to the back page. Nor did I expect when I pulled the card out, after all this time, to see my own name there from so long ago. But there it was: Karen Swallow, printed in the large, round letters of my childhood self. My name had literally been carried inside the book for these many years. The greater truth is that I have carried this book and many, many others, all these years. And they have made me who I am.

Here are some of the books that have made me who I am and that I recommend with all my heart and soul, all of which I write about in my literary and spiritual memoir, *Booked: Literature in the Soul of Me* (from which this excerpt is drawn):

Areopagitica
by John Milton

Every Christian, every citizen should read this classic work that helped lay the foundation for the First Amendment to the U.S. Constitution.

Jane Eyre
by Charlotte Brontë

This book helped me learn how to be myself, the person God created me to be, rather than anyone else

Great Expectations
by Charles Dickens

This magical story is delightful in every way, yet it teaches some important lessons, too, about humility,

Tess of the D'Urbervilles
by Thomas Hardy

I'm a sucker for tragic tales, and this novel has all the elements of a classical tragedy. It makes my heart hurt so good!

Death of a Salesman
by Arthur Miller

This play is a veritable exposé on how the American Dream went wrong. It's so powerful and so instructive—and another tragedy.

Madame Bovary
by Gustave Flaubert

Until I read this novel my sophomore year in college, I did not realize how infected I was by a Romantic worldview and how that worldview would have doomed me to a life of discontentment and unnecessary pain. This book changed my life.

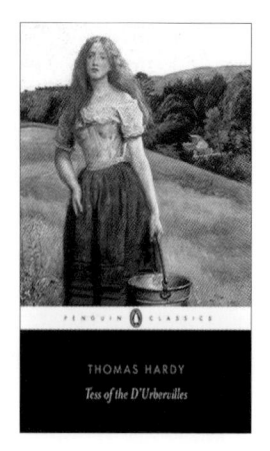

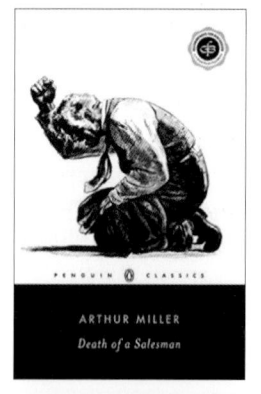

new testament studies
N.T. Wright

WHEN PEOPLE ASK ME WHICH BOOKS HAVE BEEN the most help in nearly fifty years as a biblical scholar, I often surprise (and I suspect disappoint) them: the books I consult most often are the dictionaries. This naturally includes the wonderful Lexicon of New Testament Greek completely re-edited by F. W. Danker on the basis of the older *"Arndt and Gingrich"* with which we all grew up in the 1970s.[1] Danker's new edition, a quantum leap forward in terms of all the evidence he supplies for one word after another, arrived providentially just before I began work on *The New Testament for Everyone*, in which I translated the whole New Testament and commented on it passage by passage.[2] But the book which stands out is *The Oxford Classical Dictionary*. A wise aunt gave me the first edition for Christmas when I was fifteen; it was my proudest possession. Now the fourth edition is at my elbow to help me check things I thought I knew and probe the many things I didn't but needed to.[3]

Acts: An Exegetical Commentary by Craig S. Keener

Tools like these are of course simply the foundation. Reading the New Testament seriously means understanding first-century history, and every aid to that is worth its place on the shelf. One recent work which deserves mention along with those dictionaries is the extraordinary four-volume commentary on *Acts* by Craig Keener.[4] Craig knows more about the classical world than almost any other biblical scholar alive, and he puts that encyclopedic knowledge to excellent use. But history needs not only detail but *interpretation*:

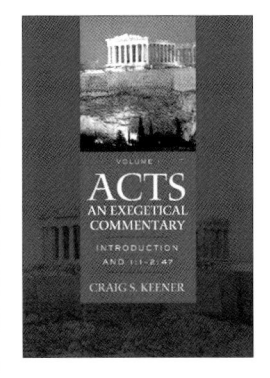

different angles of vision to probe into the past, and different insights to bring us back to the present. The books I have chosen here have done both of those things for me and I hope they will do the same for others.

Two absent friends must simply be mentioned. Albert Schweitzer was one of the greatest human beings of the twentieth century, and his big books on Jesus and Paul are worth reading partly for the energy of the writing and partly because they are so right in some ways and so wrong in others. Both halves of that claim have been enormously influential on New Testament scholarship ever since.[5] The point for which he is perhaps best known—the suggestion that first-century Jews and Christians, and Jesus Himself, thought the world was going to come to a complete stop very soon—was a major misunderstanding. The origins of this view are to be found, not in the world of so-called "apocalyptic" Judaism, but in the turbulent world of late nineteenth-century European thought, when "God" had been banished to a distant "heaven" so that any divine action in the world would involve destroying the world and doing something totally new, and when many thinkers had grown tired of Hegelian "progress" and were talking of the world's end.[6] But Schweitzer saw so many things so clearly, and expressed them so vividly, that he is always worth reading. He is one of my heroes, albeit with feet of clay.

Another scholar of whom I would say the same is Ernst Käsemann, Professor in Tübingen in the 1960s and 1970s. His commentary on Romans, owing more than a little to Schweitzer, remains a powerful reminder of the turbulent currents of faith and life in mid-century Germany.[7] Unlike many other scholars, Käsemann was wrestling with the details of historical exegesis at the same time—in the same breath, often enough!—as he was addressing questions of faith and public life, and though that sometimes makes him difficult to understand it provides a multifaceted education in biblical theology, not least when we find ourselves disagreeing. Above all, he reminds us that Paul, and especially Romans, *matters* urgently and vitally for the church and, even more so, for the world.

The Aims of Jesus by Ben F. Meyer

This brings me to the six books I would urge everyone with any interest in the New Testament to get to know. I name them in the order I met them.

Ben F. Meyer was one of the most learned scholars I have ever met. He spoke most of the major modern languages and read most of the ancient ones too. He brought to his historical work not only a passion for detail but also the mind of a trained philosopher; it was through him that I first heard of Bernard Lonergan and realized that many of the puzzles of New Testament scholarship needed to be addressed at the level of philosophical, particularly epistemological, presuppositions. Though Ben published comparatively little, his book *The Aims of Jesus* ought to remain standard fare for anyone wanting to engage the subject. It was published in 1979, just when I was starting to take an interest in historical study of Jesus alongside my work on Paul.[8] (The British publisher, SCM Press, took it on from Fortress Press in America, but John Bowden, the SCM editor, clearly didn't like its positive line. He gave star billing instead to a book on Jesus by the theologian J. P. Mackey, which has made precisely no impact.[9] Bowden went on to write a book himself called *Jesus: The Unanswered Questions*, though in fact Meyer had already answered most of them.[10]) In particular, Meyer opened my eyes to the relevance of the Scrolls and other relevant Jewish writing for understanding not just this or that saying but the whole world of second-Temple sectarian Jewish thought, and shone a bright spotlight on the centrality of the Temple itself in that world—something which Ed Sanders would then make central in his own groundbreaking *Jesus and Judaism*.[11] But Meyer, in my view, saw further than Sanders into the heart of how the Jewish theology of that world actually worked, with the Temple as the center of the cosmos and the Messiah and his people as constituting or even building some kind of new Temple. And the question implied by his title—the *Aims* of Jesus—raised a perfectly good historical question in a way that Jesus-study had not usually done: what, after all, was Jesus trying to accomplish? Traditional views had assumed that Jesus, as the incarnate Son of God, simply went about revealing Himself as divine and straightforwardly following a pre-planned agenda to die and rise again for the sins of the world. Nontraditional views had focused on the "did He or didn't He" questions: did Jesus do this healing, say this parable, make this journey, or didn't He? The assumption on the one hand was that Jesus was a divine figure dispensing wisdom; on the other, that he was an ordinary Jewish teacher with some new ideas. Meyer saw that things must have been stranger, and more compelling, than either: Jesus wrestled with difficult issues (the early church hardly invented scenes like Gethsemane, or the cry of dereliction from the cross), and seems to have had a particular plan to do certain things,

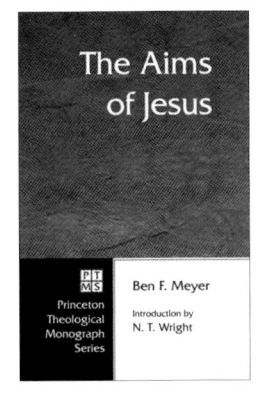

symbolic actions that resonated powerfully in the world of His day, culminating in the direct challenge to the Temple which was bound to lead to His death. Meyer's conclusion, taken out of context, might sound like a casual remark from a preacher: Jesus' aim was summed up when Paul said "He loved me and gave Himself for me." But in Meyer's work this has taken on the radical depth of patient historical study and textual analysis. His Jesus was a real human being making real, and utterly costly, decisions, for which the best explanation was a kind of radical love that embodied the love of Israel's God Himself.

The Language and Imagery of the Bible
by G.B. Caird

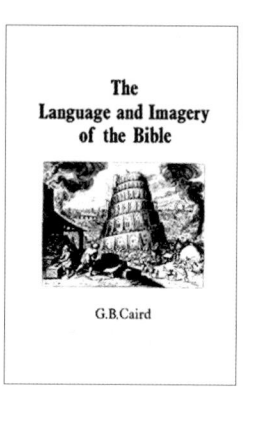

Questions, though, remain: what did Jesus say about the future? In 1980 my own teacher, George B. Caird, published his justly famous book *The Language and Imagery of the Bible*.[12] Written in an accessible style—Caird had the enviable ability to say complicated things in clear, taut prose—there was a lifetime's scholarship distilled into this detailed study of how the biblical writers used words and images and how, in particular, their rich poetic and metaphorical language ought to be read. The book proceeds through a series of detailed studies fascinating in themselves (the section on parables is especially important even though I don't think Caird followed his own insights quite far enough), building up step by step to the final three chapters. I saw George Caird not long after the book had been published, and he asked me what I thought; I replied that it seemed to me that he had wanted to write those three last chapters and had found it necessary (and also fruitful) to work through the earlier material as the foundation. He was delighted: this had indeed been his intention. The three chapters in question are on the language of history, the language of myth, and the language of eschatology. Here Caird was taking aim not only at Rudolf Bultmann but at the larger penumbra of works of which Bultmann's were typical. The word "myth" had been popular in the 1960s and 1970s, conveying to many the idea that "these things didn't really happen but they are still very meaningful:" Bultmann, famously, had "demythologized" the New Testament, declaring that one could not believe in all these extraordinary stories now that we had modern medicine and the electric light. This kind of analysis muddled up quite different categories: the "powerful deeds" of Jesus on the one hand, the language of "beasts coming up from the sea" and "the sun and the moon being darkened" on the other. For Bultmann, the "mythological" language was then a code for a kind of personal spiritual experience, the existential "decision" of faith. Caird, a longtime student of Jewish apocalyptic literature in a way that Bultmann and his followers never were, saw that apocalyptic and prophetic language was indeed code, not "literal description," but that it was code, not for "spiritual experience" but for (what we would call) events of political or social significance. When Isaiah spoke of the sun and the moon being darkened, he was describing the fall of Babylon and investing that event with (what we might call) its "cosmic" significance. This in turn leads to a reevaluation of the language of eschatology: neither Jesus, nor Paul, nor the early Christians in general, were expecting the literal "end of the world," but major world-changing events including obviously the fall of Jerusalem. Like all the best books, this one cries out for much more work to be done to fill in the new paradigms which it opens up. Sadly, Caird died before he could take this further, but I and others have done our best to follow down the road where he was pointing.

Colossians Remixed: Subverting the Empire
by Brian Walsh and Sylvia Keesmaat

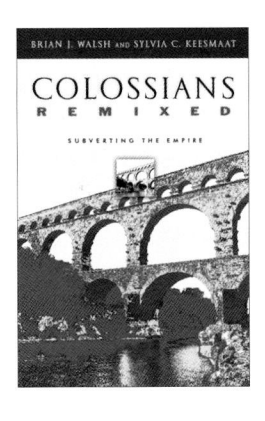

One of the reasons I was emboldened to do this was my friendship with Brian Walsh, who refused to let this somewhat conservative British scholar get away with bracketing out social and political meanings from exegesis and theology. I learned a great deal from Brian over the years, and when he married my former student Sylvia Keesmaat they set up a biblical, theological, and practical synergy that has not only said new things but said them in new ways. Brian and Sylvia have enlivened many seminars and publications, but perhaps their best known joint work is the study of Colossians.[13] I claim some credit, in that when Brian and I first met I was working on the Tyndale Commentary on Colossians, and we read through Paul's text and mine together, stimulating in Brian a lifelong interest in that letter even though—as in many academic friendships—we now disagree about some details. Anyway, *Colossians Remixed* grows out of several other contexts: Sylvia's own expert scholarship on first-century history and culture, Brian's longstanding pastoral, cultural, and evangelistic work with people from many different backgrounds in Toronto, and their shared passion for poetry, liturgy, and drama. The book explodes into life with different voices, different questions and points of view, different literary genres coming together to create the vivid impression of walking in on a lively seminar which has spilled over into a student common room with people coming in off the street and saying "How on earth can you say that?" or "Surely nobody today believes that kind of thing," or "What would that mean for inner-city life today?," and with others trying out poems, short stories or anecdotes to help discover what Paul himself was getting at in this short but vital letter. It's a risky way to write but Keesmaat and Walsh pull it off with poise and aplomb. At the heart of it all is the great poem of Colossians 1:15-20, with not only the very high Christology—Jesus as the one in whom all the fullness of deity has come to dwell—but also Jesus as therefore Lord of the whole world, sovereign over all powers and forces of whatever sort that might claim to rule in His place. For Brian and Sylvia this cashes out directly in terms of Christ and Caesar in the first century and Christ and "the empire" in the twenty-first, with "the empire" being a shorthand for the massive political, economic, and military systems of our own day that tyrannize over millions, that despoil the earth, that not only keep many in poverty but cause that poverty in the first place, and so on. Nor is this a naïve, shallow, knee-jerk political reaction; the critique is carefully researched, thought, and argued through, emerging from the book's many internal conversations. Some will object that such contemporary concerns are distorting the historical exegesis; but after generations in which the political implications of the New Testament have normally been muted one can hardly object if a text which was designed to be explosive in the first century turns out to be explosive in our own day as well.

Solidarity and Difference A Contemporary Reading of Paul's Ethics by David Horrell

In our own day, indeed, one of the greatest challenges in the church and the world is the combination of social cohesion with specific identity. The modernist dreams of a unified society—a single universal way of life, darkly symbolized for some in the ambitions of global empire against which Walsh and Keesmaat so strongly protest—are challenged, it seems, by the question of the "identity" of this or that social, cultural, linguistic, ethnic, or other category. And, indeed,

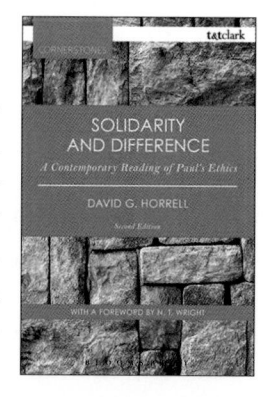

What New Testament Studies Books You Should Read & Why 149

by the putative "identities" of more and more individuals who, resenting being forced into the straitjacket of other people's expectations, insist on "being themselves" even if it means breaking off from other groupings. This standoff is a classic symptom of the split between what has sometimes been called "modernism" and "postmodernism," and though those labels are themselves fluid they name a sociocultural reality which, it seems, presented a challenge in the first century as well as today. And though the letters of Paul have often been assumed to speak of an otherworldly salvation which would make such questions irrelevant, a strong case has been made for seeing Paul as himself articulating and addressing the problem. That is what David Horrell has done in his remarkable book *Solidarity and Difference*.[14] Horrell brings a sociologist's eye and an exegete's fine-tuning to the examination of the Corinthian correspondence in particular, representing among the best of an entire wave of studies in which Paul's letters are mined for what they tell us about social and cultural issues in the first urban churches. Should the church be an example of "solidarity" in which everybody thinks and acts exactly the same? Is that what "unity" means, in the body of Christ or in the wider community? Or is individual identity important as well, and if so how? At what point does "difference" make a difference? How do we know which differences matter, and how do we handle those which do and those which don't? As soon as this question is asked it should be obvious that Paul comes at such matters again and again in his letters, and that he engages with the questions from a robust theological viewpoint. Horrell is to be congratulated for raising, shaping, and framing the whole area, even though in my mind at least questions remain as to whether he has fully appreciated the way in which Paul's call for a radical holiness of life must be seen as something of a middle term, both challenging an easygoing "solidarity" (unity cannot trump holiness) and questioning the exaltation of any and every "difference" (local cultures and lifestyles may embody deeply unholy practices, and they cannot be validated by appeal to the dignity of difference). The sociological study of Paul, and of the whole New Testament, is here to stay, and Horrell's book is to be seen both as a central achievement in the genre and as a stimulus to further probing of such questions.

The Temple and the Church's Mission: A Biblical Theology of the Dwelling Place of God by G.K. Beale

One central image for the solidarity of the church in Paul's writings was the Temple (e.g. 1 Corinthians 3:9–17), and this brings us to one of the major innovations in the last two decades. What is sometimes called "Temple-theology" has made its way from the periphery of New Testament scholarship into the center; the hints were already there in Ben Meyer's work, but it has come of age, and my next choice is both a good example and a great starting point. Gregory K. Beale is a seasoned scholar who knows his way expertly around the second-Temple Jewish world as well as the New Testament, and in his book *The Temple and the Church's Mission* he has drawn attention to some at least of the ways in which the Temple functions in early Christian thought.[15] For generations scholars of the New Testament have largely marginalised this theme, perhaps because it seemed too "Jewish," too "ritualistic," or even too "churchy;" but these are mere prejudices. For a first-century Jew, the Jerusalem Temple was not an "example" of something else. It was the place where heaven touched earth, where the twin circles of the good creation met and were held together by the powerful grace of the One God. What's more, for many Jews reading Israel's scriptures, the wilderness Tabernacle and then the Jerusalem Temple which followed it were not simply meeting places between heaven and earth, between God's space and human space; they were *small working models of new creation.* Precisely by holding heaven and earth together they were saying, "This is what the One God intends to do in the end; to bring heaven and earth together, so that the earth will be filled with the divine glory as the waters cover the sea." For Beale (so I have been told) this exploration began when he was working on his remarkable commentary on Revelation and pondering the fact that the Holy City in chapter 21 is a giant cube, reflecting the structure of the Holy of Holies—making the entire "new heaven and new earth" the larger "new temple."[16] The basic point of Beale's book, as well as providing a wealth of second-Temple evidence for ancient views of the Temple, is to stress that from the start the divine intention was to fill the entire cosmos, with the Tabernacle and then the Temple as a foretaste: an effective sign and symbol, in other words, of the mission to the world for which Israel was called, which was fulfilled in Jesus as Israel's Messiah, and which by the Spirit (described in Temple-terms in the New Testament) is now carried forward. Beale's is one of the best known of several recent works to explore this and related themes, which I believe are full of potential for many aspects of biblical theology, not least the early Christian view of Jesus and the Spirit.[17]

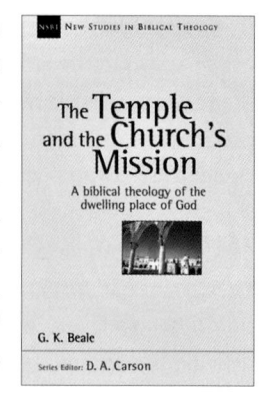

Echoes of Scripture in the Gospels
by Richard B. Hays

The early Christian view of Jesus is the subject of my final choice. Richard B. Hays came to prominence in the 1980s with his dissertation on Paul's narrative theology and then with his equally groundbreaking book *Echoes of Scripture in the Letters of Paul*.[18] Half a lifetime later, with many other books to his credit, he has turned his attention to the four Gospels, and after a short initial survey has now produced a further "Echoes:" *Echoes of Scripture in the Gospels*.[19] The book is remarkable in many ways, and I have written about it more fully elsewhere.[20] What Hays has achieved is nothing short of revolutionary. For nearly two hundred years students have been taught that whereas John's Gospel gives us an unambiguously "divine" Jesus, Matthew, Mark, and Luke give us the "human" Jesus. The implication has long been that John was written later, after the church had developed its view of Jesus towards a "high" position unknown to the first Christians (and to Jesus Himself). Of course, many writers have pushed back hard against this, but it has remained the dominant view. But if Hays is even half right this must be abandoned. We are here offered a detailed study—not indeed of all the echoes of Scripture in the Gospels, since that would demand a far longer book, but of dozens of key, telltale passages where Hays argues with great plausibility that the very different ways the four evangelists use Israel's scriptures in relation to Jesus shows that each of them saw in Jesus the living, personal embodiment of the God of Israel. The argument invites supplementation, not least because Hays gives almost no attention to the ways the Gospels use Scripture to interpret Jesus' death. But this book, as well as being written in a flowing and elegant style which belies the haste of its production when the author was facing a life-threatening illness, is a breathtaking achievement which will be cited in coming generations as a moment when a particular and powerful tide began to turn.

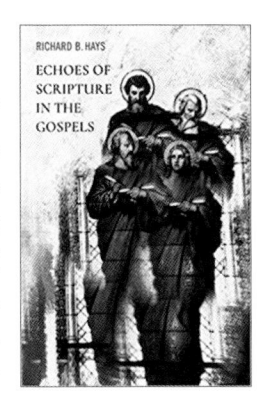

The last half century has been full of remarkable work on the New Testament. Like the eleventh chapter of the Letter to the Hebrews, I am tempted to say "time would fail me to speak of . . ." and go on to mention many others.[21] But this short essay is intended as a tribute not only to those who write books but to those who make sure that the wider public know about them, buy them, read them, relish them and spread the word. That is how hearts and minds are challenged, changed, and shaped for the work of the Kingdom. Thank you to Byron Borger for all you have done, for all you do.

Endnotes

1. F.W. Danker ed., *A Greek-English Lexicon of the New Testament and Other Early Christian Literature*, 3rd. edition (Chicago: University of Chicago Press, 2000).
2. See *Matthew for Everyone* and the other volumes, published by SPCK in London and Westminster John Knox in Philadelphia, starting in 2001; and the complete translation itself, published in 2011 as *The New Testament for Everyone* (London: SPCK) and *The Kingdom New Testament* (San Francisco: HarperOne).
3. S. Hornblower, A. Spawforth and E. Eidinow, eds., *The Oxford Classical Dictionary*, 4th edition (Oxford, UK: Oxford University Press, 2012).
4. C.S. Keener, *Acts: An Exegetical Commentary*, 4 volumes, (Grand Rapids: Baker Academic, 2012-2015).
5. A. Schweitzer, *The Quest of the Historical Jesus* ("complete edition"). (London, UK: SCM Press, 2000 [1906]); idem, *The Mysticism of Paul the Apostle* (London, UK: A & C Black, 1931). I discuss the first in *Christian Origins and the Question of God, vol. 2, Jesus and the Victory of God* (London and Minneapolis: SPCK and Fortress Press, 1996), 3-11, 18-21, and the second in *Paul and His Recent Interpreters* (London and Minneapolis: SPCK and Fortress Press, 2015), 34-38.
6. See my article "Hope Deferred? Against the Dogma of Delay," forthcoming in *Early Christianity*.
7. E. Käsemann, *Commentary on Romans* (Grand Rapids: Eerdmans, 1980 [1973]); discussed in *Paul and His Recent Interpreters* 46-57, 145-150.
8. B.F. Meyer, *The Aims of Jesus*, now in a new edition in the Princeton Theological Monographs Series: San Jose, CA: Pickwick Publications, 2002. I introduce this work in the "Introduction" to the second edition. Meyer's work on method is well worth consulting also: *Reality and Illusion in New Testament Scholarship: A Primer in Critical Realist Hermeneutics* (Collegeville, MN: Liturgical Press, 1994).
9. J.P. Mackey, *Jesus, the Man and the Myth: A Contemporary Christology* (London, UK: SCM Press, 1979).
10. J. Bowden, *Jesus: The Unanswered Questions* (London: SCM Press, 1988).
11. E.P. Sanders, *Jesus and Judaism* (London: SCM Press, 1985).
12. G.B. Caird, *The Language and Imagery of the Bible* (London: Duckworth, 1980). Second edition: Grand Rapids: Eerdmans, 1997. I describe and discuss the work in the Foreword to the second edition (xi-xxviii).
13. B.J. Walsh and S.C. Keesmaat, *Colossians Remixed: Subverting the Empire* (Downers Grove: InterVarsity Press, 2004).
14. D.G. Horrell, *Solidarity and Difference: A Contemporary Reading of Paul's Ethics*, 2nd edition (London, UK: T & T Clark, 2015 [2005]). I discuss this work in the Foreword to the second edition (xi-xv) and in *Paul and His Recent Interpreters* 285-304.
15. G.K. Beale, *The Temple and the Church's Mission: A Biblical Theology of the Dwelling Place of God* (Downers Grove: Inter-Varsity Press, 2004).
16. G.K. Beale, *The Book of Revelation* (Grand Rapids: Eerdmans, 1999).

17 See e.g. *PFG* ch. 9. Out of many recent works in this area one might instance the essays collected in L.M. Morales, *Cult and Cosmos: Tilting toward a Temple-Centred Theology* (Leuven: Peeters, 2014).

18 R.B. Hays, *The Faith of Jesus Christ: An Investigation into the Narrative Substructure of Galatians 3:1–4:11*. 2nd edition (Grand Rapids: Eerdmans, 2002 [1983]); *Echoes of Scripture in the Letters of Paul* (New Haven: Yale University Press, 1989).

19 R.B. Hays, *Reading Backwards: Figural Christology and the Fourfold Gospel Witness* (Waco, TX: Baylor University Press, 2014); *Echoes of Scripture in the Gospels* (Waco, TX: Baylor University Press, 2016).

20 See N. T. Wright, "Pictures, Stories, and the Cross: Where do the Echoes Lead?," *Journal of Theological Interpretation* 11.1, 2017, 53–73.

21 All right, just one: speaking of Hebrews, I must mention D.M. Moffitt, *Atonement and the Logic of Resurrection in the Epistle to the Hebrews* (Leiden: Brill, 2011).

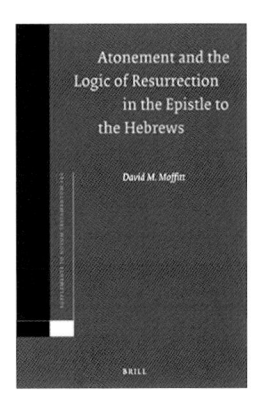

POETRY
Aaron Belz

THE CALLING OF A BOOKSTORE PROPRIETOR in the twenty-first century is a noble one. To sell books in the new millennium is implicitly to argue for genres almost completely ignored by both popular readership and mainstream media. A poetry book that sells over 2,000 copies, for instance, is considered successful. Why is that? And what, if anything, should we do about it?

These days we talk about *information*. It appears on our phone screens, laptops, tablets, on the sides of our buildings, on billboards, on tickers at the bottoms of our television screens, on our car dashboards and smart watches—a deluge of information. The digitization and global sharing of it may be new, but the volume of it isn't. Information appears, and it disappears. Every day it points its million arrows in a million new directions.

Information is happening in smaller and smaller increments. Beginning twenty years ago with the "blog post" and trending currently as "captions" and "tweets," the most popular forms of verbal communication are practically atomic. Quotes. Memes. Comments. In one hundred years we have devolved from novels and symphonies to tweets and three-minute pop songs. Debate has moved from open letters and editorials to rapid-fire and rapidly forgotten Twitter wars.

Information enters through your eyes the moment you wake up. Your phone is your alarm clock, and, reaching to silence it, you see numerous notifications that have arrived overnight. Many people have liked the information you've added to the internet. Some have commented on it or shared it. Many have posted information of their own. "Friends" are everywhere, doing everything, and you're being passively alerted.

Then it's off to work. Many of us work in information, arranging it, sending and receiving it, recording it, shaping and developing it, using it to promote an institution or product. We work in information the way miners work in mines. We breathe it even when it's toxic. It is our medium. And no matter what we do for a living, we constantly communicate: email, text message, message board, chat, Google search. And when we have down time, we peruse Facebook or Twitter, Snapchat or Instagram. Words, words, words.

Who has time to read? Poetry's purpose in the new information economy is to stop us grasping after meaning, to prevent us gasping for air when we already have the oxygen we need. T. S. Eliot sounds like he's talking about the internet when he writes, "Words strain, / Crack and sometimes break, under the burden, / Under the tension, slip, slide, perish, / Will not stay still. Shrieking voices / Scolding, mocking, or merely chattering" (*Four Quartets*, "Burnt Norton"). Against this cacophony he posits "love" which "is itself unmoving" and "timeless."

That Eliotic "love" is *poetry*. It is, as he says earlier in the same poem, the "still point of the turning world" where "there would be no dance, and there is only the dance." It is the fulcrum of human life, where desire and ambition, both so amplified by communications technology in the information economy, resolve in silence. It is the gravitational center of contemplation and prayer. People who don't regularly visit the "still point" eventually risk losing their minds.

Another analogy for poetry might be horizontal versus vertical. While the noise of life, commerce, friendship, consumer activity, politics, community organization and cultivation, manual labor, and corporate drudgery is *horizontal* and exists on largely the same plane, the still point, or poetry, or prayer, is *vertical*. It is lonely and quiet. It transcends the madness of worldly life. All good art should accomplish this purpose.

The best art does it sneakily, so you don't feel as though you're treading upon holy ground; instead, you may feel as though you're with a familiar spirit who knows you intimately. You may feel as though you've entered a strange alternate universe. You may feel as though you've fallen into a dream. The best art hypnotizes you, and your spirit awakes.

Repetition, rhythm, the flattening of words into mere sounds, sensual evocation, and intertwined threads of song give a poem the physical presence of a rosary. In fact, a rosary works in much the same way: it is prayer *as* a tangible object. Liturgy works the same way: it is prayer or Scripture spoken *en masse*, often robotically, sometimes in a foreign tongue. It is sound not for sound's sake, but as incantation to broker supernatural experience.

Poems break through the deafening white noise of modern life in different ways. Some use surprise, sudden juxtaposition, or a defamiliarization of language; some use a more sensuous, songlike approach. Here are a few examples of what I'm talking about to get your poetry collection started.

The first two are poets of surprise. Surprise takes the form of comic, manic, or abstract, fragmentary poetry. The out-of-place idiom or misapplied cliché—a sentence begun and then stopped halfway, a line break in an odd place, an inappropriate tone or word choice—any sort of grinding of language's gears tends to upset the reader. It displaces the reader and forces her or him to reset coordinates. Turbulence in language compels the reader to decide why certain norms are in place to begin with.

Houseboat Days by John Ashbery

The modern master of discomposition is John Ashbery. His perfectly idiomatic thought-trains have such unpredictable tracks that hundreds of scholars disagree about his method, or they compare it to dreaming. Yet he's won almost every literary prize in the Western hemisphere. The canonical Ashbery includes his debut collection *Some Trees* (1956), his Pulitzer Prize-winning *Self-Portrait in a Convex Mirror* (1976), a later work, *Hotel Lautréamont* (1992), and other equally worthy works too numerous to include here.

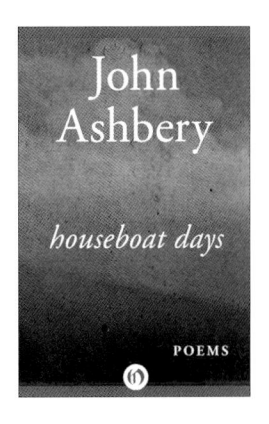

Here's an excerpt from the middle and end of "And *Ut Pictura Poesis* Is Her Name," which originally appeared in *Houseboat Days* (1979). It begins as a sort of cockeyed *ars poetica*:

> Now,
> About what to put in your poem-painting:
> Flowers are always nice, particularly delphinium.

But the narrative soon breaks down:

> She approached me
> About buying her desk. Suddenly the street was
> Bananas and the clangor of Japanese instruments.
> Humdrum testaments were scattered around.

And while this may seem an obviously absurdist antinarrative, words jostled free from their expected settings, the poem's concluding passage is *almost* straightforward:

> Something
> Ought to be written about how this affects
> You when you write poetry:
> The extreme austerity of an almost empty mind
> Colliding with the lush, Rousseau-like foliage of its desire to communicate
> Something between breaths, if only for the sake
> Of others and their desire to understand you and desert you
> For other centers of communication, so that understanding
> May begin, and in doing so be undone.

An absolutely breathtaking documentation of the poet's mind at work, and not at all absurdist. From the clatter of the former arises the latter. Or say, only in the decontextualized and perhaps disconcerting imagery of the former can the latter moment occur. For me, this merits reading and rereading year after year. It stands as a reminder of what can be done with language. It is the quantum physics of poetry.

Most of John Ashbery's poetry functions this way for me.

Partly: New and Selected Poems, 2001–2015
by Rae Armantrout

Another poet of surprise is Rae Armantrout. Although she's been publishing books since 1978, her profile has really risen the past ten years. A good place to start is her 2009 collection *Versed*, which won both the Pulitzer and the National Book Critics Circle. Another good option is the recent collection from Wesleyan, *Partly*.

Turning to page 33 of *Partly*, I find "Voices." This is what I love about Armantrout:

What Poetry Books You Should Read & Why 159

> You're boring, people.
>
> America doesn't want
> to watch you sleep.
>
> America doesn't want to hear you
> think about tacos.

If a television commercial were having a midlife crisis, this would be its internal monologue. In other poems, such as "Make It New," she refers to consumerism more directly:

> Shaking the parts of speech
> like fluff
> in a snow globe—
>
> the way sleep scrambles
> life's detritus.
>
> Each poem says,
> "I'm desperate"
>
> then, "Everything
> must go!"

This is what Robert Bly calls *leaping* poetry. It begins with a tangible, seeable simile ("like fluff"), expands to a recognizable analogy ("the way sleep"), then out of nowhere announces poetry's twofold message: "I'm desperate," and "Everything must go!" So weird and wonderful; I'm left wondering, is this true? Despite its imaginative leaps, it feels right. Is this the poet's *ars poetica*? After all, the title alludes to Ezra Pound's famous modernist dictum. Also, could music such as *sleep scrambles* and *life's detritus* arise more naturally?

Whatever the case, I could read Rae Armantrout's lithe, bizarre poems all day long and never get bored.

They're also sexy. Bookseller-sexy, I mean. Word nerd-sexy:

Scumble

What if I were turned on by seemingly innocent words
such as "scumble," "pinky," or "extrapolate"?

What if I maneuvered conversation in hope that
others would pronounce these words?

This wonderful speculative detour ends with a question: "What if there were a hidden pleasure / in calling one thing / by another's name?" In fact, there must be. It isn't just surprise that delights us. It's the upending of something we'd taken for granted, the fanciful twisting of a reality we hadn't thought to question. We find ourselves wondering why things are called what they are in the first place. One of my very favorite John Ashbery poems begins with the question, "How funny your name would be / if you could follow it back to where / the first person thought of saying it [?]" Great question. How much of our verbal environment do we fail to question?

Neruda and Vallejo: Selected Poems
edited by Robert Bly

One thrilling way to question language is to try reading poetry written in a language other than your native tongue. For most of us, that means reading poems in translation.

Poems in translation are notoriously hard to discuss, though, because who wrote them? For example, I've treasured Robert Bly's translations of Peruvian poet Cesar Vallejo for more than twenty years, even though I've heard they're as much Bly as they are Vallejo. Someone told me Clayton Eshleman's translations are better, but I find them flat and uninspired. I conclude that I have a personal attachment to Bly's Vallejo, *per se*.

I suppose it was 1993 or 1994 when I first picked up *Neruda & Vallejo*. Robert Bly was, or would soon be, my professor at NYU. He was a jolly and frank man, apple-cheeked and barrel-chested, and seemed to have walked to class from the Minnesotan woods. He wore a colorful Native American vest. He reeked of body odor and loved to hug his students with his strong frontiersman's arms.

What Poetry Books You Should Read & Why 161

He would read a poem to us, wait a couple of beats, and read the same poem again. And sometimes a third time.

I describe Bly's charisma as evidence that he might not be the most impartial or academic translator. When he translated, he must have been in the translation. I don't think Bly wrote anything at all without his own powerful musk at work.

Which is all to say that although this book with "Neruda & Vallejo" in large pink letters on its cover and spine, containing translations by not only Bly but James Wright, John Knoepfle, and Douglas Lawder, served as my introduction to a poet who would become immeasurably important to me, such service may have been corrupted by oddball, biased, or otherwise intrusive philosophies of translation. I may have fallen, at least to some degree, for the translators' charm rather than for the pure fire of the original authors.

By way of counter-caveat, the book *does* contain all the original texts on its facing pages, so readers can enjoy them in Spanish or try their own hands at translation.

But it was the *translations* with which I, personally, fell in love:

This afternoon it rains as never before; and I
don't feel like staying alive, heart.

The afternoon is pleasant. Why shouldn't it be?
It is wearing grace and pain; it is dressed like a woman.

This afternoon in Lima it is raining. And I remember
the cruel caverns of my ingratitude;
my block of ice laid on her poppy,
stronger than her crying "Don't be this way!"

My violent black flowers; and the barbarous
and staggering blow with a stone; and the glacial pause...

Whew. Vallejo! I read these lines and wondered, how can this exist? Another:

I feel that God is traveling
so much in me, with the dusk and the sea.
With him we go along together. It is getting dark.
With him we get dark. All orphans...

These are just the beginnings of poems so perhaps you'll read them to their ends on your own. Here is perhaps my favorite, "The Anger that Breaks a Man Down Into Boys," in its entirety:

> The anger that breaks a man down into boys,
> that breaks the boy down into equal birds,
> and the bird, then, into tiny eggs;
> the anger of the poor
> owns one smooth oil against two vinegars.
>
> The anger that breaks the tree down into leaves,
> and the leaf down into different-sized buds,
> and the buds into infinitely fine grooves;
> the anger of the poor
> owns two rivers against a number of seas.
>
> The anger that breaks the good down into doubts,
> and doubts down into three matching arcs,
> and the arc, then, into unimaginable tombs;
> the anger of the poor
> owns one piece of steel against two daggers.
>
> The anger that breaks the soul down into bodies,
> the body down into different organs,
> and the organ down into reverberating octaves of thoughts;
> the anger of the poor
> owns one deep fire against two craters.

I read this aloud to someone the other day and he said, "Sounds mathematical." At first I thought, what an odd response. But it's correct. Vallejo is actually an algebraic poet, creating a syntax full of variables and assigning to them what appear to be slightly incorrect values. To wit, the first two stanzas of "Poem to be Read and Sung":

I know there is someone
looking for me day and night inside her hand,
and coming upon me, each moment, in her shoes.
Doesn't she know the night is buried
with spurs behind the kitchen?

I know there is someone composed of my pieces,
whom I complete when my waist
goes galloping on her precise little stone.
Doesn't she know that money once out of her likeness
never returns to her trunk?

Funny to imagine singing this, especially the closing line: "But she does look and look for me. This is a real story!" But I love it *so much*. I wouldn't have become interested in writing my own poetry if not for Vallejo via Bly, or at least not interested in the way I became interested in it, with a passion for strange, surprising syntax that references love and God amid a din of microsymbols. Moments of enlightenment in a whirlwind of worldliness.

Perhaps more importantly, Bly's Vallejo gave me a voice I'd never heard before in literature. It sounded so personal and direct, while at the same time keenly aware of its own limitations, and it also clunked, strangely. All I wanted was a poetics that was unafraid to clunk. I felt I could be at home there.

So there are three good reasons to walk into the poetry section of the bookstore. Those, plus you might meet a good old-fashioned bookstore proprietor. If you do, ask him what poetry *he* recommends.

The Vallejo portion of this essay originally appeared on *TheOperatingSystem.org*.

POLITICS
Eric Bryan

THE SECOND GREATEST LIE EVER PERPETRATED against humanity is that we can get ourselves out of the same mess we got ourselves into. It is difficult to determine, based on Scripture, whether this was a lie initially told us by the Evil One or whether we conveniently told it to ourselves. Regardless, it is a lie that came to fruition as early as the first moments after our great Fall from a harmonious relationship with God, when we, according to Genesis 3, sewed fig leaves together in an effort to cover our shame. Cain believed the lie again when he took the life of his brother; the peoples of Babel believed the lie once more when they tried to build a tower to make a name for themselves; and over and over again the lie is told. From Egypt and Africa to Greece and Rome, to China and India in the East, and back through Russia, Europe, and finally over to the New World, we have told ourselves this lie again and again, and believed it—that humanity, by its own devices, can redeem this world that has so obviously fallen into division and violence. In the modern world, as in the ancient, this lie enacts a tragic play in which (often times well-meaning and earnest) leaders and activists work to overcome injustice, unrest, and violence by means of secular social and political agendas. But try as we might, the ship cannot be un-sunk.

Historically, Christianity has combatted this lie, which we may call the sociopolitical deception, with the proclamation that it is not by any human means that the world can be redeemed. It is only through divine incarnation—through the living and literal body of Christ—that the world will be set right. William T. Cavanaugh identifies the Western iterations of this lie, forwarded by political philosophers such as John Locke and Thomas Hobbes, as a forgery of the body of Christ, arguing that both the modern state and the Church "ultimately have the same goal: salvation of humankind from the divisions that plague us."[1] As a result, many of the aspirations of the sociopolitical deception are in line with the kinds of justice and redemption hoped for by Christians, but the means matter, especially when we have such an end as redemption in mind. If there is any truth to this line of thinking, then it becomes rather difficult to answer the question *why read books about politics?* with any satisfaction, and whatever we decide, the answer must certainly not be "because politics will save the world."

We might turn to the more practical, less theoretical writing of Amy E. Black for further guidance. She offers the straightforward perspective that politics ought to be viewed "as a means for demonstrating love in action as a witness to the world."[2] This is an admirable and Godly reason to read about politics. The difficulty is that Christians have historically been so very bad at following through with Black's view. As Black herself puts it,

> Unfortunately, far too many discussions of Christianity and politics end in shouting matches instead of constructive dialogues. An environment that encourages simplifying controversies into two positions, "us" and "them," creates instant enemies, as if anyone expressing an opinion on a political question must be preparing for war. When Christians speak hatefully of another believer, they sin against their Christian brother or sister and erode the unity of the church. When Christians speak with hatred toward someone outside the church or intentionally cause dissension, they harm the reputation of the church as a community of love in the world.[3]

It is interesting to note that Black published her commentary in 2008, long before—the span of the entire Obama administration, in fact—the volatile political climate of today. We must regretfully acknowledge that Christian discourse on politics and social change has not improved. It has grown much worse.

Since the 2016 presidential campaign, the polarizing political climate has grown worse not just between Christians and non-Christians, but amongst Christians. Christians on either side of the election have begun looking at the other side and saying something to the effect of, "How could anyone call themselves a Christian and vote for [*fill in the blank*]?" The problem with questions like this one is that they are not questions at all; they are commentaries on a person's spiritual well-being. The mentality behind such questions signals more than just a divergence of political opinions and ideologies within the Christian church; they signal a rupture of the unity and communion that God calls us to.

The problems that lead to this rupture are nuanced from one church community to another, but broadly speaking, there are three fundamental issues that need to be addressed. First, we must recognize that our problem is not that we are arguing about politics and social reform in the Christian church; our problem is that we are *not* arguing about these things. This must sound quite odd indeed, especially in our modern age when conflict is seen as something to be avoided or defused rather than something to be embraced, but godly, redemptive conflict is something quite set apart from the bickering and quarreling that Paul condemns in his letters.[4] Bickering and quarreling are in fact the poor forgeries of proper, godly argument and Spirit-filled conflict. Those forgeries lead to isolation, bitterness, and misunderstanding. The real thing looks a lot more like learning than bickering.

Godly, redemptive conflict does not mean allowing our anger to rule us. It means the opposite. We are indeed to be slow to anger, slow to speak, and quick to listen. To that end, we must strive to treat every argument or conflict, whether with another believer or with someone outside the Church, as though we are having that argument while waiting in line for the Communion Table, because, whatever else we may be doing at one time or another, we are always waiting in line for the Communion Table. When we argue before the Table, our conflicts are transformed from something confrontational into something much more confessional. A confessional heart is the heart that knows it does not have the final say in what is good or bad for our country or city; a confessional heart puts its prospect for the redemption of the world in the hands of our risen Lord rather than in our own wisdom; and a confessional heart is one that does not do harm to others for the preservation of its own sense of justice, because a confessional heart knows that justice must proceed not through our own understanding but through the Christ of the Communion Table. It is thus before the Table that the Christian church in the United States will remember how to argue in a godly, redemptive way.

A second fundamental issue is the impact of conventional and social media in a globalized world.[5] In an article published not long after the 2016 election, Barry Corey, president of Biola University, had this to say about media and the Church:

> American Christians, like all Americans, are being conditioned by the rhetoric of division. It's the air we breathe on 24-hour cable news, on social media, and in the click-bait articles that favor un-nuanced and polarizing headlines. How can a 20-minute Sunday sermon on charity

and forbearance compete with 20 hours a week of cable news fear mongering and its polarizing spin? It's clear that many of our hearts have been formed more by the liturgies of radio talk show hosts than the lessons of Jesus.[6]

It is perhaps too easy these days to criticize the media, so I will try to make my comments relevant by addressing the reasons why media is so appealing to our hearts: in a word, justice. It might not always be obvious, but our hearts and minds are built for justice, which means we long for justice in everything we do, whether we are Christians or otherwise. Regardless of their political leanings, the various forms of contemporary conventional media (whether TV, radio, internet, or whatever), promise to bring us that justice in the form of relevant information. Likewise, social media promises the opportunity to *participate* in that justice by giving us the ability to share our convictions with a large, if absent, audience. Ultimately, media cannot keep its promises; and thus media, perhaps especially social media, begins to work upon us like a drug: there is never enough of it; it doesn't feel good even though we want it; and we cannot stop consuming it until, ultimately, it consumes us. It would be unfair of me (and would possibly show my age!) to say that all social media is a bad thing, but I will say that, when it comes to difficult and important topics, one face-to-face conversation over a cup of coffee is worth more than all the Facebook posts we could ever write.

In a speaking engagement just before the 2016 election, Timothy Keller spoke about the third issue contributing to division in the church. He registered concerns that Christians were in danger of building their identities upon a foundation of political and cultural allegiances rather than upon the person of Christ.[7] Keller's concerns resonate with Corey's observation that Christian hearts are being formed more by the media than by liturgies. The tragedy of the secular political and social agenda seems to have penetrated our own ranks: Christians have been enticed by the sociopolitical deception; we have begun to believe that the redemption of the world can come from human means rather than from the body of Christ.

Perhaps we should not ignore the fact that the common denominator in our three fundamental issues is politics itself. Perhaps politics itself is the problem, after all. Perhaps the answer to the question *why read books about politics?* is simply the dissenting voice: *you shouldn't!* Perhaps the answer is to abandon the sociopolitical world altogether. After all, when our hopes are rooted in the redemption and communion of saints offered by the death and resurrection of

What Politics Books You Should Read & Why 169

Christ, the equality and social justice offered by sociopolitical activism seems rather a low bar. Why strive for mere earthly unity when you can have real Communion? Why strive for social justice when you can have a world so just and righteous that the word *justice* need not be so much as uttered? Why seek equality when you can celebrate relationships that will surpass even our best estimations of familial intimacy? Should we not merely reject and altogether abandon the sociopolitical realm because it offers such a low bar? Not according to Scripture. Keller points out that throughout the Old and New Testaments God is constantly calling His people to works of what we might now call "social justice."[8] N.T. Wright has likewise contextualized our work toward social justice here on earth in the larger tapestry of Christ's renewal of the world.[9] Both of these arguments point, I think, to the way God has chosen to save the world.

One of the most important beliefs held by all of Christendom, despite doctrinal differences, is that God, in His wisdom, allows us to be a part of the Great Narrative of His redemption of the world. That means that we have a role to play in the greatest rescue mission in the history of the universe; it means we have to operate behind enemy lines, *in* the world but not *of* it; it means that we must speak the language of those whom the Lord will rescue; it means that we must be able to see, and work towards, the one true body politic—the body of Christ, so that we can proclaim that there is something far greater than we could ever hope for or imagine in the political agendas set up by the world in which we live. All this brings us to the question relevant to this chapter: Why read books about politics?

... because the best forgeries are those that look exactly like the original.[10] The real weakness in all of the Evil One's lies and forgeries is that they are too close to the real thing to be of any lasting distraction. The Truth cannot help but be a dim reflection in the tarnished and distorted image of the forgery. In the case of the sociopolitical deception, the one constant from the time when Adam and Eve sewed fig leaves together to Rousseau's Social Contract to the protests in Ferguson, Missouri to the Presidential election of 2016 is that on some level, regardless of political leaning or even of religious convictions, we all know that something has gone very, very wrong with the world we live in, and we all have the conviction somewhere in our hearts that we are called to something better.[11] The End, to put it another way, is a good one. The means by which we get there, however, make all the difference between Heaven and Hell.[12]

We read books about politics not because politics will save the world; we read books about politics to be well equipped to reveal the truth behind the forgery, to show the world that the body of Christ is the true redemptive force, to be an example of the loving kindness that far surpasses anything the Social Contract could ever aspire to. Most of all, we read books about politics because, as bad as the second greatest lie of all time might be, there is an even greater lie that we were told long, long ago, and that we believed: "You will not surely die."

But, thankfully, that is not the end of the story.

God gives us the opportunity to play a role in the Grand Narrative that is unfolding. Here are some books that might help us play our part well:

***Theopolitical Imagination: Christian Practice of Space and Time* by William T. Cavanaugh**

This little book is not for the faint of heart, but its provocative reading of the relationship between Church and State pays great dividends in the end. Cavanaugh's purpose is to expose and correct what he sees as the misconception that the secular state saved the West from the religious wars waged by the Church. Rather, argues Cavanaugh, the secular state envisioned by post-medieval political philosophers is a simulacrum of the body of Christ. It was furthermore the secular state, not the Church, that shed so much blood, and the Enlightenment merely justified the state's existence by putting the blame on the Church. As Cavanaugh puts it, "What I hope to have shown... is how the dominance of the state over the Church in the sixteenth and seventeenth centuries allowed the temporal rulers to direct doctrinal conflicts to secular ends."[13] In other words, the secular states, for the sake of acquiring and maintaining power, appropriated the language and posture of doctrinal differences in the Church, such as the disagreements between Protestants and Catholics on the substance of communion bread and wine, to justify the violence necessary for establishing and defending state power.

The one weakness of Cavanaugh's approach is that he does not go back far enough in history. The state's appropriation of the Church might have reached a climax in the Enlightenment period, but it had been going on for many centuries before that. Nation making during the medieval period regularly appropriated the language and vision of the Church to unify otherwise diverging, localized governing bodies, particularly those in the medieval north, where Germanic and Norse paganism offered a much more pluralistic religious—and consequently political—milieu that was unsuitable for the centralization of government.[14] Christianity offered a unified alternative to that milieu, and ambitious leaders made use of it. Cavanaugh is not ignorant of these historical valuations, but his unwillingness to engage them fully permits a too generous view of the pre-Enlightenment church, both Protestant and Catholic. Nevertheless, Cavanaugh's observations are sound and provocative as far as they go.

Generous Justice: How God's Grace Makes Us Just
by Timothy Keller

Timothy Keller is no doubt one of the most influential and popular Christian writers alive today. His work in the inner city and his vision for social reform have permeated a great number of Christian ministries. *Generous Justice* can be seen as the concise articulation of Keller's vision in specific reference to social and political thought. He spends much of the first half of the book arguing that both Scripture and theological thought call Christians into service of the poor and socially outcast. He is also more willing to see the value in working alongside the secular sociopolitical agenda than, say, Cavanaugh, who wants ultimately to set up the Church as a renewed public space. Keller rather suggests that the Christian must not be afraid of working with social and political agents to bring about the justice called for in Scripture. He nevertheless warns against becoming too closely aligned with any one political or social agenda: "No current political framework can fully convey the comprehensive Biblical vision of justice, and Christians should never identify too closely with a particular political party or philosophy."[15] The costs of doing so are great, for "if we tie the Bible too tightly to any particular economic system or set of public policies, it bestows divine authority on that system."[16]

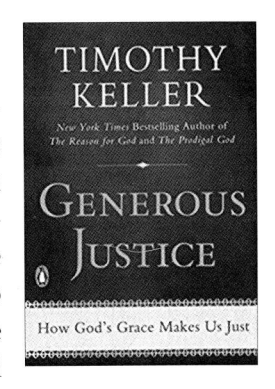

Like most of Keller's books, this one is easily accessible, grounded in Scripture, and most useful for practical application. It would be best made use of in a church reading group geared towards leadership training or small-group discussions. For someone looking for a deeper theological discourse on politics, they should perhaps look more towards Cavanaugh and others of that ilk.

Beyond Left and Right: Helping Christians Make Sense of American Politics, by Amy E. Black

Amy E. Black's objective in this volume is to equip Christians to participate in the political arena in the United States, whatever one's denominational or political convictions. Her book is not partisan in the traditional liberal-vs.-conservative sense, yet she believes that Christians ought to participate in the political arena for the purpose of serving our neighbors and glorifying God. To this end, Black's book succeeds. Black also wants to reconfigure the assumptions Christians often take into political discourse by offering correctives to some of the commonly held beliefs about Christianity and America. She holds that the United States is in fact not a Christian nation as is proclaimed by many on the right. It is in fact dangerous, argues Black, for American Christians to associate Christianity too closely with their nation or a political party:

> When evoking God and country or God and politics, Christians must walk a very careful line. Associating the message of Christ with the actions of a secular state ultimately dilutes the gospel and may adversely affect our Christian witness. It seems wise to approach political discussion with great care and tact, resisting the temptation to play the "God card" as a cover for seeking to further our own political interests.

Black also presents various data from voting surveys and linguistic analyses of important speeches and political documents throughout history, which affords her some insightful information on assessments of what Christianity in American politics really looks like. At bottom this volume will be at its best with the Christian individual who feels themselves called to a more active sociopolitical life but who doesn't know how to begin. It offers a balanced and critical look at what Christianity looks like in America and gives guidance for how to approach politics from a godly perspective while avoiding some of the common pitfalls of joining religion and politics in the United States.

Life Together by Dietrich Bonhoeffer

If we are to be an example of the benefits and blessings of the body of Christ, then we must have some understanding of what that system of life will look like. The best way, in my opinion, to learn about what it means to live "in the body" is to participate in Christian communal living of some kind, such as staying for a time at one of the L'Abri fellowships or even participating in a neighborhood-based church. I am fortunate to have lived at the Dutch L'Abri for two periods in my life— once as a single person in my late twenties and once with my wife and our first child. For obvious reasons the experiences were quite different from one another, but both taught me (and later my family) the value not just of worshipping, thinking, and living together, but of what a friend of mine calls "B-time interactions"—those idle moments we consider to be less important, such as when you're taking out the garbage, or cleaning the bathroom, or absently throwing rocks at a can while you wait for dinner. Dietrich Bonhoeffer's *Life Together* captures those aspects of Christian communal living and much more. Perhaps most helpful is his understanding that communal living means learning how to embrace solitude as much as community, and that confession, communion, and ministry are inherently communal acts. Bonhoeffer proclaims that community is essential to an understanding of Christianity, as "Christianity means community through Jesus Christ and in Jesus Christ. No Christian community is more or less than this. Whether it be a brief, single encounter or the daily fellowship of years, Christian community is only this."[17] And yet the mandate of the Christian community is not to isolate itself from the world but to celebrate its community in the midst of the world, for by this the world will know the message of Christ.

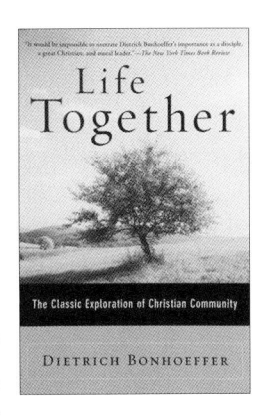

The Man Who Was Thursday by G.K. Chesterton

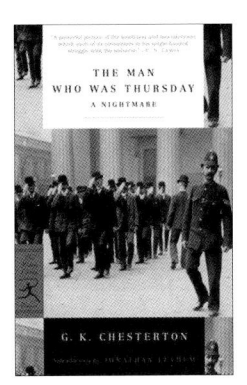

No one ever believes me when I tell them that reading a detective novel will bring them closer to God, but everyone always pays a little closer attention when I say it is a detective novel by Chesterton. He is sometimes called the "Prince of Paradox"[18] because he is so fond of expanding the deeper meaning of things by confining that depth to a cleverly contorted, backward, or upside down statement. (It would be annoying if he weren't so good at doing it!). In classic Chestertonian style, this entire novel is upside down, starting with the nonsense title, *The Man Who Was Thursday*, and not finishing until the last syllable is impressed upon the minds of his readers. That is well and good, but the value of Chesterton's novel on a list of books to read about politics is more difficult to explain because doing so would ruin the story for the readers. At risk of such an offense, I will only say the barest amount: the most obvious way that this story relates to politics is that it unfolds a contest between anarchy and civil governance, and the hero of the story—or at least we will call him the detective, for he is not the hero—is charged with defeating anarchy in Europe. So much is true, but there is a deeper, more paradoxical reason for recommending this book: earlier in this essay I shared my concerns about the usage of such questions as, "How can anyone call themselves a Christian and vote for [*fill in the blank*]?" We should indeed be concerned about such questions, but there is an even more frightening question that Christians are likely to ask as the sociopolitical deception continues to take hold of our society. That question is, "How can God truly be God and allow [*fill in the blank*] to happen?" We need not conjure apocalyptic imagery to validate this prediction. We need only look at history, even recent history, to see that God allows all manner of evil and chaos to take hold of the social and political world. It is easy to be afraid in those times, when evil and chaos seem to be in charge of the world's great nations, and it becomes difficult to make the argument that God is indeed in control. At one time or another in our lives, we all are likely to look at the social and political landscape and ask this question. Some of us will carry the burden of asking it many times. I will say no more about this little novel by G.K. Chesterton than that it helps us towards an answer to this sometimes difficult question.

Endnotes

1 Cavanaugh, *Theopolitical Imagination: Christian Practices of Space and Time* (Bloomsbury T&T Clark, February 1, 2003) 9.
2 Amy E. Black, *Beyond Left and Right: Helping Christians Make Sense of American Politics* (Grand Rapids: Baker, 2008), 27.
3 Ibid., 26.
4 2 Timothy 2 and 1 Cor. 3. See also Romans 14.
5 For more on Globalization, see William T. Cavanaugh, *Migrations of the Holy: God, State, and the Political Meaning of the Church* (Grand Rapids: Eerdmans, 2011), 39-41.
6 Barry H. Corey, "Lovingkindness: A Post-Election Path for Christians in America," *Christianity Today* (November 9, 2016). Accessed 3 March 2017. http://www.christianitytoday.com/edstetzer/2016/november/post-election-path-for-christians-in-america.html.

7   Timothy Keller, lecture, *Movement Day* (New York: October 25-27, 2016). Accessed 3 March 2017. http://movementday.com/videos-2016/.
8   See chapters 2 and 3 of Keller, *Generous Justice: How God's Grace Makes Us Just* (New York: Penguin, 2010).
9   N.T. Wright, "Jesus is Coming, So Plant a Tree," *Surprised by Scripture* (New York: Harper Collins, 2014), 83-107.
10 I heard this saying many years ago from a radio program on a different topic. It has stuck with me ever since, though I'm ashamed to say I cannot give an accurate reference to the speaker.
11 I would argue that this truth has been a principal factor in the demise of the Postmodern/Post-structuralist movement, but that is an argument for another time.
12 Niccoló Machiavelli was the first Western thinker to argue for consequentialism, casually stated as "the ends justify the means," though it is possible, as Rousseau suggested, that Machiavelli's *The Prince* was a book of satire. It is not insignificant that he is also one the earliest and strongest supporters of the sociopolitical deception in the Western world. See William E. Johnston's interesting article entitled "The Crisis of the West: Machiavelli, Rousseau, and the Imperative of Salvation," *First Things* (June 1990). Accessed 29 July 2017. https://www.firstthings.com/article/1990/06/the-crisis-of-the-west-machiavelli-rousseau-and-the-imperative-of-salvation.
13 Cavanaugh, *Theopolitical Imagination*, 42.
14 Many works could attest to this point. For a recent assessment, see Sverre Bagge, *Cross and the Scepter: the Rise of the Scandinavian Kingdoms from the Vikings to the Reformation* (Princeton: Princeton University Press, 2014).
15 Keller, *Generous Justice*, 163.
16 Ibid., 164.
17 Dietrich Bonhoeffer, *Life Together* (New York: Harper & Row, 1954), 21.
18 See a lovely essay by J.D. Douglas, "G.K. Chesterton, the Eccentric Prince of Paradox," *Christianity Today* (1974; repr., 2001). Accessed 31 July 2017. http://www.christianitytoday.com/ct/2001/augustweb-only/8-27-52.0.html.

science
Michael Kucks

SCIENCE AND FAITH: WHAT A GREAT TOPIC! THERE IS so much of interest to ponder. We are living at a time in history when scientists are feeling especially pleased with themselves and want to invest some of that good feeling to answering some of the great questions:

>Does God exist? *and* Where did we come from?

One question is from the field of metaphysics and one is from the field of physics. Scientists have direct credibility to speak to the question from physics. (Where did we come from?) They have indirect credibility to speak to the metaphysical question. (Does God exist?)

Scientists have every right to feel pleased with themselves. The successes of science are all around us. Dedicated scientists work diligently to understand the fundamental rules of the physical world. Some do it on a theoretical basis using mathematics and computers. Some do it on an empirical basis working in laboratories using carefully controlled experiments. These two, taken together, form what we have all been taught is the scientific method. Theory and experiment go hand in hand to uncover the repeatable patterns of nature. One of the best examples of these two sides of science is the story of the periodic table of the elements. Chemists made very careful observations of reactions and properties of materials, and in the nineteenth century Dmitri Mendeleev constructed the first periodic table based on the repeated patterns. In the twentieth century theoretical physicists came up with the mathematics of quantum mechanics. Application of that math gave verification of the structure of the periodic table. Theory and experiment coalesced to produce a consistent picture of the elements. The scientific method requires both. That's how scientific knowledge is advanced.

Then engineers take all of that scientific understanding and make items used by the rest of us. Engineers make the innovative items we use daily and buy as Christmas gifts. Engineers are the "bridge" between the pure scientists and the end users (you and me). So pure science finds its way into our daily lives.

My point is that science speaks with such force these days because it touches so many of us. When a paradigm is so successful, people ascribe to its practitioners a certain amount of credibility. Scientists have this kind of "success cred." Physicists like Stephen Hawking get to speak into the theological issue of the existence of God based on scientific "cred." He has written several books in which he concludes that God does not exist, in his opinion. But he is a physicist and not a meta-physicist! John Lennox, author of the book *God and Stephen Hawking: Whose Design Is It Anyway?* takes Hawking to task for his attempt at metaphysics. It's a very interesting perspective on Hawking's arguments against the existence of God.

As I have interacted with this topic over the years, it has become clear that people take several different approaches:

1. The theological/biblical approach
2. The philosophical approach (metaphysics approach)
3. The scientific/mathematical approach (physics approach)
4. The historical approach

Most of the time people take several of these approaches simultaneously. No wonder confusion abounds! But I do believe in intellectual liberty. What I mean by that is that each person is free to decide what kinds of arguments will convince him. Just because some of these approaches are convincing to me does not mean that they must be convincing to someone else. We each have freedom in that regard. Good conversation occurs when people share what they find convincing. The hope is that it will convince someone else. It does no good to claim that the rules of logic dictate what must be convincing. Two people looking at the same data and using the same rules of logic can come to different conclusions. It happens all the time. Just look at the last few presidential elections. Plenty of similarly Ivy League-trained individuals came down on opposite sides of the political divide when discussing presidential politics. The issue is weight. Each intellectually free person is able to assign whatever weight he wants to any particular piece of data. Two people with the same data at hand can come to different conclusions precisely because they assign a different weight to each piece of data. Different weights make for different conclusions. While it is good to know the rules of logic, because they are part of what makes an argument convincing, they do not guarantee agreement!

So, what about faith and science? Are the two fundamentally contradictory or can they peacefully coexist? Or do they support each other? There are many who would argue that faith deals with issues that are outside the realm of science, and vice versa. So it is said they are logically disconnected. I have never liked that kind of thinking. I believe the two are inextricably intertwined. Here's why. Faith is believing something that I cannot see. Instead, faith is believing something I am told. Faith is relational at its core and science is objective. By objective, I mean that the way one person relates to the natural world is exactly the same as the way any other person relates to the natural world. There is no individuality to science. Gravity treats everyone the same. Science discerns the patterns in nature that apply equally to everyone all the time. That's what I mean by objective. Faith, on the other hand, is all about the subjective. A man has a relationship with God and God tells that man something. Faith is when that man believes what he is told, based on relationship and not based on measurement or observing patterns in nature. Instead the man has confidence in the pattern of relationship that indicates God is trustworthy in what He says. While these sound very different, I believe they are connected.

One of the things that God has said is that He is a God of order and not of chaos. The world He created is orderly and follows definite patterns. In fact, science is only possible if this is true. If the world were fundamentally chaotic, with no patterns and no cause/effect relationships, then science would be impossible. Science can only exist because there is order in the natural world and men have the capacity to discern it. So science actually affirms a statement by God. That builds "cred" for God. When scientific observations, or historical investigations, or philosophical arguments confirm what God has said, then the subjective credibility of faith is strengthened. This is far from proof. But every instance of confirmation builds greater "God cred." My point is that science can actually be used to affirm, or deny, a faith issue. Faith and science can work together; they are connected through the concept of credibility.

Since science has shown unequivocally that nature is orderly and follows patterns, it is also possible for science to describe what is normal. When patterns repeat predictably, then they become normal. Rare events are odd by comparison. It is very difficult to do science on rare events. Remember, science looks for patterns. It takes several occurrences of something before a pattern can be observed. If an event has occurred only once, then no pattern can be discerned. This is one of the big distinctions between theory and experiment. Theory can predict singular events. But until they are observed, the theory is just a theory. Only experiment and observation can validate a theory.

So, science can tell us what is normal and, therefore, it can tell us what is abnormal. Science, therefore, has a few important tasks it fulfills:

- Discerning patterns in nature by careful observation
- Forming mathematical models to describe those patterns
- Discerning what is normal behavior in nature
- Commenting on what is abnormal in nature

The second item on the list is interesting. Scientists make use of math all the time. Many would say that math is the language of science, much to the chagrin of many students. Why is this? Why should nature care about math? Why should math be so well-suited to capturing the details of nature? Many notable scientists have wondered at this, Einstein among them. We may not be able to answer the why question concerning math, but one thing is for sure: science has shown beyond doubt that math is a powerful tool in both discerning patterns and describing normal behavior. But what about the fourth item in the list? Can math be used in discussing abnormal events? Sure! In fact, that is precisely what the mathematics of statistics is all about. Statistics helps to determine if something is odd or normal. High probability events are normal and low probability events are abnormal or odd.

One of the great practitioners of mathematical physics (combining observation and theoretical modeling) was Isaac Newton. He applied his skills to one of the first patterns observed in nature. The stars in the sky rotate in a circle through the night. Normal is for the stars to stay in fixed positions relative to each other as they rotate. The abnormal observation was of a few "rogue" stars that wandered among the others. They were not fixed in their positions relative to the other stars. Centuries of observation and careful theoretical work were performed to figure out these wandering stars. Elaborate geometrical schemes were concocted along with philosophical and theological arguments for the wandering stars. It wasn't until Newton and his idea of gravity came about that a simple mathematical expression was able to describe the wandering stars and predict their movements through the night sky. What was initially abnormal had finally become normal. Science does that. It moves the unexplained, abnormal observations into the realm of the normal and patterned and natural. But it takes time, careful observation, and clever thought.

Some scientists believe that every observation can be moved from the abnormal category to the normal category if given enough time for careful observation and thought. That's quite an assumption! First, it assumes that every phenomenon in nature will repeat, given enough time. But might it not be true that some phenomena will occur only once in all of time? In that case there can be no pattern discerned. Science is out of luck. Singular events are outside of the scientific method. But how does one know if an event is singular? Certainly, there are events that occur rarely, but do repeat on a long time scale. Comets are a great example. Some comets only pass near Earth rarely. So rarely, in fact, that no one human lifetime can span the repeat cycle. That is where the historical perspective on this issue of God and faith becomes so important. There are natural phenomena that can only be studied when different generations of careful observers record their observations. Then, when enough observations have been collected, it is up to the generation of that time to look for patterns and to try and develop the mathematical model. The best known comet, Comet Halley, has a period of about seventy-five years, just about one observer's lifetime. Lesser known comets, such as Comet McNaught, have periods approaching 93,000 years! Such a long period makes collecting information on that event rather difficult. Here we need to make a distinction between phenomena that are singular and categories of phenomena that are singular. Comets, as a phenomena, are certainly not singular. There have been many sightings over the centuries. Once Newton's gravity concept was introduced it became possible to understand the comet phenomenon, even though there are particular comets that will only be observed once every 93,000 years. Details about that particular comet are going to be slow in developing. But even Comet McNaught supports the scientific understanding of the categorical phenomenon of comets. Comets that appear only once and never return to our solar system are singular events in themselves, but they are part of the comet category, which science can study.

But what about truly "categorically singular" events that will never repeat? Do such things really exist? Well, the origin of the universe seems to be a categorically singular event. We do not expect to see other universes being created, ever. So, the one event that is most important to the discussion of science and faith happens to be in this very special situation of being a categorically singular event. This makes any claims by scientists about where we came from much less credible since singular events are outside of the scientific method. Remember, that method requires both theory and experiment. Singular events cannot be subjected to controlled experiments or repeated observations. Therefore, they are beyond the reach of the scientific method. They enter the realm of metaphysics.

Any good scientist will quickly object to this last statement and remind us that science can deduce much about singular events by making use of mathematics and theory. Computers can calculate so much and so quickly that modeling very complex systems has become a specialty field. Remember all those computer models of the weather patterns one hundred years from now and how we are all going to burn up? There's only one problem with using computer models for singular events: there's no way to verify that the models work! Models are developed with lots of real data, and the models then have to be able to backtest and reproduce the old results. Otherwise the model is no good. The more old data one has, the better the chance that the model can predict the future. But with categorically singular events there is only one data point! Backtesting is not very convincing with only one point to compare. But the effort can be made, should be made, and has been made. The current model for the origin of the universe is the Big Bang model, and computers have simulated the first minutes after the big bang. There have been some very impressive results. The model shows the formation of fundamental particles which then bond together to form atoms and molecules. That's a very good showing for a computer model. It argues very strongly for the Big Bang theory. But recall that real science requires both theory and experiment. Computer models are still just theory. They are not experiments. So while the process is important and worthy of effort, it is not the scientific method. For a very interesting look at singular events and the power of math and models, take a look at Stephen Hawking's book *A Brief History of Time*.

Let me wrap up this discussion with my own perspective. I like to use the biblical/theological approach combined with the science/math approach. Faith is believing what God told us. He says He created the universe in six days. I know there are many believers who take a different view on the timing issue. But they always offer an "alternative" interpretation and argue that the six days can be taken in some less than literal way. All of that simply says that the most straightforward interpretation is six literal days. So, I'll go with that interpretation as the clearest representation of what God said. Others can argue about what God meant!

There is no scientific theory that supports any scenario in which the universe could come into being in six days. Science says that normal processes of nature and a Big Bang require something like ten billion years to bring us to where we are today. So, a six-day origin of the universe would clearly be an abnormal event according to science. Remember, that is one of the purposes of science, to declare what is abnormal. When the Bible declares an event that is scientifically abnormal we typically call it a miracle. Miracles are abnormal

What Science Books You Should Read & Why 183

events that nonetheless are claimed to occur. The Bible records many miracles. It also tells us why miracles occur. Miracles build "God cred"!

> Woe to you, Korazin! Woe to you, Bethsaida! For if the miracles that were performed in you had been performed in Tyre and Sidon, they would have repented long ago, sitting in sackcloth and ashes.
> —Luke 10:13 (NIV)

Jesus declares that the miracles He performed should provide credibility for what He said about these cities. If science shows that something abnormal has occurred (the universe exists and we exist) and God says that He did it, then science is connected to faith and builds credibility for God and His word. What does science say about origins? Is the origin of the universe normal? Is life normal? That is precisely the domain of Stephen Hawking. He trusts his math because math has been so tremendously useful in his pursuit of scientific knowledge. He concludes that yes, the universe and life itself are normal. Let me borrow his scientific trust in math and let me turn to a different area of science: biology. The math I want to use is much simpler than Hawking's M-theory. Let's see where that math takes us.

Probability is a well-defined area of mathematics and involves counting possible arrangements of events and determining the likelihood of any of them coming to pass by random chance. Biology has determined that very specific proteins are necessary for all forms of life. Proteins are molecules made up of sequences of amino acids. Those sequences are critically important to the biological activity of the protein. For a protein molecule to possess the quality of being alive it must be folded on itself in a very particular way. It is that folding that makes a protein molecule able to perform its function in a living cell. If the molecule gets unfolded (or denatured) then it loses all of its ability to perform life processes. So, there are two related aspects to living proteins: they must be made up of very definite sequences of amino acids and they must be folded correctly.

These two aspects are related. It is the sequence of amino acids that determines how a protein folds on itself. If the sequence is wrong, then the folding will either not happen at all or will happen in the wrong way. In a living cell, proteins are made by DNA and RNA molecules and as they are being made there are other molecules, called "chaperones," that actually guide the folding process during the construction of the protein. It is truly amazing. Without the chaperone molecules the protein is left in a denatured state and must try to fold all by itself. Short protein molecules (about 40 amino acids) can actually do it. That's because the number of possible ways a short protein can fold is rather limited. The configuration space is rather small. Random fluctuations in the molecule can bring about the correct folding as the parts of the protein that are supposed to stick together come close to each other. But for long proteins (400 amino acids, a more typical size in living organisms) the ability of the protein to fold correctly all by itself is greatly reduced. That's because the number of possible configurations is enormous and the chance for parts of the molecule that are supposed to stick together to get close is limited by all the rest of the molecule getting in the way.

Now for the math. Remember, we trust math in the sciences and we trust what it tells us. We've all heard of the probability of rolling a die and having the number 3 come up. The probability is 1 in 6. That's because there is only one 3 on a die and there are a total of 6 numbers possible when we roll. 1 in 6 is a probability of 16.7%. So if we roll a die 6 times we would expect a 3 to come up once. Of course it doesn't work that way every time. But if we perform the experiment many times the results should be in line with this probability calculation. If I wanted to know the probability of rolling a 3, 5 and 2 in any order, then I would take the probability of each event alone and multiply the probabilities together: 16.7% x 16.7% x 16.7% = 0.4657% Notice that the probability gets smaller. But if I don't care about the order in which I roll each number, then the probabilities get bigger since there are a number of ways, or a number of permutations, that I will accept. I could accept 3, 5, 2 or 3, 2, 5 or 5, 3, 2 or 5, 2, 3 or 2, 3, 5 or 2, 5, 3. Since any of these is acceptable I increase my chances. My new probability is: 0.4657% x 6 = 2.79%

This is a simple example of probability and it can be extended to include our protein molecule. Instead of rolling a die, I can think of reaching into a bag containing amino acids and picking one out at random. There are 20 different amino acids used in living proteins. So to construct a living protein by chance I have to reach into a bag containing the 20 amino acids, pick one out at random, and stick it on the molecule. Remember that a typical protein has 400 amino acids. The sequence is very important. Any sequence is not acceptable. I need a very specific sequence so that it will fold correctly. So we do the calculation like we did above: (1/20) x (1/20) x (1/20) x (1/20) x ... 400 times or (1/20) raised to the 400 power. That comes out to be: 10^{-520} or we can say it would take 10^{520} tries to get one right protein sequence. That is a huge number. So let's see if we can knock it down a bit with some more math. Let's take all of the atoms in the visible universe (about 10^{80}) and imagine that they are all amino acids. We are putting the odds very much in favor of evolution by making this assumption. Then we'll put 400 "bags" of 20 amino acids each (8000 amino acids altogether; or 10^4) into imaginary boxes spread throughout the universe. Then inside each box we'll again imagine that the amino acids are trying to combine together to form a single protein molecule with a specific sequence by picking one amino acid out of each bag. All of these experiments are going on simultaneously. So, that would give us 10^{76} boxes spread throughout the universe all doing experiments to get a single protein molecule. That lowers my number of times I need to run the experiment to 10^{444} instead of 10^{520}. So, every instant in time when I run the experiment I do many simultaneously, and I still need 10^{444} periods of time to get one correct outcome.

So, what is a reasonable amount of time to do an experiment? Let's imagine that the amino acids in each box can rearrange themselves and try a sequence of 400 in a "Planck time." A Planck time is the shortest time known to science. It is 10^{-44} seconds. Another way to measure Planck time is in years. Since there are roughly ten million seconds in a year (10^7), a Planck time can be stated as 10^{-51} years. So, we imagine that every Planck time there are 10^{76} experiments where boxes of amino acids are testing combinations of 400, and it will take 10^{393} years for one particular protein molecule to be formed. Again, we are giving every advantage in the calculation to the random processes of evolution.

The current theory is that the universe is 10^{10} years old (ten billion). That's not even close to the amount of time it would take for amino acids to randomly create a protein molecule (10^{393} years). Even if we did manage, by chance, to come up with one correct protein sequence, then we still have to fold it to make it alive. That is another probability that takes a long time. Then we need other protein molecules to be formed, since one protein does not make life. Then they all need to get from whatever box they are in to the same box where they can interact and possibly make a single living cell. At each step the probabilities get smaller and smaller.

The point of all this math (math that scientists trust to tell them about what is normal and what is abnormal in nature) is that it tells us quite clearly that life is abnormal. There is no mathematical probability for life to spontaneously arise from dead atoms and molecules in the age of the universe predicted by the Big Bang theory. In more basic terms, the math says that life is a miracle. So, here we have the math that scientists trust saying the exact same thing that God says about the origins of life: it is a miracle, and God says He did it. The math gives us another example of "God cred." If science wants to deny that math and instead argue that life is normal, then science has undermined its most fundamental tool: math. And if science chooses, in this case, to ignore the math, then why should any of the rest of us take seriously the mathematical claims of science, such as Hawking's M-theory, which is his basis for concluding that God does not exist and life is normal? Science can't have it both ways! It can't ignore the math that says life is impossible by natural processes and at the same time claim that Hawking's math must be believed.

One final comment needs to be made on this topic. I have been intentionally using the term "science" when discussing the view that God does not exist and that the universe, and life, came about by natural and normal processes of nature. But it would be more accurate to say "scientists" instead. Science itself, as a discipline, does not take a stand on this issue. Individual scientists do. Throughout history there have been many notable scientists who believed in God's existence. There have also been many scientists who believe that God does not exist. So, within the practice of science the issue is divided. Those who would like to argue that "science" proves that God does not exist must ignore those scientists who disagree and must rewrite history to minimize any from the past who believed in God. Be assured that science does not speak with a unified voice on this issue.

Here are some books that I recommend to investigate this issue of science and faith further:

The Genesis Flood: The Biblical Record and Its Scientific Implications by John Whitcomb and Henry Morris

This is the book that really got the whole faith and science topic rolling. Morris was a civil engineering professor at University of Louisiana and later the head of the civil engineering department at Virginia Polytechnic. Morris and Whitcomb wrote an extensive apologetic for the literal interpretation of Scripture using all of the tools of science and math to give credibility to God and His Word. The modern discussion of this topic owes so much to this book. It is certainly worth the time to read both from an historical perspective and for the science it contains. While this volume focuses primarily on geology and paleontology, it covers these topics with great skill and practical knowledge.

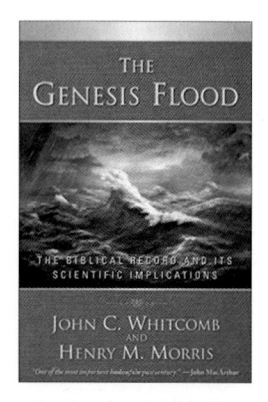

Evolution: A Theory in Crisis by Michael Denton

This book is so well written and so well documented that it cannot, and should not, be ignored. The author Michael Denton is a biochemist and an agnostic. He does not write from a Christian worldview. Instead, he writes about the scientific evidence for "intelligent design" in biology. The references in his book are numerous, and his ability to describe very technical details of biology and biochemistry is noteworthy. He makes the complex very accessible.

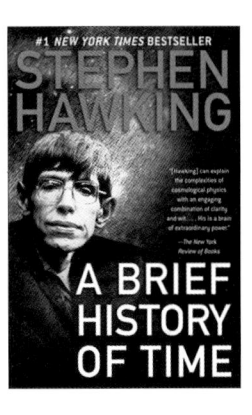

A Brief History of Time by Stephen Hawking

This was Hawking's first book on cosmology. In it he discusses modern physics and describes the complexities of general relativity and quantum mechanics in layman's terms. He progresses to the discussion of unified theories that combine both gravity and quantum mechanics, as well as black holes as an example where both gravity and quantum effects coexist. Eventually he moves to the Big Bang model and the origin of the universe. In the book he declares several times that God is no longer needed since we have the scientific knowledge that he describes. This book was one of the most influential in terms of promoting the idea that science proves God is dead.

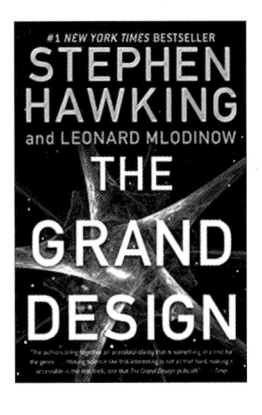

The Grand Design by Stephen Hawking and Leonard Mlodinow

This is Hawking's follow up book to *A Brief History of Time*. It encapsulates much of his theoretical work over the years since he published the first book. In it he describes his mathematical model for the universe, which he calls M-theory. He postulates that M-theory predicts that there are multiple universes and that we just happen to be located in one where life arose by spontaneous generation (chance). In essence, he refutes the probability calculation put forth in this article by saying that there are many universes where amino acids are trying to combine into a protein, and we live in a universe where the attempts were successful. There are many more universes where the attempts were unsuccessful. It is an interesting look at where math can take the mind.

God and Stephen Hawking: Whose Design Is It Anyway? By John Lennox

John Lennox is an Emeritus Professor of Mathematics at Oxford University. He speaks and writes on the issue of faith and science. In this book he takes a very philosophical approach in evaluating the arguments put forth by Hawking in *The Grand Design*. It is a great example of two approaches to the topic colliding. Hawking takes the purely mathematical/scientific approach and makes philosophical statements as conclusions. Lennox takes the philosophical approach and argues that Hawking's conclusions are amiss.

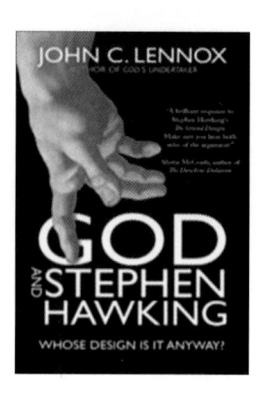

The Delusion of Disbelief: Why the New Atheism Is a Threat to Your Life, Liberty, and Pursuit of Happiness by David Aikman

David Aikman is a former *Time* magazine correspondent, author, and professor of history at Patrick Henry College. While his book is not focused on science at its core, he does respond to what he calls the "four horsemen of the apocalypse," by which he means Sam Harris, Richard Dawkins, Daniel Dennett, and Christopher Hitchens. Each of these authors produced a book that concludes that God does not exist and that the world would be a better place without religion (especially Christianity). For reference, the four books are: *Letter to a Christian Nation* by Sam Harris, *The God Delusion* by Richard Dawkins, *Breaking the Spell: Religion as a National Phenomenon* by Daniel Dennett, and *God Is Not Great: How Religion Poisons Everything* by Christopher Hitchens.

Aikman takes the historical approach to the argument and does a masterful job of answering these four critics. It is an excellent example of the historical approach and the value of knowing what has happened in the past!

SOCIOLOGY
Bradshaw Frey

Matthew Desmond's *Evicted* caught my students by surprise. It was a study of rent and eviction in Milwaukee, especially as it affected the poor. He compiled a stunning array of information on eviction nationwide. He collaborated with a regional university to study landlord practices, pricing, and laws affecting renters in Milwaukee. But what my students found compelling was that he lived for months in the poorest neighborhoods as a renter himself.

One student quipped, "A sociology book I couldn't put down, that's pretty rare!" Indeed. Desmond, a Harvard sociology professor, conducted his research more like the participant observer typical of an anthropologist. I first encountered the book when I surfed onto C-Span's "Book Notes" one evening. Desmond was speaking to a packed bookstore audience in a Washington, DC neighborhood. He spoke of the plight of the poor and their need for housing. He spoke of a tremendous lack of adequate housing and the small fraction of the poor who live in government subsidized housing. He spoke of landlords good and bad. But mostly he told stories.

The stories he told gave his research an authenticity lacking in many studies. This wasn't the uber-rational social scientist dispassionately sifting through data gathered anonymously (though that work had been done and was referenced throughout the text). These were real people in a real city interacting with real landlords and in many cases really suffering. There was nothing antiseptic about the study. It was earthy—that is, on the street, in the trailer, in the tenement earthy. People weren't just political statistics to be tossed back and forth by policy wags. They were people whose life circumstances, some self-generated and some sadly innocent, had put them into apartments or houses that were unfit for people.

Desmond found that eviction *always* led people to more severe housing circumstances. He found that eviction on a person's record (now immediately available to landlords online) shut them out of most possibilities and forced them down the housing chain. His study showed that as incarceration is to African-American men so is eviction to African-American women. One in five African-American women will be evicted in her lifetime. As incarceration impacts future life possibilities for those incarcerated, so eviction does. It appears to be another dimension of "the new Jim Crow."

This is far from a black/white issue. Desmond had spent months living in an unraveling trailer park. Most of the residents there were white and absolutely living on the edge. Their stories and circumstances were quite similar to those who lived in urban ghettos. For those of us whose lives are lived in the middle class and above these were stories seldom heard or even imagined.

Was this sociology or some sort of social activism? Was this an academic study or a compelling docudrama? Desmond's speech on "Book Notes" had the zeal of an enthusiastic preacher and yet he is a Harvard sociologist. This was either a "new" style of sociology or the unraveling of the modernist ideal. No scientific aloofness, this was a passion for justice delivered with academic clout—exactly what my students longed to read.

Our college is located in the perfect laboratory for sociology, a distressed, postindustrial, rust belt small town. Over half the properties in our downtown are not owner occupied and a third of our people live in government housing. As in Milwaukee, there is a lot of money to be made off the poor. My students generated a study of eviction in our town. It culminated with interviews of people in the community who had been evicted. My students were convinced afterwards that eviction was one of the least understood yet most compelling problems of modern America. They were also convinced that what Desmond reported in *Evicted* was not just a national epidemic illustrated by his experience in Milwaukee. It was a reality in our own community. They prepared a presentation on their findings and presented it to a room packed full of their peers during "Justice Week." They were convinced. Now that's a great sociology text! That's the power of a book well-conceived and well written, even in sociology! It also seems representative of a transformation taking place in the way sociology is imagined and the way it is written about.

Sociology is an ancient discipline, though its birth is typically assigned to the late Enlightenment period between 1830 and 1850. This modern birthdate is not because people haven't been studying societies for millennia, but because it wasn't until that late date that the "scientific" study of sociology was introduced. One of the agendas of the Enlightenment was to replace superstition and tradition with hard scientific learning. This new study needed to displace traditional disciplines such as philosophy and religion with scientifically generated information.

By the mid-twentieth century this approach to sociology had become reified in the approach of structural functionalism, or simply functionalism, possibly best embodied by Harvard sociologist Talcott Parsons. As modernity consumed more and more of the American imagination, students on university campuses flocked to sociology departments to major in the discipline that offered them the broad horizon of this new world.

However, this was an activistic generation, and the promise of justice, peace, and harmony of a finely tuned modernist society somehow got lost in statistics, data, and funded studies. As early as 1960, C. Wright Mills in his final book, *The Sociological Imagination*, warned of sociology graduates who would simply become part of the bureaucratic machine because of their close proximity to the modernism foundational to both. Such concerns were harbingers for things to come in the discipline. Could a human science (as was transpiring in economics) simply become a mathematical, scientific discipline of data wags? Was there not more to "human" societies than just the scientific?

For decades the health of 60s-era sociology departments has been on the decline. In whatever way the discipline was able to capture the imagination of folks in the 60s, it had let go of it by the 2000s. As a discipline birthed by modernity, it comes as no surprise that the rumblings of postmodernity have been hard to ignore. The assault of the French linguistic philosophers on the metanarrative of science has certainly fragmented the world of sociology. One of the most stunning developments of this fragmentation is the "emperor has no clothes" text of Aldon D. Morris. Morris, a prestigious sociologist himself from Northwestern University, exposed the ideological biases of the early days of the discipline in a stunning way. A scientifically neutral, facts-only discipline has little room for such an exposition. Boston University sociologist Julian Go, in a review of the Morris text, claimed, "This changes everything." What was it that changed?

THE "EMBARRASSING CASE" OF W.E.B. DU BOIS

Morris' 2015 text, titled *The Scholar Denied: W.E.B. Du Bois and the Birth of Modern Sociology*, describes a sociological guild so enamored with a racist social Darwinism that they both ignored and conspired to subvert Du Bois' work. For students of race in America this may not be surprising, but for champions of the "science of society" this work is severely damaging. Their commitment to an unbiased scientific sociology was not strong enough to overcome their own prejudice—which is, of course, exactly what champions of the Enlightenment aimed at.

The story begins with Du Bois' own quest to become an elite academic. Following his graduation from HBC Fisk University in only three years, Du Bois found his way to Harvard. Not given credit for a legitimate bachelor's degree, he was required to do additional years of study at Harvard. His work was strongly affirmed by faculty luminaries such as William James, and he was admitted to a graduate program. The climax of his experience was his winning a scholarship to study at the University of Berlin for his PhD, which was recognized as the pinnacle of the educational world. During his stay in Germany he sensed that he was being singled out as the "new Moses" for his people back in the U.S.

Though his funding ran out just before he finished his dissertation, Du Bois returned to the U.S. to eventually finish his degree at Harvard, and entered academia with an elite education behind him. However, the educational world was no different than society at large, and though he had superior credentials he could find no teaching jobs. This was the firmly structured era of Jim Crow.

After teaching at HBC Wilberforce College for a few years Du Bois took a "research only" position at the University of Pennsylvania. The university commissioned him to do a full-blown study of the black community in Philadelphia. (The study was actually funded by a university philanthropist anxious to make political points in the city.) Du Bois did his work with scientific precision and his work was quite possibly the first scientific study of its kind worldwide. The result, *The Philadelphia Negro*, was a model of scientific sociology for decades to come. Nonetheless, Du Bois was still not offered a teaching position at the university and chose to go to HBC Atlanta University where he could pursue his craft more fully.

It's at this point that Morris upsets the sociological applecart. In the telling of the history of American sociology, the University of Chicago is acknowledged as the first school with a sociology department and the first to generate a "school" of sociology—directed by Robert Park—especially as they studied the immigrant reality in Chicago. The Chicago School's text, *The Polish Peasant in Europe and America*, was hailed as a groundbreaking work in scientific sociology establishing the University of Chicago as the first school of sociology by the 1920s.

Here's the problem: Du Bois' work on *The Philadelphia Negro* more than twenty years earlier had already established this research methodology. Not only that, for nearly a decade after the turn of the century Du Bois had been generating yearly scientific studies directed by black sociologists, graduate students and undergraduate students trained by him at Atlanta University. Then, with the scientific precision he learned in Berlin and at Harvard, he generated publications based on the fieldwork, buttressed with scientific analysis. Finally, he would host a conference at the end of the academic year when he would bring some of the most famous academics in the land to review the work and interact with the investigative team. Scholars such as Harvard's president Charles Elliot, Columbia's world-famous anthropologist Franz Boas, and Hull House founder Jane Addams all spent time with Du Bois at his Atlanta conferences. This is exactly how a "school" of sociology is built. Yet for Du Bois, no acclaim, not even any acknowledgement.

The hole gets deeper still. Morris makes a case that this wasn't benign neglect on the part of culturally-formed, bigoted academics, but intentional sabotage. University of Chicago sociologist Robert Park is Morris' focal point. Park, as Booker T. Washington's ghostwriter/publicity director, had been thoroughly acquainted with Du Bois, as Washington's key rival and critic. He was thoroughly knowledgeable about Du Bois work because one of his tasks in his role with Washington was to discredit his rival. After Washington's death Park moved to the University of Chicago, where he simply ignored any work Du Bois had done. Even as late as the 1940s Park continued to sabotage Du Bois' work, according to Morris' research.

The discipline birthed by the Enlightenment, committed to science as a way to avoid the bias and prejudice of tradition rooted in philosophy and religion, was so committed to social Darwinism and petty jealousy that it missed the very founder of its American version. Even though Du Bois was a friend and colleague of classical sociologist Max Weber (Weber visited Du Bois on a trip to the U.S., offered to have Du Bois' seminal work *The Souls of Black Folk* translated into German, and recruited Du Bois to write for his journal), he was ignored by the guild built on Weber's work.

It is not Morris' intention to challenge the methodological orthodoxy of sociology. His work was done to reclaim the rightful place of Du Bois as the founder of American scientific sociology, and he does so brilliantly. Nonetheless, one can't miss the irony of a discipline so steeped in the scientific and yet unable to see the "facts" clearly available for a century. Such a work clearly displays the power of "prescientific commitments" to the scholarly project. As such it also begs the question of how the discipline should proceed and what a person should read to get her or his bearings.

To Change the World: The Irony, Tragedy, and Possibility of Christianity in the Late Modern World by James Davison Hunter

Fortunately, we live at a time when sociologists are emerging who are not only people of faith but also write from a faith-grounded perspective. While many could be noted, two are very important to read. James Davison Hunter, the founder of the Institute for Advanced Studies in Culture (IASC) at the University of Virginia, has generated a massive amount of research and writing. I will note one book in particular out of many, as well as his work to found and direct the award-winning journal "The Hedgehog Review," that has brought together a prodigious array of scholarship. Hunter says he has found it impossible to be restricted to strict disciplinary boundaries. When investigating an issue he says he never lets sociology stand alone. He always investigates an issue by supplementing sociology with intellectual history and religion. This three-pronged approach allows him to explore critical social issues in a more human and comprehensive way.

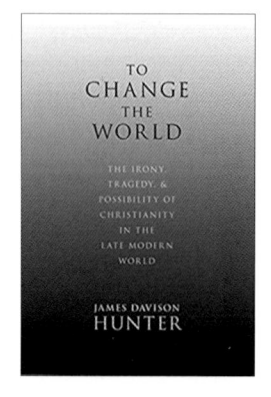

His approach may be clearly illustrated in his 2010 book, *To Change the World: The Irony, Tragedy, and Possibility of Christianity in the Late Modern World,* where he powerfully brings these three disciplines together. How societies change has long been a focal point of sociology. Here Hunter takes on the premise that evangelical Christians will change the world by the means played out in the mission movement of the previous two centuries. He claims that, though well-intentioned and committed, evangelizing groups are missing a deep understanding of how societies actually change. As such, they spend much time and money on techniques destined to be ineffective in the long run.

After a lengthy examination of how people of faith in fact have gained influence in the past, he tries to help the reader understand how elite institutions disproportionately impact a culture. Finally he describes a way forward that seems to give Christians a way to stand in the midst of a society where they've lost most of their meaningful influence. This is an impressive piece of analysis spanning centuries, not to mention scores of the foundational thinkers of the West. However, there needs to be additional conversation about an analysis that leaves little room for the historical irony of "the first will be last and the last first."

Moral, Believing Animals: Human Personhood and Culture by Christian Smith

A different approach to wedging a scholarly shim into the discipline is the work of Notre Dame sociologist Christian Smith. (Ironically both Hunter and Smith attended the same tiny, evangelical Christian college for their undergraduate degrees.) Smith conducted an award-winning study of youth and religion in America. Published as a trilogy of books titled *Soul Searching, Souls in Transition,* and *Lost in Transition,* Smith used mixed method research to both survey and interview his way to possibly the most comprehensive understanding of American youth and religion ever attempted. These books were widely read and discussed, as they showed us how faith was actually functioning in today's youth and young adults.

But Smith's work aims at something deeper, more foundational. He would like to reconfigure the theoretical approach to sociology. His first salvo was fired in his *Moral, Believing Animals: Human Personhood and Culture.* He contends that the real social order contains elements long seen as marginal in historic sociological study. Drawing on traditions that understand morality as a universal category, Smith contends that constituent to the human enterprise is that people are moral and believing. His point is that there is no least common denominator way of understanding humans that doesn't include the uniqueness of each person's believing and therefore their moral commitments. Such foundations don't emerge primarily in empirical studies but in the narratives we live by. His approach necessitates a sociologist identifying their underlying moral beliefs as a starting point for explaining their research. This is a categorically different way of approaching "religion" or any other issue long studied by the discipline.

Sociology, to be sure, has always been interested in religion. The founders of the discipline understood religion to be a central phenomenon in social life. Many studied and wrote about it. Founder Émile Durkheim was intensely interested in what might replace religion as modern societies eclipsed it. Max Weber, though not personally interested in his family's Lutheran faith, believed religion had been central in the emergence of capitalism. And of course Karl Marx lamented the power of religion to keep poor workers from understanding the nature of their oppression.

Habits of the Heart: Individualism and Commitment in American Life by Robert Bellah

Many of the "deans" of the discipline in our current times are quite religious. Peter Berger is a lifelong Lutheran and Princeton sociologist Robert Wuthnow a Presbyterian. Both have written extensively about religion. The late Robert Bellah (ironically a Cal Berkley sociologist and Episcopal lay preacher) found religion an impossible thing to ignore in his seminal works *Habits of the Heart* and *The Good Society* (written with a team of stellar sociologists). In both books the role of religion in American society was examined deeply.

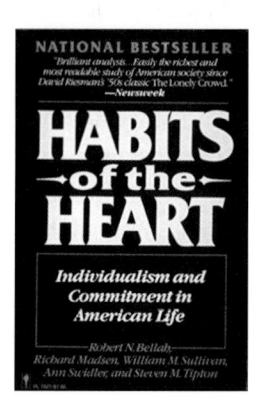

Incidentally, Bellah made an early splash in the study of religion with the study of American civil religion titled *The Broken Covenant*. This spawned an ongoing examination of how religion had indeed turned its focus from a deity to deifying a nation. Standing in the tradition of and trying to answer the question Émile Durkheim had asked nearly a hundred years earlier.

What Is a Person?: Rethinking Humanity, Social Life, and the Moral Good from the Person Up by Christian Smith

But Smith wants to explore the roots of sociology in a way that studies religion and everything else differently. As a matter of fact, Smith objects to the rut professional sociology has fallen into. His *The Sacred Project of American Sociology* describes a discipline religiously committed to a perspective, hardly keeping with scientific investigation or even scholarly investigation of any sort. He charges the discipline with a type of disciplinary political correctness that marginalizes most perspectives not toeing the line. Smith here unleashes a diatribe against an exclusionary discipline not always interested in an accurate approach to our culture or a fair study of it. And as a frontline sociologist his critique is compelling.

But his most impressive work is developed in his text simply titled *What Is a Person?* Smith is developing a theoretical approach he calls critical realist personalism. In the second chapter of the text he draws on three different philosophic traditions to craft his theory. In the first, critical realism, Smith contends that "ontology must precede epistemology." Simply, being must precede knowing, even though both modernity and postmodernity would object.

He combines this with an extremely interesting grab at a philosophy almost dormant. The philosophy of personalism was flourishing in Europe in the mid-twentieth century between the world wars. Many prominent proponents, such as Martin Buber, wrote from this perspective. Possibly its most important student, Martin Luther King, Jr., encountered the philosophy while a seminary student. Directed by a supportive professor, he chose Boston University for his PhD so he could study with America's luminaries of personalism.

Finally, Smith draws on what he calls "antiscientific phenomenology" and especially on the work of Canadian philosopher Charles Taylor. Actually, Taylor seems to be one of the main animators of the entire project.

While parts of this text are quite dense, certainly aimed at scholars, the object of his theorizing is quite approachable. He is aiming at a social theory that allows a person to posit the centrality of categories such as "the good" and "human dignity," often marginalized in orthodox social theory.

Gang Leader for a Day: A Rogue Sociologist Takes to the Street by Sudhir Venkatesh

No matter if these books seem too theoretical for your sociological reading interests. This is a fantastic time to be reading sociology. If you'd like to get your feet wet in some "applied" sociology, there's plenty to sample. For instance, Sudhir Venkatesh's *Gangleader for a Day: A Rogue Sociologist Takes to the Street* is an implausible story of a young graduate student at the University of Chicago misunderstanding an assignment and being thrust into the world of Chicago's drug gangs. Realizing that he has access to a world seldom encountered by academics, Venkatesh spends the next few years inside the gang trying to understand a world dramatically misunderstood by the media and the university alike.

Just Mercy: A Story of Justice and Redemption
by Bryan Stevenson

Or if you have an appetite for justice, it would be hard to go wrong spending a week on death row as Bryan Stevenson narrates his work with inmates who have no one to represent them. His New York Times bestselling book, *Just Mercy,* will move you to tears as you encounter both the hopelessness of many trapped in the criminal justice system (some wrongly) and the glimpse of hope that can restore even in severe circumstances. When Stevenson acknowledges that the brokenness of the inmates and the system are in a profound way his brokenness, the reader senses she's been able to glimpse a profundity not often available to us. This book also provides a fine introduction to Michelle Alexander's *The New Jim Crow: Mass Incarceration in an Age of Colorblindness.*

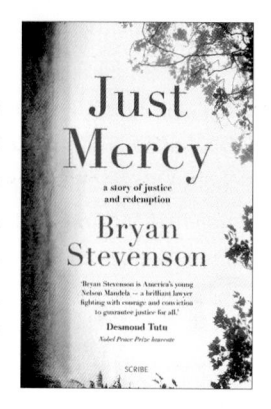

If the power of sociology is to more deeply understand the nature of our society and its institutions, then there's no end to the reading that awaits us. Books such as these can empower us to see our societies in their brokenness and their goodness. They can deepen our appreciation as citizens and our resolve as change agents. I can't imagine a better time to peruse the sociology section of a bookstore comprehensive enough to include one. There's much to read and much to change!

URBAN PLANNING
Tom Becker

I IMAGINE YOU, READER, BEGINNING MY CHAPTER in one of three places: somewhere you'd rather *not* be, like a train, a loud dorm, or a prison. Or somewhere you've been *wanting* to be, like Myrtle Beach, a coffee shop, or a cabin. Or somewhere you call *home:* on a couch, in your bed, or in your bathtub. I read in the bath, and I'm not ashamed.

Are you aware of where you are and how it affects you? If a jellyfish asks a fish, "What is water?" Does the fish answer back, "It's what we live in, silly." Or does he say, "Eek! A talking jellyfish!" He ought to say the former because talking creatures ought not surprise him in the least. To the point, how aware are you of your immediate, *material* surroundings?

The three books I now recommend will pique your awareness of your emplacement. They will do much more than that; they will build for you a mental framework for understanding how places work best for human flourishing. And if you're like me, decently aware of your surroundings, these volumes will become your friends, speaking meaning and direction into your life as good companions always do.

Each of the three are readable, approachable, and wonderfully practical, and I will present them in the chronological order they came to me. They will get you started on a "theology of place." Thankfully, each one offers an outstanding and, in some cases, an extensive bibliography for delightful rabbit trails.

Before I crack these open, though, I present three highly recommended Honorable Mentions. The only reason they didn't make the cut was their tendency to be cranky, long, and technical, respectively.

Let's start with the cranky one. *Home From Nowhere: Remaking Our Everyday World for the 21st Century* by James Howard Kunstler. This is the book that a stranger recommended to me in 1998 at a worship service in St. Louis. My family and I were visiting New City Fellowship as part of a Francis A. Schaeffer Institute week of intensive cultural apologetics. When this fellow discovered in our small talk that I was writing my ethics paper for Dr. Peter Jones on gentrification, he went ballistic on me. He told me in no uncertain terms I had to read Kunstler. He was right. This book codified clearly why I felt so much angst simply living in St. Louis' West County. It wasn't just the occasional death-defying bicycle jaunts on Mason Road that rattled me. It was the constant sense of disintegration of life's most basic elements. Though my family and I lived in a dense, walkable campus, we had to drive forty-five minutes to buy a carton of milk. Everyone, it seemed, lived in their cars. I was exhausted and didn't know why. Then I sat with Kunstler, the suburb-hating Thaddeus Stevens of the New Urbanist movement. His soulmates who wrote *Suburban Nation* smoothed out the furrows he dug up with his rants against car-driven cultures and they offered hopeful ways forward. I'll get to that book shortly, but I first must say: I can remember no more vivid epiphany than reading Kunstler, save my spiritual conversion itself. Having been raised in a very small town that was physically integrated, tight-knit, and walkable, he showed me why much of American habitation made me queasy.

Now to the long one. *The City in History: Its Origins, Its Transformations, and Its Prospects* by Lewis Mumford. For the past ten years or so I've been plodding through this bible of place-making. At 575 pages long, I find it debilitating that Mumford quips in his tiny introduction: "This [first-hand acquaintance with places] has limited me to Western civilization, and even there I have been forced to leave out large significant tracts: namely Spain and Latin America, Palestine, Eastern Europe, Soviet Russia." If only he'd gotten his act together! Published in 1961, Mumford's *Cities* is *The Silmarillion* to Jane Jacob's *Fellowship of the Ring*. That makes the rest of us, writers and readers alike, hobbits. Though this book is foundational for grappling with how and why humans settle and erect their idols to self and gods, it is quite laborious. Each of its eighteen chapters could be a small, immensely annotated book.

The third Honorable Mention goes to the slightly more technical one: *Where Mortals Dwell: A Christian View of Place for Today* by Craig G. Bartholomew. Picking this one over Jacobsen's *The Space Between* was sort of like choosing between *Revolver* and *Rubber Soul*. Not because they're nearly indistinguishable and could've been lashed together as a double LP album; rather, they both deal magnificently with the God-origins of place. Bartholomew's bent, though, is more philosophical. If you want a thorough and engaging what-the-Bible-says-and-implies-about-space book, his first section is for you. His second section deals with the approach to materiality in the Western philosophical tradition, grounded as it is on historical theology. Excise his third section on "A Christian View of Place Today," and you've got the basis for Jacobsen's entire book. I ultimately chose Jacobsen because he writes in line with his vocation as a pastor. Choosing one over the other leaves me unsatisfied, but I'll trust you to make the best choice for yourself.

Back to the Big Three books on place, space, and what Jesus would build. Step into Byron's shop, and let's head over to his Architecture section. Byron knows that architecture, the design of buildings, can't be properly understood in a vacuum. Buildings inhabit places. They must take geology, topography, history, and currency seriously if they're to be useful, appreciated, and sustainable. He recognizes that all structures must be *in*-placed. So, he stocks books on town design, aesthetics, the history of inhabitations, and the philosophy that drives the built environment. Incidentally, he offers the biggest and most lovingly curated such section you're likely to encounter in a bookstore owned by a Christian.

Suburban Nation: The Rise of Sprawl and the Decline of the American Dream by Andres Duany, Elizabeth Plater-Zyberk, and Jeff Speck.

The first book I'm pulling off for you is *Suburban Nation*. Duany, Plater-Zyberk, and Speck (herein DPS) managed to create a subtly illustrated, finely documented, and winsomely reasoned book you can read in a couple of days. Like a great novel, it will propel you through the history of American sprawl into a discussion of the future of cities and concluding with a trove of surprisingly detailed applications. For instance, Appendix A is "The Traditional Neighborhood Development Checklist." Short of a Traditional Neighborhood Ordinance they wish more municipalities would adopt (chapter 11), they offer the checklist to civic leaders and developers who have the opportunity to build a town from scratch. All sorts of elements are taken into consideration, such as the regional context, nearness to rivers and parks, traffic patterns, and streetscapes, down to the exact dimensions that are best for buildings' setbacks. Their point is to bring living towns back that are not car-dominated. If you grew up in a small town, as I did, or if you enjoy visiting a place like Lititz, Pennsylvania or San

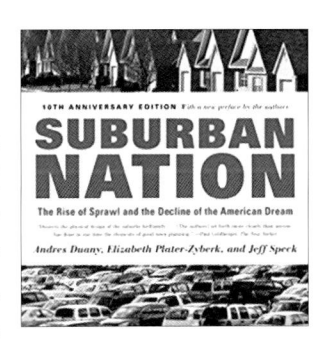

Louis Obispo, California, you will know there's something special about them. You may be tempted to say, "quaint." What is the magical element?

DPS show quite clearly the common factor is mixed-use zoning. Their first nine chapters document how our culture decided to subsidize automobile travel, opening up the great frontier that is our land. And key to that development was designating the various spheres of life to their own space. Because industry is loud and messy, we created industrial zones. There are zones for everything from public schools, to commerce (the shopping center) and the subdivision. A common trope among Americans is that post-WWII suburbia demonstrated our prosperity: more of us had cars. We built out because our cities were deteriorating. We did what Henry Ford predicted: "We shall solve the City Problem by leaving the City."[1] Didn't racism, though, play into "white flight"? Don't get Kunstler started on that question!

Speaking of the curmudgeon and cars, I am, paradoxically, a real car guy. I can name any model and make coming at me within a quarter of a mile. It's just a weird obsession I have along with reading in the tub (usually *Autoweek* magazine). I never realized until I read Kunstler and DPS that our federal government royally subsidizes our auto dependence. DPS rely on a study that demonstrates "government subsidies for highways and parking alone amount to between 8 and 10 percent of our gross national product, the equivalent of a fuel tax of approximately $3.50 per gallon."[2] That is, if we were to add in the "soft" costs of our car addiction such as pollution mitigation and road emergencies, gas should cost $9.00 a gallon at the pump (year 2000 prices). And this doesn't even begin to call into question the cost of lives lost and medical treatments. The leading cause of death among teenagers is automobile fatality. In sprawling environments, children are separated from playgrounds by highways, the elderly are forced to rely on substandard public transportation, and commuting becomes an assumed, albeit stressful, part of everyday life. Are we a freer country for having offered our wrists to the golden handcuffs of suburban sprawl?

DPS would say we are willing slaves. But we are free to build our way out of this mess by building new towns that take their cues from places built before cars were king, to retrofit subdivisions to a more breathable existence, and to imagine what it would mean to both preserve land and build better cities.

Their book inspired me to take college students on architectural tours of Seaside, Florida. You may know this idyllic town from Jim Carrey's film, *The Truman Show*. Designed by the DPS team, Seaside was built on the coast in the panhandle of Florida halfway between Jacksonville and Pensacola. For a few years, I was taking students to a weeklong Christian conference in nearby Laguna Beach. I went again in 2017 and offered the same tour: a thirty minute ride up the coast through mid-century developments and into the Main Street of Seaside. Granted, at its inception, the town looked too perfect, and in fact it has become mostly a resort town. The wonderful thing about Seaside, though, is that it's a delightful and invigorating mixed-use town. It's not gated, it offers a lot of carefully designed, functional public space. It just feels like the kind of place you want to visit or move to. And it's dense, walkable, with incredible sight lines.

The Death and Life of Great American Cities
by Jane Jacobs

DPS make no bones that Seaside can or should be replicated in any place, but they have proven that there is a hunger, perhaps a societal turn, toward integrated towns. When I moved to Lancaster, I was heartened to witness Charter Homes, a construction company, embracing the new town philosophy. One of their developments, Florion Hill, built on Traditional Neighborhood Development (TND) principles, is built purposely to tie into the town of Mount Joy, adding to its historical grid. Their design team clearly took a play from the city life coach herself, Jane Jacobs.

In her seminal book, oft-quoted by any and all New Urbanists, Lady Jane explores the ecosystem of cities. Take the chunky volume off Byron's shelf, the one that says "Modern Library" on the dust jacket. Random House has published multiple versions since she wrote it in 1961. If my tiny preview doesn't whet your appetite for a thorough read, I've not done my job. The four main sections give you an idea of what you're in for: The Peculiar Nature of Cities, The Conditions for City Diversity, Forces of Decline and Regeneration, and Different Tactics. In the end, the sense you get from Jacobs is that she respects the city as a living organism.

Perhaps an analogy will help. Several summers ago my doctor friend looked at my face and shook his head: painful sores with blisters were running up my jaw to my temple, my teeth hurt, my tongue was swollen, I had difficulty swallowing, I had a slight fever, and I was low on energy, yet couldn't sleep well. He called his Physicians' Assistant in, and they both shook their heads. "This guy is really sick. He has a bunch of stuff." They weren't sure what to do; I was already on antibiotics for a sinus infection. I really did have several conditions at once: sinus infection, thrush, and an outbreak of shingles! To assist my body in healing itself, I was given Ambien, and Steve prescribed a steroid to accelerate the retreat of the shingles. I rested and eventually healed. The root cause of my condition, though, was stress that came as a result of overworking while nursing a common cold. Steve's job was to create conditions for my body to heal itself.

Similarly, cities are as complex as our bodies. Their troubles are complex, and so are their contributions. So much is going on and could go wrong. And yet, at their core, human habitations have a biology of their own. How, then, can we create conditions that allow them to flourish? That is the central question Jacobs addresses.

And she does it with chops: a New Yorker writing on architecture throughout the 1960s, she is also the author of *The Economies of Cities* (1970) and *Dark Age Ahead* (2005). She lived in Greenwich Village and came to love its unique beauty, diversity, and walkability.

Her book is at once inspiring and polemical. In discussing why sidewalks matter, she describes a woman yahoo-ing at her as she makes her way to a bus stop. Making eye contact with her, the lady shouts, "That bus doesn't run here on Saturdays!" By pantomime gestures, she directs Jane in the right direction. "This woman was one of thousands upon thousands in New York who casually take care of the streets," Jacobs reflects. Similar stories of life-on-life hint at a hunch we all have but may never have named. Namely, that human density is not problematic in and of itself. In fact, it might also be full of glorious possibilities.

Eyes on the streets; clear demarcation of healthy public space; private enterprises; strangers enjoying the sights; children playing safely on sidewalks lined with parked cars as barriers; neighborhoods folding into larger city districts; criminal elements dissipated instead of congregated; diverse populations living in symbiotic interdependence. These are all part of the city ecosystem that is ever shifting, ever emerging, and somehow ever imposed upon by goofy urban planners.

Which leads to her polemic: Jacobs is no modernist in the sense that she lives by a fixed philosophy of what should be best for people. Too often, the architects and city planners were those with a utopian vision. Fair enough, but those visions rarely comport with the nature of things. How may 1970s urban renewal downtown projects turned cities around? They certainly didn't work in

What Urban Planning Books You Should Read & Why 205

Detroit or Atlanta, or in my small city of Lancaster where we're still recovering from the brutalism imposed upon a couple city blocks. What went wrong?

Observing the contribution a church youth center and a corner bar make to night life in a neighborhood, Jacobs puts it this way: "The preferences of Utopians, and of other compulsive managers of other peoples' leisure, for one kind of legal enterprise over others is worse than irrelevant for cities. It is harmful."[3] Cities themselves must lead the way for planners (not the other way around).

It is her observation of the system that is most impressive. She will not go into the deeper reasons cities have problems. Things like sin and redemption are not the purpose of her book, but I imagine Jacobs reading through Francis A. Schaeffer's five-volume series and saying, "That guy understands how reality works." You hear people like Schaeffer, C.S. Lewis, and my Old Testament mentor Jack Collins talking like that often: God made the world to function a certain way. A cow moos. That is his glorious calling in life. Penning him up and shooting him up with hormones and antibiotics only does a number on his digestive system. A cow, by its very nature, is meant to graze. The Creator in the Bible sets things up a certain way and his purpose in Christ is to restore all things to their natural condition in a world that, regrettably, is bent and torn. Christ came to redeem cows (free them from human degradation), to redeem people, and in so doing to redeem places like cities that are, by their very nature, not evil, just thoroughly messed up. I don't know if Jane was a believer in this Christ, but she surely drew conclusions that are consonant with a Christian theology of place. If this was never her intent or purpose, Eric Jacobsen indeed makes it his own.

The Space Between: A Christian Engagement with the Built Environment by Eric O. Jacobsen

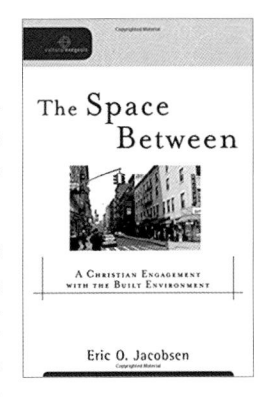

The Space Between came to me after having read Kunstler and Jacobs. In fact, I had read Jacobsen's smaller introduction to the subject, *Sidewalks in the Kingdom: New Urbanism and the Christian Faith,* and was thrilled to see a fellow believer synthesize the disciplines that had meant so much to me: place and theology. I only wish I had written it myself, so I admit to a tinge of jealousy. This second book of his, though, is one only he could write. Not only is he wise in the ways of New Urbanism, he also pastors a downtown church in Tacoma, Washington. He wrote the book while still living in Missoula, Montana which must've been a fascinating laboratory.

As I said in my introduction, his book is a how-to for living out biblical principles of community without ignoring one's emplacement. It's amazing to me, really, that many of my fellow Christians talk of community with barely any reference to geography. Well, Pastor Eric doesn't do that. Part I seeks to answer four questions: who are you, where are you (now we're talking!), what are you, and when are you?

You can see where he's going with this: he agrees with Kunstler that we can't buy community and takes him "one step further in saying that we cannot even build community. [It] requires wisdom, grace, and time." These two gents should have lunch together.

Jacobsen also mentions Seaside, its promise and shortcomings. The anti-Platonism in me is glad to hear him say, "What we cannot do is reject our communities to purse some kind of abstract and idealized community that is devoid of human messiness."[4] Going headlong into the messiness, his Part II encourages winsome Christian engagement in family, politics, and church. He ends the book commending sustainability and love in Part III. I read it with bated breath and a pounding heart.

The Row House Forum, being an extension of the household Becky and I have cultivated in Lancaster since 1999, is an experiment in such *lived* theology. We simply cannot separate the work of apologetics and mission from the messiness of a noticeable human presence. We cannot love without knowing our neighbors. I've dedicated my life to the notion that Christian cultural engagement is like a contact lens: it must be *permeable*. People, ideas, and cultural contributions must not only flow out from the believing community; they must also flow in. And our lives must be fully within the sight lines of our fellow earthlings. We can' t avoid, build, or create culture. We are *in*-culturated. And the question we must ask, and one which Jacobsen answers adroitly is this: how are we cultivating our embodied lives for the sake of the world in the name of Christ?

It makes sense that Byron Borger has been pushing the books of Jacobsen, Bartholemew, and Jacobs for years. His thirty-five years of *BookNotes* and electrified book plugs notwithstanding, his real estate is telling. As you drive through the hamlet of Dallastown, Pennsylvania on Main Street, you are bound to miss the store the first time. Your attention may be drawn to the late nineteenth-century Lutheran church across the street, a staple of many Pennsylvania towns. Then you swing back into the alley and find the tiny car park. You're now looking at a back garden and patio. You enter what looks like a home, and it is. It's Byron and Beth's residence. The place is crammed wth books organized by subject. Look out the windows. You will see that Lutheran church spire, neighbors walking by on the sidewalk, and a mighty oak shading the back garden where you left your car.

If you're lucky, you'll get a few minutes to yourself to peruse the shelves before Byron himself finds you. And then the encyclopedic frenzy of friendliness begins. The saddest days in New York are the ones when Tim Keller is not preaching, some say. The same can be said for a visit to the Borger's shop without Beth or Byron. Regardless, I double-dare you to *not* spend a hundred dollars.

You and I are encased in built environments all the time. And they are built by humans with a specific intent. To be aware of both our settings and their intended purposes is to be an observant human. We are more than rats scuttling around in a maze chasing bits of cheese. These three books by DPS, Jacobs, and Jacobsen get behind the intent of design. I love them because they codify for me my experience in the settings God has graciously placed me in. By their guiding light, I've become more human, I suppose, and I trust you will too.

Endnotes

1   Henry Ford, 1922, *Suburban Nation*, 135.
2   Stanley Hart and Alvin Spivak, *The Elephant in the Room: Automobile Dependence and Denial.*
3   *The Life and Death of Great American Cities*, 52.
4   *The Space Between*, 100-101.

vocation

Steve Garber

IN LATE AUGUST, EVEN WITH THE FAN BLOWING, it was too hot. But I was coming to the end of a summer of writing, sitting at my desk in our third floor apartment in Pittsburgh's East End, looking at the small bookshelf in front of me, aware that these books were my books—in their different ways they had formed me, heart and mind.

Married for two short years, I was newly aware that I was slowly entering into a long-loved love . . . for the first time I was working as if my life depended on it, because it did . . . and I was finishing a thesis, though at that moment I was unaware of what mastering it would mean for the rest of my life . . . and I saw this small collection of books in a way that I never had before. They were ones that I had lived with and through, thinking with their authors, wanting their authors to teach me, opening myself to them in ways that I had never before known.

At the time I had a small library, pretty portable as it needed to be, and I knew each one. A couple of boxes and a strong back was all I needed to move my books from one apartment to another in those early days of finishing college, getting married, and starting off in life. Many years later there are thousands of books that fill the shelves of our life, upstairs and downstairs, and in between too. Every room has a bookcase, and some spots are especially honored because they provide floor space for overflow.

We love books, all kinds of books—for young and old, some very serious and some very playful. Some we call "children's books," but those who know, know that only the very best books can be for children, because if they are good enough for children they are good enough for everyone; there are shelves of novels, new and old, and some novelists even get a whole shelf; some are photo essays, remembering people and places that are important to us for many reasons; there is cultural analysis of all kinds that fill shelf after shelf; another bookcase is full of deeply devotional literature that runs back over the centuries; biographies and autobiographies take several bookcases, a genre that I have loved for all my life; and yes, there are shelves and shelves of philosophy and theology, some almost ancient and some just off the press.

I don't know all these books in the way that I knew those first books, but in their very different ways they are me, reflecting my loves and longings, nourishing my hopes and dreams; sometimes cutting me to the core of my being, calling me to be more than I am and want to be; sometimes taking me to places that I simply want to be, offering me imaginative rooms that are big enough that I can be lost in the cosmos for a brief, shining moment. To say it simply, my vocation is indistinguishable from my life among my books. The truest learning only happens when words become flesh, because that has to be for us to understand them; but it is its own wonder when that happens.

The Reading and Writing of Books

My earliest memories are of my mother sitting with my brother and me, reading. My father was very busy with a graduate degree, and I remember cuddling with her, hearing her read and read. Not so many years later, still a little boy, one of the first heartache moments of my life involved reading a book. We lived in Davis, California then, and early in the fall of my first grade year our teacher promised that if we would learn to read before the Thanksgiving break, we could take our little "Dick and Jane" readers home, showing our parents what we could do. I worked at it, mastering its complexity, full of expectation that sometime soon I could read to my family. For what is still an inexplicable reason, she reneged on her promise—and I still remember the hurt to my heart.

A year later we lived in Shafter, CA, my father having finished his studies, taking up what would be his work for the rest of his life as a research scientist for the University of California. In the local Richland Elementary School, I was placed in a class with kids who became my classmates for years to come, and some are still my closest friends. By second grade I had moved beyond Dick and Jane, and was reading more interesting stories—enough so that my teacher asked me to go around to each of the other classes, and read a book aloud to the other second graders. It was all very innocent, and I did not think much about it at the time, but remembering those years, I now know that it was a small part of the story of my life, my love for books as a thread making its way through my life.

Two years later, the school's annual visiting author was Leo Politi, the renowned writer and illustrator whose books now fill one shelf in our home. Before anyone had ever imagined a word like "multicultural," Politi offered the world book after book telling the stories of children from the tribes and tongues that made California "California." Little Juan longing for the swallows to come back to the mission at San Juan Capistrano... Moy Moy and her friends following the New Year's dragon through the streets of Los Angeles' Chinatown... Stephen and Lucia, the Portuguese brother and sister from Monterrey who delighted in the annual migration of the monarch butterflies through the trees of their backyard... the little Italian boy named Leo on his ranch near Fresno who loved the West with its cowboys and Indians, and more and more, each one full of beautiful watercolors telling their own tale of the people and places of California.

And yes, when I began taking my children to the library years later, I found Politi's books, and read them to another generation. When these little ones became adults, they began giving me his books as Christmas gifts, and we now have most of what he wrote—and it all began with a librarian who took the initiative to bring an author to "show and tell" the simple truth that real people write books.

Two more years passed, and another author came. Walking from my class to the cafeteria one day, in a long, straight, no-nonsense line, I saw a row of books in the glass case outside of the library, one jumping out to me called *Little Britches: Father and I Were Ranchers*. Before the day was done, I had that book under my arm, and read it all the way through, swallowing it as fast as I could—and by the time Ralph Moody came for his visit a couple of weeks later, I had read all the books in his autobiographical series. Looking back, I am sure that my interest must have interested the librarians, because the day before he came they asked if I would like to meet him after school, to have a more personal time with him—and my parents were invited too! So we all found our way to the Richland Elementary School library, and had a short, but momentous meeting with the great author himself. In my copy of *Little Britches,* I have a photo of Moody and me sitting on the table in the library, with his inscription, "To my Colorado friend, Steve...." Like Politi's books, Moody's have their own shelf, prominently displayed in our living room. Life goes on, and my learning went on. Not every year did I meet an author, but that I did as a boy was formative for my own love for books. And that Politi and Moody were good writers mattered too, as I was not then, nor am I now, embarrassed at all over the quality of their writing, the goodness of their gifts to me and the world. Their stories drew me in to worlds that I wanted to understand, to experiences of life that I could understand. Good authors do that, always and everywhere they do that.

A Learning That Matters

Before my last year of high school, I spent the summer in Colorado, as I had done for most of my life. Born in a high mountain valley under the Sangre de Cristo range, my grandparents' love for me, and cattle, kept me coming back to my birthplace for the years of my growing up. That seventeen-year-old summer was important for a couple of reasons that have shaped me for the rest of life, and both had to do with uncharacteristically rainy days and alfalfa.

My work that summer was mostly haying, as the cowboys call it; cutting hay, winnowing it, letting it dry, and then baling it. But twice that summer we had more rain than Colorado typically gets—most afternoons, early on, it rains for fifteen minutes, and then the sky is blue again for another day—and so we could not bale the hay until it dried out. On one of those days I met my wife Meg in Rocky Mountain National Park, a moment that runs through everything that I am, everything that I have been and will be; and the Park is a place where we have returned again and again in our life together. On the other rainy day I decided to go into the local university to see if I could find a journalism professor. By that time I had given up all hope of high school glory on the football field—whatever hopes were fancifully imagined, one fall day I was taken off in an ambulance, and the orthopedic surgeon told me to stop playing—so I began writing about sports, instead. My first try was as the correspondent for the area newspaper, reporting on our high school's athletic teams, being paid by the inch for my labor; but in the same year I became the sports editor for the high school newspaper. I enjoyed it enough to become the editor at-large my senior year, which was what took me to the University of Northern Colorado in Greeley on that rainy day, hoping to find someone to learn something from.

After knocking on several doors, I eventually found myself in the office of William Hartman, chairman of the journalism department at UNC, and to my great surprise the author of the standard textbook for high school journalists across the country, a book simply titled *Journalism*. That I had come looking for someone like him must have surprised him, because he invited me for lunch at the faculty club, which I did with some awkwardness and much pleasure. And before we were done, he invited me to come to his class two weeks later, to "lecture" with all of my seventeen-year-old wisdom, speaking to his summer school students who were high school journalism teachers from throughout the state. Looking back on this, I smile, having no idea at the time that I would spend much of my life speaking in universities and colleges across America, often to their faculties about the nature and direction of a learning that matters.

And then I entered into college, having a draft lottery number that kept me "safe" in those volatile years of Vietnam. In my first year as a journalism major, I was required to read in journals within the discipline. One day in the library, I was struck by these words, jumping off the page at me: "The media today not only needs those who have the ability to communicate, but those who have something to communicate." All of my thoughts about the next years of my life were upset, in one fell swoop. My educational career was mapped out: I would do this, and then that, and then this would happen, and I would be that for my life. But those few words would not leave me alone. I could see that they were describing a world I did not yet know, and I began to ponder deeper things, ideas that I had not yet explored—the word "worldview," for example, began echoing its way through my mind over the next weeks and months. A year earlier someone had offered it to me as a way of making sense of life and learning. I was intrigued, but had no idea what it would mean for me and my life. But a few months later, reading the journal, caught by the words, I began to rethink what I was doing, and why.

So I decided to go to a college where "worldview" mattered, explicitly, choosing a liberal arts institution all the way across the country, Geneva College in Beaver Falls, Pennsylvania. That it was also where my parents and grandparents had gone to school was important, but the driving motivation was that I was promised a way to learn about the whys and wherefores of life in the world, to study in a place where I could develop "something to communicate."

Geneva was all that and more, and so much of the way I think was formed among those people in that place, but over the year I began to think about things that colleges simply are not very well equipped to help young people understand—and I dropped out. Students did things like that then, exploring the world all over the world, trying to find their place in it; looking back, I am sure that it was in the air of the early 1970s, and I breathed it in, deeply. And so I went back to California, and lived for a year in a commune in Palo Alto, where together we published magazines observing and analyzing culture. Intimidated by people older than me who had read more than me, I did not write anything at all that year, finding my satisfaction as the managing editor, making sure everything got done when it was supposed to get done.

That year was critical in my growing up. I began to see as I never had that ideas have legs, that worldviews become ways of life. But of everything I thought about in those counter cultural moments—living between the university communities of Palo Alto and Berkeley, often stepping into the city of San Francisco itself—the deepest insight that began to rumble through my mind was that the way we define ourselves as human beings shapes everything else in life. Love and sex, politics and economics, the meaning of history, the arts, everything we know grows out of our view of the human person. And I wanted to know more about that, especially digging more deeply into what I believed about human nature... which took me to another commune, this one in Europe, known by a very simple name: *L'Abri*.

Those years away from school mattered then, but in retrospect they matter even more now in so many ways that have formed my commitments about who I am and what I do—yes, the vocation that is mine. "Extra-academic education" as it was, my years away from formal education were crucial in making sense of the next years of my life, lived within the rigors and contours of degrees and more degrees as they would be. To say it simply: I learned to learn about things that matter.

How did that happen? In those days and months at L'Abri I met people and ideas that shaped me for my life. Francis and Edith Schaeffer, Donald Drew, Hans Rookmaaker, Os Guinness, Jerram Barrs, each one a real person with a real life, but also each one writing about the world that I wanted to understand. Their lives intrigued me, because I could see enough to know that their words were not abstractions, but were being made flesh. No one was perfect, nothing was perfect, but for the young pilgrims of the world like me, there was enough reality to persuade us that the ideas at the heart of L'Abri could be lived into in ways that made sense of life. There was an honest integrity that was its own apologetic for the meaning of faith, for the very possibility of faith.

BOOKS FOR LIFE

After two years away, I finally returned to college, having learned something about learning that is still central to my beliefs about pedagogy, i.e. if you know what you want to learn, you can find a way to learn it. In the end, we are the learners, and learning is our responsibility—and so my final years as an undergraduate were ones full of hope for what might be learned. The books I began reading while away from school gave me lenses and categories for my reengagement of learning back in school. Not everything was exciting, but what I found was that with the right questions, any course could become honestly interesting. So I took up readings in intellectual history, the history and philosophy of science, psychology, sociology, theology, and more, pressing myself to think things through in a way that I had never imagined. I even went to the academic dean with ideas for courses, persuading him that my friends and I would pay good money to be able to learn about this and that, intellectual interests that had captivated me—I was sure that they would captivate my friends. He agreed, and we did.

That next summer I returned to California, and at its end made my way through Colorado for days with my family. On the banks of the Poudre Canyon, I tried for the third time to read *The Dust of Death* by Os Guinness, and I began to understand his analysis and argument, finally. Towards its end I read these words, and they caught me: "Christian social analysis must first of all analyze what is wrong, but also redefine what is desired." That seemed right, and an idea was birthed as I watched the water cascade down the mountain canyon, trout sometimes visibly swimming downstream. It was the summer of 1975, and we were coming into the Bicentennial Year of America, 1976—I began thinking about where we had gone wrong as a country, and what might be done to correct it. Audacious, yes, but I was a young man, dreaming dreams. When I got back to school I gathered my friends and favorite professor, and we began planning toward an event in the spring which we called Reshaping the American Dream. For most of the next year that vision made sense of much of what I thought about, and worked on.

That winter I was with these same friends for dinner one night, and Dr. Peter Steen joined us. A professor at-large traveling the highways of western Pennsylvania, teaching students wherever he could find them about the meaning of everything, I mentioned that I had a question that mattered to me. So very typical of Pete, as we knew him, he asked, "Have you read *Where the Wasteland Ends?*" Nope, I had not, but I made my way to the library and found Theodore Roszak's book, a critique of the Enlightenment epistemology, especially probing its cultural consequences. As I read, I begin to see into my question in ways that opened up avenues for analysis that guided me through my final year of college, forming the backdrop for my senior honors thesis . . . which was written into my master's thesis two years later . . . which then was written into my doctoral dissertation ten years later . . . which has become the long thread coursing its way through my teaching and writing in the years since. That almost-happenstance dinner in the cafeteria was a conversation with consequences . . . for my life, and over the years for the lives of many others.

More could be said about the gifts of good people like J.I. Packer and John Stott, whose writing nourished me in the most important ways in those years; over time their beliefs about God and the world are ones that I have taken into my deepest places, forming my dispositions and desires in ways I know and do not know. One more time, their books taught me; but their lives persuaded me, words becoming flesh as must be.

The Best Bookseller in America

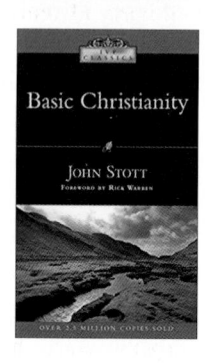

And now I want to draw in my long friendship with Byron Borger, whose own vocation in service of the vocations of others is my reason for writing. Born in different places to different families, somehow we both found our way into long lives full of a love for books. He became a bookseller, an apostle and evangelist for reading the best books; I became a professor, bringing books into the classrooms of my life, longing for them to give life to the learning of my students. I first met him when he was cutting his vocational teeth among university students, with undying passion, giving his heart away with the hope that these emerging adults would grow into men and women with an unusual commitment to things that matter most. Though we were not in the same places in our university years, we had many of the same influences. In a wonderful way, in a profound way, my teachers were his teachers, and his teachers were my teachers. As we began to get to know each other, it was clear that we both loved books. For Byron, the conviction that students should read the right books for the right reasons became his *raison d'être,* committed to the hope that students would form lives of moral meaning—where what ought to matter did matter —forming in them an unusual integrity of heart and mind. Those years of living his life among students grew into a life with his long love Beth, together giving their lives to the same end, with the same hope, born of the same passion. Differently done, that is my story too.

And those books that were me, filling the small shelf on my desk? They were all published by InterVarsity Press, the distinctive "IVP" marking the spine of each book—and that day I knew that I owed them something. Lots of life happened in the next years, with a growing family and a deepening sense of who I was and what I was to do. In the surprising ways that vocations are unfolded, finding ourselves in and through the callings that become us, most of twenty years later I offered their senior editor a manuscript, which became *The Fabric of Faithfulness,* a book first written for someone like I had been, a twenty-something with questions that had no easy answers; its many printings surprised the publisher, and have made me smile. As it was read far and wide, Byron being a tireless promoter, it became a book for everyone, young and old alike, each of us hoping as we are to form habits of heart that sustain a vision of vocation in us and for us. When I was ready to publish another book, Byron was the principal reason that I offered my work again to IVP; he persuaded me that they would serve me and the world with the most integrity, which they have. So many years ago now, sweating on that summer day in August, knowing that I was implicated by the work of IVP, I had no idea that someday I would write my own books under their imprint, offering my thinking to the next generation, pilgrims as students always are, slowly making their way into the world with their own unique hopes and fears, commitments and questions, just as I had once done.

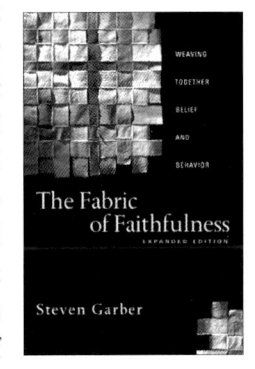

A couple of years ago, I was invited to a dinner in downtown Washington with IVP's publisher. Around a large table a group had gathered to honor another writer who was in town to lecture on his recently published book. We talked about many things, and along the way Byron's name came up, honored by us all, every one of us in awe of his life and labor. The publisher said, without a blush, "We think that Byron Borger is the best bookseller in America," and he went on to explain his commendation. No one could disagree, because that is plainly true for all with eyes to see. No one knows books, and loves books, as does Byron.

For the years of his life Byron has served the wide world with his deeply-formed commitment to a reading that educates us in the most important ways, teaching us to see the world as it really is and to care for it in its complexity—calling all of us, hearts and minds twined together, into vocations that are born of a love for God and for God's world, which when all is said and done is the very meaning of a good life for everyone everywhere... for him, and for all the rest of us.

overstock
About the Authors

ANDI ASHWORTH is the author of *Real Love for Real Life: The Art and Work of Caring*. She and her husband, Charlie Peacock, are Co-founders/Directors Emeritus of Art House America, with Art House branches in Nashville, Dallas, and St. Paul. Andi also serves as editor-in-chief of the Art House America literary blog.

TOM BECKER earned his MDiv from Covenant Theological Seminary, studied at L'abri, and was ordained in the Presbyterian Church in America. After serving several years in campus ministry and a few more teaching, Tom founded the The Row House—a monthly forum for cultural engagement. He is the author of *Good Posture: Engaging Current Culture with Ancient Faith*, lives in the very walkable city of Lancaster with his wife Becky, and has five grown children. *TheRowHouse.org*

AARON BELZ holds an MA in Creative Writing from New York University and a PhD in American Literature from Saint Louis University and has also published numerous essays, reviews, and academic papers. His books of poetry include *The Bird Hoverer* (2007), *Lovely, Raspberry* (2010), and *Glitter Bomb* (2014). He resides with his wife Araceli Cruz, also a writer, in Hillsborough, North Carolina, where they both serve on the board of the town arts council. For more information about Aaron or his writing, visit *belz.net*.

BYRON K. BORGER, along with his wife Beth, owns Hearts & Minds, an independent bookstore in Dallastown, Pennsylvania, where they have sought to offer a wide selection of fine books designed to inspire readers to relate faith to all areas of life. They travel often, serving many organizations with book displays, and much of their business is on-line where they serve customers all over the world. He is an Associate Staff of CCO and has received an Honorary Doctorate through Geneva's Higher Education Degree program. He also was the editor of *Serious Dreams: Bold Ideas for the Rest of Your Life.*

Eric Bryan received his PhD from Saint Louis University and is currently Associate Professor of English at Missouri University of Science and Technology, where he teaches courses on mythology and folklore, linguistics, fantasy literature, and early British literature. He has published articles on Old Norse-Icelandic folklore, historical linguistics, and medieval conversion narratives, and he is co-editor of a forthcoming volume entitled *Pragmatics and Proverbs in the Medieval North* (ACMRS 2018). During his nine years at Missouri S&T he has received four teaching awards. He also serves as a ruling elder at Grace and Peace Fellowship in St. Louis, Missouri.

Ned Bustard is a graphic designer, children's book illustrator, author, and printmaker. Books he has written, illustrated, or edited include *It Was Good: Making Art to the Glory of God*, *Squalls Before War: His Majesty's Schooner Sultana*, *History of Art: Creation to Contemporary*, *The Reformation ABC's*, *Bigger on the Inside: Christianity and Doctor Who*, and *Revealed: A Storybook Bible for Grown-Ups*. He is creative director for Square Halo Books, Inc., curator of the Square Halo Gallery, and serves on the boards of the Association of Scholars of Christianity in the History of Art (ASCHA) and The Row House. *WorldsEndImages.com*

Matthew Dickerson is the author of *The Daegmon War,* a three-volume fantasy novel featuring *The Gifted* (2015), *The Betrayed* (2016), and *Illengond* (2017). He has also published a medieval historical novel *The Rood and the Torc: the Song of Kristinge, Son of Finn* (2014), as well as several works about J.R.R. Tolkien, C.S. Lewis, and fantasy literature, and also books of narrative nonfiction on fly-fishing, trout, and ecology. He is a professor at Middlebury College in Vermont.

G. Tyler Fischer has been the Head of School at Veritas Academy in Lancaster County, Pennsylvania, since 1997. He received a BA in history from Grove City College and a MDiv from Reformed Theological Seminary. He serves on the board of the Association of Classical and Christian Schools. He has been involved in numerous curricular projects. Most recently, he edited *Teaching Beauty: A Vision for Music & Art in Christian Education.* He was

About the Authors

the managing editor of Veritas Press' *Omnibus* Curriculum. He was also a contributor to *Perspectives on Family Ministry* and *Perspectives on Your Child's Education,* which were published in 2009. Ty and his wife, Emily, are the parents of four daughters: Maddy, Laynie, Karis, and Elyse, and the proud owners of one "periodically obedient" puggle, Roxy.

BRADSHAW FREY is a professor of sociology at Geneva College in Beaver Falls, Pennsylvania. His work has focused on the nexus between academia and a mill town. In particular he has investigated the history of race and economic development in towns like the one where Geneva is located. With a friend and three former students he founded a community development corporation and an LLC to work on the redevelopment of a distressed mill town. Before teaching at Geneva he worked for the CCO in campus ministry. He has three grown children and five grandchildren.

STEVEN GARBER is Professor of Marketplace Theology and Leadership at Regent College, and director of Regent's new graduate program, the Masters of Arts in Leadership, Theology, and Society. For many years the Principal of The Washington Institute for Faith, Vocation, and Culture in Washington, D.C., his conviction that faith coherently make sense of the whole of life brought forth the books, *The Fabric of Faithfulness* and *Visions of Vocation,* and is the context for his work as an advisor and consultant with a diverse range of businesses, foundations, and educational institutions. He is married to Meg, and they live between Vancouver and Virginia, enjoying the beauty and wonder of both worlds.

DAVID P. GUSHEE is Distinguished University Professor of Christian Ethics and Director of the Center for Theology and Public Life at Mercer University. One of the premier ethical thinkers in American Christianity, he is the author of twenty-two books. He serves as President-Elect of the American Academy of Religion and President of the Society of Christian Ethics. He is the interim pastor of the 1,400-member First Baptist Church of Decatur, Georgia.

DENIS HAACK is co-director, with his wife Margie, of Ransom Fellowship, a ministry that seeks to help Christians develop skill in discernment, applying the Gospel creatively to all of life. A visiting instructor at Covenant Theological Seminary in practical theology, he lectures regularly at conferences, retreats, and L'Abri Fellowship on culture, film, and Christian faithfulness. He is the editor of *Critique*—in which a notice for Hearts & Minds Bookstore appears regularly, so that readers will know the best place to order the books he reviews. *RansomFellowship.org.*

MICHAEL KUCKS is an associate professor of physics and math at Patrick Henry College in Northern Virginia and is head of their Economics & Business Analytics program. He received his PhD in physics from Lehigh University and has taught at Franklin & Marshall College as well as in various industries. He encourages his students to read broadly, think clearly, communicate mathematically and, above all, to use Excel. He and his wife, Mary, have four grown children and three grandchildren.

KAREN SWALLOW PRIOR, PhD, is an award-winning Professor of English at Liberty University. She is the author of *Booked: Literature in the Soul of Me* (T. S. Poetry Press, 2012) and *Fierce Convictions: The Extraordinary Life of Hannah More—Poet, Reformer, Abolitionist* (Thomas Nelson, 2014). Prior's writing appears at *Christianity Today, The Atlantic, The Washington Post, First Things, Vox, Think Christian, The Gospel Coalition, Books and Culture,* and other places. She is a Research Fellow with the Ethics and Religious Liberty Commission of the Southern Baptist Convention, a Senior Fellow with Liberty University's Center for Apologetics and Cultural Engagement, and a member of the Faith Advisory Council of the Humane Society of the United States.

MIKE SCHUTT is director of the Christian Legal Society's Law Student Ministries and Associate Professor at Regent University School of Law. Mike directs the Institute for Christian Legal Studies, a cooperative ministry of CLS and Regent Law. He serves as editor of the *Journal of Christian Legal Thought* and host of the *Cross & Gavel Audio* podcast. His book *Redeeming Law: Christian Calling and the Legal Profession* (InterVarsity, 2007) is a vocational exhortation for lawyers and law students. Before entering academia, he practiced law in Fort Worth, Texas. He serves on the boards of trustees for LeTourneau University and Worldview at the Abbey, and he lives in Mount Pleasant, Texas with his wife Lisa. He has three grown children and four grandchildren.

CALVIN SEERVELD is emeritus professor of Philosophical Aesthetics at the graduate Institute for Christian Studies in Toronto. Among other books he has written *Rainbows for the Fallen World* (1970/1980), *The Greatest Song, in critique of Solomon* (rev. 2nd ed. 1988), *Take Hold of God and Pull* (rev. 2nd ed. 1999), *Bearing Fresh Olive Leaves* (2000), *In the Fields of the Lord, A Seerveld Reader,* ed. Craig Bartholomew (2000), *How to Read the Bible to Hear God Speak* (enlarged ed. 2003), *Biblical Studies & Wisdom for Living,* with five other volumes of lectures and articles on art edited by John Kok (2014), and *Never Try to Arouse Erotic Love Until—* (forthcoming).

DANIEL SPANJER has worked as a mechanic, commercial fisherman, grant administrator, golf course greens keeper, and, in April, 2016, he successfully defended his dissertation at the University at Albany, SUNY. He has taught at Nyack College, University at Albany, and is currently the Chair of the Arts and Science Department and Professor of History at Lancaster Bible College. He also serves the college as the director of the Alcuin Society, a scholarly organization which serves campus faculty. Dr. Spanjer has published several essays for the new *Encyclopedia of Christianity*. He is married to Tara Spanjer and they have three daughters: Meghan, Emily, and Katelyn.

GREGORY WOLFE is the founder and editor of *Image*—one of America's leading quarterly journals. During the 2016-17 academic year, he served as Senior Fellow with the Institute for Catholic Thought and Culture at Seattle University. From 2004-2016 he served as the founding director of the Seattle Pacific University MFA in Creative Writing program. He has served as a judge for the National Book Awards. In 2013 he launched a literary imprint, Slant Books, through Wipf & Stock. Wolfe has published essays, reviews, and articles in numerous journals, including the *Wall Street Journal, Washington Post, Commonweal,* and *First Things.* His essays have been anthologized in collections such as *The Best Christian Writing* and *The Best Catholic Writing.* Among his books are *Beauty Will Save the World, Intruding Upon the Timeless,* and *The Operation of Grace.*

N. T. (TOM) WRIGHT is Professor of New Testament at the University of St. Andrews, Scotland. He taught New Testament in Cambridge, McGill and Oxford Universities for 20 years before becoming Dean of Lichfield, Canon of Westminster Abbey, and finally Bishop of Durham (2003-2010). Wright has written over 80 books at scholarly and popular levels, and has lectured and broadcast around the world. He is married to Maggie and they have four children and five grandchildren. He is still trying to improve his golf game.

SQUARE HALO
Books You Should Read & Why

The Beginning: A Second Look at the First Sin
"[A] very readable and engaging discussion on the nature and consequences of the original sin using the biblical accounts as his primary authority ... A sound background in scripture, a solid presentation of his positions, and generous application make this book a very good reference on the subject." —*The American Journal of Biblical Theology*

Bigger on the Inside: Christianity and Doctor Who
Like the TARDIS itself, the fantastically popular series *Doctor Who* is bigger on the inside, full of profound ideas about time and history, the nature of humanity, and the mysteries of faith.

Deeper Magic: The Theology Behind the Writings of C.S. Lewis
"... a treasure trove of systematized information—a must for every C.S. Lewis fan, and all the rest of us who should be." —Norman Geisler, PhD

Intruding Upon the Timeless: Meditations on Art, Faith, and Mystery
"A collection of brief essays by the editor of *Image*, a distinguished journal of religion and the arts. A nice mix of the whimsical, provocative, and devout, as befits the variegated subject." —*First Things*

Revealed: A Storybook Bible for Grown-Ups
"*Revealed* sets out to crush any notion that the Bible is a safe, inspirational read. Instead the artwork here, historic and contemporary, takes a warts-and-all approach to even the most troubling passages, trading well-meaning elision for unvarnished truth."
—J. Mark Bertrand, novelist, speaker, and founder of the Bible Design Blog

Serious Dreams: Bold Ideas for the Rest of Your Life
Edited by Byron Borger, this collection of insightful commencement speeches is full of ideas that will help you live out your calling in God's story and pursue serious dreams.

Teaching Beauty: A Vision for Music & Art in Christian Education
"*Teaching Beauty* is a must-read for school administrators, teachers, education majors, and all who seek to encourage the next generation to engage in creativity and beauty."
—Dr. Robert F. Bigley, Executive Director of The Trust Performing Arts Center

Learn more at SquareHaloBooks.com

SQUARE HALO BOOKS ARE ALWAYS IN STOCK—AND ON SALE FIRST—AT HEARTS & MINDS BOOKSTORE! STOP IN THE STORE (234 E. MAIN ST., DALLASTOWN, PA), CALL (717.246.3333), OR ORDER ONLINE (HEARTSANDMINDSBOOKS.COM).